Good Morning
GOD

To Dad, faithful father and preacher of the Word.
Thank you for living it.

Good Morning GOD

Daily Devotions For One Year

Rick Coram

Visit Rick's website: www.rickcoramministries.com

Good Morning God – Rick Coram

Copyright © 2016

First edition published 2016

Scripture quotations are from the King James Version of the Bible

Cover Design: Amber Burger

Cover Photography: Galyna Andrushko /Shutterstock

eBook: Icons Vector/Shutterstock

Editors: Judith Forsyth and Ruth Zetek

Printed in the United States of America

Aneko Press – *Our Readers Matter*[TM]

www.anekopress.com

Aneko Press, Life Sentence Publishing, and our logos are trademarks of

Life Sentence Publishing, Inc.
203 E. Birch Street
P.O. Box 652
Abbotsford, WI 54405

RELIGION / Christian Life / Devotional

Paperback ISBN: 978-1-62245-343-6

eBook ISBN: 978-1-62245-344-3

10 9 8 7 6 5 4 3 2 1

Available where books are sold

Share this book on Facebook:

PREFACE

I magine for a moment that you are vacationing at a beautiful, secluded lakeside resort in a luxurious condo tucked in the middle of dense woods. One gorgeous morning, you step out into the sunshine, geared for a fun-filled day of watersports and recreation down at the lake. Suddenly, an ominous rattle warns you of impending danger. A six-foot rattlesnake is coiled up on the ground right at your feet. The snake is ready to strike in an instant.

Quickly, adrenaline surges above the paralyzing fear, and you jump back inside the room and slam the glass door shut. Your heart pounds rapidly as you gaze in horror through the glass at the big snake curled up on the patio. In slow motion, the rattler uncoils his big body and relaxes. But instead of slithering off the porch, the ugly serpent stretches out and decides to stay in front of the door. After several minutes, the stark reality begins to sink in. That rattlesnake is not leaving. He has chosen your condo unit as his perfect place to lie in the sun.

You've got a big problem. How are you going to get rid of that snake? Of course, there are a few options you might consider. For instance, if you have completely lost your mind, you could grab a broom and try to scare it away by screaming frantically and running at him, waving the broom. I wouldn't recommend that idea. Another option would be to try to find something like an ax, or a golf club, or a shovel, and attempt to chop the snake's head off. Obviously, that means getting really close to him, and if you miss, your bad day is bound to get a whole lot worse.

Frankly, it's absurd to consider doing battle with a huge rattlesnake using any of those inferior types of weapons. To overcome a dangerous reptile like that, you'll need to select a weapon powerful enough to do the job. Something like a broom, shovel, golf club, or even an ax would not be sufficient.

You need to get a gun. Nothing else will suffice. The last thing that needs to pass through that rattlesnake's mind is a bullet. If you want to be able to walk out of your condo in safety and security, you can't mess around with that venomous snake. He cannot be trifled with, played with, or toyed with. You need to be aggressive, militant, and decisive. So, you get a powerful weapon, point it at his head, and shoot him right between his beady eyes.

I believe that you know where I'm going with this simple analogy. Every morning that you walk outside the door of your house, there is a snake waiting for you. Although it may not be a real live rattlesnake, I can assure you that the serpent you will encounter is far more dangerous than that. He is a wicked snake called Satan (Revelation 12:9). Satan the serpent is more venomous than a rattlesnake, meaner than a moccasin, more paralyzing than a python, and deadlier than a cobra. He is the very same snake that bit our first parents, Adam and Eve, and corrupted the entire human race.

That insidious snake is still on the loose today. He never quits attacking. Even after you are saved, the serpent never lets up nor leaves you in peace. The Enemy is constantly trying to poison you. He is always waiting at your front door, coiled up and ready to strike. What is his target? The answer is simple. Since Satan has lost your soul, he wants the next best thing. The snake wants to attack your mind. He is constantly waiting for you to let down your guard so he can take a bite out of your mind.

Do you realize that the greatest and most complete computer

on this planet is the human mind? It was designed and created by Almighty God. There is no computer in this world like the incredible computer that God put inside your head. In fact, it has been said that if someone could build a super-computer to do all that the human mind could do, that phenomenal computer would be one city block deep, one city block wide, and rise up in the air as tall as the Empire State Building. Let me say it one more time ... there is no computer like the one that God gave to you and me.

Our Enemy is aware of that, and this is the reason he fights so hard and aggressively to poison your mind. Believe it or not, your mind is ground zero to Satan. It is the battleground that he wants most to seize and plant his flag on. Why does the Devil fight so hard to capture your mind? The answer is simple. *If Satan can control your mind, he can control you.* The snake wants to slither in and send spam to your computer. He is constantly working to give your computer a virus, and contaminate it and weaken you from the inside out.

It is a constant, hourly battle waged against every Christian. Think for a moment about what believers have to face every single day. The anti-Christ culture that we live in is consistently surrounding and bombarding our minds with images, words, philosophies, and opinions that are defiantly against the standards, laws, and commands of God. Every time we look at the Internet, turn on a television, glance at a smartphone, or even walk down the street, we are exposed to things that are unholy and spiritually unhealthy.

How are we to combat such a powerful and relentless Enemy? What weapon can be confidently used to stand against the venomous snake that confronts you every single day as you step outside and face the world? God has given us a supernatural weapon to use against the satanic snake that lies at our door. Our weapon is much more powerful than a gun. It is the mighty sword of the Lord. Did you get that? The weapon that is available to every blood-bought Christian is the inerrant, inspired, infallible Word of God.

In Ephesians 6:13, Paul said, *Wherefore take unto you the whole armour of God, that ye may be able to withstand in the evil day, and having done all, to stand.* Four verses later, we are specifically commanded to boldly pick up our weapon and use it daily to fight the dangerous Enemy confronting us. The Bible says, *And take the helmet of salvation, and the sword of the Spirit, which is the word of God* (Ephesians 6:17).

Whatever you fill your mind with determines how you act and live. Proverbs 23:7 says, *For as he thinketh in his heart, so is he.* If a modern-day Christian is going to survive spiritually in this ungodly generation, they must daily fill their minds with the purity and power of God's holy Word. If your mind is filled every day with Scripture, you can use it to thwart the poisonous and fiery darts that the Enemy will throw at you.

It is important for every believer to always be ready for battle every time we walk out into the world. A few years ago, there was an American Express credit card commercial that popularized the slogan, *"Don't leave home without it."* That is an appropriate attitude for every saint of God to have in this dangerous day we live in. Don't leave home without talking to the Father and spending time in His Word. Don't leave home without arming yourself for the traps and temptations the Enemy will throw at you. Don't leave home without spending time in the presence of God.

There is something healthy and refreshing about starting your day in the presence of the Lord and equipping yourself against the adversary that you will face during the day. Ephesians 4:23 says, *And be renewed in the spirit of your mind.* The Greek word for *renewed* means "to be renovated or reformed." It is a great picture of cleaning out, purging, and uncluttering the mind. What a beautiful way to start each day. Before venturing out into the world, it is a good thing for any Christian to open the Bible and let God saturate their hearts and minds with His powerful Word.

One of the greatest preachers that I have ever known has had a profound impact on my life. I have considered him one of the most spiritual people that I have ever met. One day, I asked him, "Why do you seem to be so anointed and Spirit filled?" In humility, he just smiled at me and said, "I am just a sinner saved by grace. But when I wake up in the morning, my feet never touch the floor until I have looked up and said, "Good morning God." Then I make sure I never leave my house until I have had my morning devotions."

I have never forgotten those words. What a great and exciting way to begin each day. "*Good morning, God.*" The first thing we should do each day is praise the God who has protected us through the night and awakened us to a fresh new day. "*Good morning, God.*" It is an acknowledgement to the Creator of the universe and the giver of life. "*Good morning, God.*" It is a statement of worship and love.

Come to think of it, *Good Morning God* is a great title for a devotion book. I think that I will borrow it. The volume that you are holding is appropriately titled, *Good Morning God.* It is a book of Scripture passages, inspirational illustrations, humorous applications, and devotions for all 365 days of the year (including one for leap year). It is my prayer that when you wake up, you will use this simple book as a guide to begin each morning in the Word of God. May our great heavenly Father richly bless you as you study His Word, seek His face, follow His heart, and walk in His will.

Because Jesus lives,

Rick Coram

Evangelist, Rick Coram Ministries, Jacksonville, Florida

THE GREAT CREATOR

(Genesis 1:1-25)

On September 5, 1977, NASA launched a nuclear-powered space probe called Voyager 1 into outer space. Its purpose in space is to explore the outer solar system and send back data and photos. Voyager 1 is about the size of a small car and travels at an astounding 38,000 miles per hour. In 2012, the space probe finally exited our solar system and entered what is known as interstellar space. Think about this. Traveling twenty-four hours per day at 38,000 miles per hour, it still took thirty-five years just to exit our solar system, and our solar system is just a small part of one galaxy. Astronomers now estimate that there might be one hundred billion galaxies out there. God not only created them, but He also holds them all in the palm of His hand.

The battle of evolution versus creation all boils down to this: Either there is a God, or there isn't a God. If you believe the first chapter of Genesis, it is impossible to believe in the scientific theory of evolution. All of our scientific explorations point to one abiding truth: The Great I AM is the creator and sustainer of the universe.

UNDER THE INFLUENCE

(Ephesians 5:8-21)

One time, and one time only, I had the misfortune of running out of gas. As a young preacher, I was on my way to speak at a big student rally. I was running late, and though my gas gauge warned me I was near empty, I thought I didn't have time to stop. Consequently, I passed three gas stations along the way before my vehicle started sputtering, and I coasted to a stop less than one mile from my destination. I learned a very valuable lesson, one that has relevance for the Christian life. You had better take time to stop and fill up your tank, or you will not be able to move forward.

Ephesians 5:18 commands us to *be filled with the Spirit*. The Greek verb *filled* is in the present tense and means "be continually filled." It is a daily command, not a one-time event. The filling that you receive today will not last you until tomorrow. You need to be filled with God's power every day. Remember, the *baptism* of the Holy Spirit lasts a lifetime, the *sealing* of the Holy Spirit lasts an eternity, but the *filling* of the Holy Spirit must be renewed every single day.

BLOOD OF THE LAMB

(Exodus 12:1-13)

Thousands of years of ago, God commanded the Jewish fathers to paint the doors of their houses using the blood of lambs that had been sacrificed. God specifically told them to apply the blood on the side posts and the upper doorpost of the house using hyssop, which signifies cleansing, as with a brush. They did not paint the blood on the ground, or the floor, or the doormat, but only over the door. Don't miss the great lesson here. *The Jews did not enter the house of safety by walking in over the blood; they walked in under the blood.* Unsaved people who die and go to hell are people who trample on the precious blood of Jesus. Those of us who are saved will enter the gates of heaven one day only because we will walk in under the blood.

Once they were "under the blood," the Jews were commanded to remain there. Real salvation is only possible under the blood. The Jews were not saved because they hung pretty flowers over the door, or because they nailed up a beautiful memorial picture, or put up a framed piece of poetry about the meaning of life. The Jews were saved for one reason only. The blood of the lamb was over the door.

A CHURCH THAT IS ALIVE

(Acts 2:37-47)

A man bought an exotic talking bird but returned a week later and said, "My bird won't talk." The shop owner replied, "He needs enticing. Put things in his cage so he'll feel comfortable." So the man bought a swing and a bell. Another week passed, and he returned and said, "He still won't talk." The shop owner said, "He needs more enticing." This time, the man bought a mirror and ladder for the cage. Three days later, the angry man returned and said, "He's dead. He pecked his bell, looked in his mirror, swung on his swing, and climbed up and down his ladder. Then he fell on his back, kicked his little feet up, and died. But right before he died, he did finally speak. He looked at me and said, 'Hey dummy, don't they have bird seed down at the pet store?'"

Sadly, this sounds like many modern-day churches. They have all the bells and whistles, but are dying without spiritual food. No matter what century we live in, the church of Acts is still God's perfect design. Pray today that the wind of revival will blow on your church.

HAVE YOU LOST SOMETHING?

(2 Kings 6:1-7)

If you have been married for any length of time, you'll probably agree that one of the chief purposes of staying married seems to be to help each other look for lost stuff. Surely you know what I am talking about. If your house is anything like mine, then the following words are frequently heard. "Where are my keys?" "Where are my glasses?" "Where is the remote control?" When I ask those questions, my wife, Judy, will always respond with another question. She will ask, "Where did you have them last?" Of course, most of the time, I will retrace my steps and discover that the lost item is exactly where I left it. That is a great spiritual lesson.

In Second Kings 6, a young servant of God lost his ax head, rendering him ineffective in the work of God. He immediately turned to Elisha, his master, and confessed the problem, and Elisha restored it to him. If we find ourselves lacking the cutting edge of the Spirit and the Word in our work for the Lord, it is because we have turned from Him, and it is to Him we must immediately return. The place of departure is always the place of recovery.

Victory In Jesus

(Revelation 5:1-14)

D o you know that the largest manufacturer of athletic shoes, apparel, and sports equipment in the entire world began humbly in the trunk of an automobile? One day, a distance runner from the University of Oregon named Phil Knight started selling tennis shoes door to door from his car. The rest is history. Today, Phil is the CEO of the mega Nike Corporation. Nike is a global giant that employs close to sixty thousand people. In 2015, the total revenue of Nike, Inc. amounted to about 29 billion U.S. dollars. Nike apparel and footwear is easily identified by the famous "swoosh" that is symbolic of victory.

Revelation 5:5 tells us that Christ has prevailed. The word *prevailed* comes from the Greek word, *Nike*, that speaks of victory. One day in heaven, every blood-bought child of God will put on their "Nike" robes. Our robes won't have the Nike swoosh on them, but they will be the white robes of victory, because Jesus Christ, our champion, has prevailed. They will be robes of righteousness, washed in the blood of the Lamb, the rewards of overcoming faith for those who walked in the victory of the cross.

BRING THE BOOK

(Nehemiah 8:1-12)

Preachers are always encouraged when folks shout, "Amen!" while they are preaching. I met a dear brother at a church in North Carolina, who was so full of Jesus, he simply couldn't keep quiet. I preached a revival in the church he attended, and each night he sat right in the front row with a big smile on his face and the Bible in his hands. While I preached, he didn't just shout words like "Amen!" "Hallelujah!" or even "Praise the Lord!" Repeatedly, during the course of the message, he would enthusiastically shout, "Bring it!" The first time he did this, I almost jumped over the pulpit with excitement. It was so refreshing to see someone so thrilled about the Book.

After rebuilding the walls of Jerusalem, one of the greatest revivals ever recorded occurred. Historians believe that as many as fifty thousand people may have assembled on the streets for the first service. They told Ezra to "bring the Book!" Ezra read from God's Book from six in the morning until noon. Is "Bring the Book!" the cry of our hearts today? It is the Book that stirs us to repentance and worship, and which releases the blessed anointing for revival in our lives and churches.

FREEDOM

(Romans 6:1-23)

Slavery did not end when the Jews left Egypt, when the Roman Empire crumbled, or when Abraham Lincoln signed the Emancipation Proclamation. Sadly, there are untold millions of slaves living in America today. Think about these sobering statistics. Thirty-five million people try to stop smoking each year, and 85 percent don't even last one week. Twenty-five million Americans are addicted to drugs or alcohol, and less than 10 percent will ever be set free. Forty million people in the U.S. view online pornography each week. Every single second of the day, twenty-nine thousand people in this country are watching porn on the Internet. Satan is in the business of slavery.

We don't have to be into drugs, porn, or alcohol to be in bondage. Ongoing sin of any form is slavery, and in God's eyes, no sin is better or worse than another. But, in the Spirit, God's people are not slaves to sin. This is an established spiritual fact. In Romans 6:22, Paul triumphantly reminds us that Christians have been redeemed and set free. The Greek word for *free* means "to be liberated." We are not servants of sin. We are servants of the Lord. We need to learn to walk in liberation daily.

JAWS

(Jonah 1:1-17)

One Sunday morning, a pastor preached about Jonah and the whale. When he and his family arrived home for lunch, his inquisitive young son asked, "Dad, do you really believe that a big fish swallowed a man whole, and he lived for three days?" The father lovingly answered, "Of course I do." With a perplexed look, the little guy shocked his father when he said, "I don't think that's possible." The dad replied, "Well, if God could make a man out of nothing, and make a fish out of nothing, don't you think that God could make a fish that could swallow a man?" His son looked at him and said, "Well, if you are going to bring God into it, that's different."

The big fish in Jonah was the original *Jaws*. God created a fish to swallow a man who was rebelliously running away from Him. He disciplined him out of love. How could being swallowed by a whale be an act of love? Well, if the fish hadn't been there, Jonah would have drowned. God's discipline brings us to a place where we must rely only on Him to get us back into His will, His plans, and His purposes.

January 10

Peculiar People

(1 Peter 2:1-12)

It seems like almost every single day on the calendar now is recognized as some kind of wacky national day of celebration in America. Today is January 10. It has been designated as Peculiar People Day, the day to honor or celebrate someone who is considered peculiar. By definition, a peculiar person is one who is abnormal, odd, strange, weird, or unusual. According to those who celebrate this strange holiday, you need to find a person who is peculiar and do something nice for them today. Hey, I've got a great idea. Why don't you take a fellow believer to lunch today? After all, every blood-bought Christian is a peculiar person according to the Bible.

That is what Peter calls us in First Peter 2:9. The Greek word *peculiar* found in that passage has a very different meaning from the English dictionary version. Literally, it means "a purchased possession." God's people are peculiar because Jesus Christ has purchased us once and for all with His precious blood. He has set us apart as belonging to God forever. This is one holiday every Christian can joyfully celebrate – and not only today. We are eternally peculiar, blood-bought people of God, set apart for Him alone.

COURAGEOUS CHRISTIANS

(Daniel 3:8-28)

The definition of the word *courage* is not what it used to be. In the 1940s, *courage* was used to describe the men who braved the bloody beaches at Normandy. During the 1960s, *courage* defined the valiant troops who endured the steamy jungles of Vietnam. In the early 1990s, *courage* was the word for the men and women who fought in Operation Desert Storm. In the 9/11 tragedy, firemen and policemen who rescued victims from burning buildings epitomized *courage*. But in this generation, people who change their gender or come out of closets are called courageous and are even given awards. The times have certainly changed.

An act of true courage took place twenty-five hundred years ago in ancient Babylon. Three Hebrew teenagers stood for God, even when they were thrown into the furnace. But they weren't alone. Do the math. Three went into the fire, four were seen in the fire, but only three came out. Where is the fourth man? He is still in the fire. When you have to go through the fire, Jesus is waiting for you, just as He promised. Real courage – the kind that endures the trial – is absolute faith in the eternal presence of Christ, no matter what the circumstances.

JANUARY 12

STAY ON TRACK

(2 Timothy 4:1-8)

One January, after overindulging in holiday fare, it was time to get back into shape. So, on my first road trip, I spent forty-five minutes one afternoon on the hotel treadmill. On my way back to the room, I passed the vending machines. I confess that I have a serious addiction to Reese's Peanut Butter Cups. That orange-wrapped chocolate-and-peanut-butter candy is hard to resist. In a moment of weakness, I succumbed to pressure. I went to my room, got a dollar, returned, and bought a Peanut Butter Cup. The next day, I was prepared. When I went to the treadmill, I already had a dollar in my pocket. On the following day, I didn't even go to the treadmill. I went straight for the machine. I guess you could say that I got off track.

The Enemy wants to knock you off track on your spiritual course and prevent you from completing the race. More often than not, it's the little things, the seemingly unimportant choices, that most easily distract us and lead us astray. Paul, at the end of his life, told Timothy, *"I have finished my course."* Don't quit. Be disciplined. Stay on track and finish God's course for your life.

JANUARY 13

DON'T COMPLAIN

(Numbers 20:1-13)

It has been said that Moses was the pastor of two million people, and all but two of them were backslidden. The history of Israel's pilgrimage from Egypt to the Promised Land was filled with griping, grumbling, and complaining. It seems the people always had a water problem. At the Red Sea, they complained because of too much water. When they reached Marah, they griped because there was bitter water. In Numbers 20, the group was grumbling because there was no water. God told Moses to command the rock to release water. But the great leader was so frustrated that he hit the rock with a rod instead. He most likely used the rock to resist the urge to use the rod on the gripers' heads.

Moses shouldn't have responded like this, but the griping angered him, and his act of disobedience cost him the blessing of entering the Promised Land. Sadly, the people of Israel forgot that God had always provided. This is what happens when we complain instead of giving thanks. The Devil wants you to focus on your few burdens rather than on your thousands of blessings. Rejoice today. God will provide.

JANUARY 14

FULFILLING YOUR PURPOSE

(Luke 19:1-10)

One gorgeous spring day, I prepared to grill some burgers when a wasp started buzzing around me. For several annoying minutes, that dangerous insect interfered with my cookout, and I was relieved when it finally flew away. We often wonder what purpose a small and pesky bug like a wasp can possibly have. Whenever you see one, all you want to do is run for a can of Raid insect spray or a rolled-up newspaper. But a wasp is a biological control agent. Wasps are predators of worms and parasites. Without wasps, important crops like tomatoes and oranges would be attacked, and prices would skyrocket. It is amazing that every creature God created has a purpose.

The story of Zacchaeus beautifully portrays the desire of a man who desperately wanted to see Christ. As the children's song says, "He climbed up in a sycamore tree." All the sycamore tree did was stand there, but when the moment was right, it lifted Zacchaeus up to Jesus. That was the single most important purpose of the tree. Everything and every person has a purpose, including you. It may seem inconsequential, but the smallest action or word that lifts up Jesus transforms lives forever.

TO SPANK OR NOT TO SPANK

(Proverbs 23:13-28)

When it comes to punishing your kids, where do you draw the line? Should you just give them a time-out? Should you lecture them? Or should you simply squeeze their arm and speak firmly to them? Parental discipline is a divisive issue. Some pediatric experts agree that spanking is absolutely necessary, but in a recent CNN study and report, the majority of experts disagreed with spanking. One psychologist even suggests that spanking may cause future mental issues. When I was a boy, my parents only checked with one expert when it came to discipline. They obeyed God.

The Bible does not teach child abuse, but it does teach godly discipline. Paraphrased, Proverbs 23:13 says that a correct and loving spanking will not kill a child. In fact, God's Word clearly teaches that a proper spanking will ultimately do a child good. Unfortunately, a child does not have to be taught to lie, cheat, and steal. We have to teach them to do what is right. We raise our children according to God's Word. Just as He disciplines His children, so we must discipline those in our charge according to the same godly principles of love and wisdom.

THE DEVIL IS DEFEATED

(Colossians 2:6-23)

The most lopsided football score in history happened a hundred years ago when tiny Cumberland College played mighty Georgia Tech. That spring, Cumberland's baseball squad had shocked Tech and beat them 22-0. When football resumed in the fall, the Cumberland team took the field feeling cocky and confident. Before the game, they enraged Tech by taunting them. But Georgia Tech beat Cumberland 222-0. It was 63-0 after the first quarter, and Cumberland's best offensive play of the day lost six yards. That game is still recognized as the greatest defeat of all time. How easily we remember worldly defeats, but we often lose sight of the fact that these cannot compare with the humiliating defeat that Jesus Christ put on the Devil.

Colossians 2:15 describes a picture of a great Roman victory parade. When Rome conquered a nation, they always celebrated. Crowds cheered as trumpets blew, and the victorious army led the chained prisoners and spoils of war down the streets. When Christ died and rose again, He stripped Satan of his power and authority and publicly humiliated him. We are all a living testimony to his defeat. We must live as captives freed, celebrating the victory of our conquering King and His eternal victory.

SEND DOWN THE FIRE

(1 Kings 18:21-39)

When I was in college, I preached a revival in a dry church. Challenged, I decided to speak one night from 1 Kings 18 on the revival fire on Mount Carmel. The church in question was remodeling. The platform carpet had been removed, exposing the plywood and framing. Wires hung down from the microphone plugs and electrical outlets. During the sermon, I emphatically said, "Send down the fire!" As I said those words, I accidentally stomped on one of those plugs. Literal fire shot up from the hole. Thankfully, it quickly disappeared. But I will never forget the result. That crowd came to life. After the service, I had a talk with the Lord and said, "Father, I wanted to be on fire, but I didn't want my pants to be on fire!"

In 1 Kings 18, the nation of Israel had compromised and drifted far from God into idolatry and immorality. The prophet Elijah proposed a contest of fire with 450 false prophets. Their false, dead gods didn't produce fire, but the living God did. Every church should pray that same prayer today. "Send down the fire!" The holy fire of God alone can cleanse us, bring us to real repentance, and ignite us.

JANUARY 18

ETERNAL LIFE

(John 5:17-30)

A young boy attended a revival crusade and heard the evangelist preach a powerful message on the subject of hell. It severely scared the boy and made him doubt his salvation. On returning home, he was so frightened he put his feet up on the couch because he thought that the Devil was hiding beneath it. His very wise father counseled him and showed him John 5:24. That verse promises eternal life to those who hear the Word and believe. After he read the verse, the excited youngster exclaimed, "I heard it, and I believe it!" Then the boy put the open Bible underneath the couch and said, "There, Devil, read it for yourself, and leave me alone."

Jesus specifically calls it everlasting (eternal) life. If you could lose your salvation, it would not be called eternal life. There is absolutely nothing that a blood-bought child of God can do to be unsaved. Your salvation is not based on your behavior, it is based on His blood. If you hear and believe, you are saved, and Satan cannot steal that away from you.

JANUARY 19

NO SECRETS

(Ecclesiastes 12:1-14)

It is amazing that so many people in this generation feel the need to document every detail of their life on the Internet or smartphones. One New Year's Eve, an eighteen-year-old guy named Jacob attended a party and drove home intoxicated. He hit two parked vehicles on the drive home. Nobody would have known about it except that, foolishly, Jacob couldn't keep a secret. He told it to the entire socially connected world. Jacob posted his exploits and bragged about hitting the parked cars on his Facebook page. A policeman discovered it and charged Jacob with the crime.

The real tragedy is that humanity boasts about their sins. Instead of confessing them to God in repentance, they brag about them to the world. We may think that God is unaware because we haven't confessed to Him, but one day, every sin concealed and "kept secret" from God will be revealed. Everything cloaked in acceptability will be exposed for what it really is – sin. Those secrets won't be revealed on the Internet or displayed on a computer screen. Instead, the mighty God who sees them all will bring them out into the full light of His righteous judgment and call us to account.

DON'T GET HUNG BY THE TONGUE

(James 3:1-12)

There are almost 650 muscles in the human body, and the tongue is one of them. Scientists tell us that it's one of the strongest muscles because it is made up of many muscle groups. That may be true. I believe its strength comes from being constantly exercised. The average person speaks between ten thousand and twenty thousand words per day. Our tongues are always in motion. The little preschool song says, "Be careful, little tongue, what you say." Paraphrased, that means, don't get hung by the tongue.

The Word reminds us that the tongue can be a very damaging force. James compares it to a destructive fire, a wild beast, and a deadly poison. That is why it is so important to ensure that our tongues are under the control of the God who made them. When you visit the doctor, one of the first things he does is check your tongue, because it provides a wealth of information on many health conditions. The Bible also says that *out of the abundance of the heart the mouth speaketh.* Each day, stick out your tongue and let the Great Physician examine it. It can reveal the condition of your heart and what needs to be done to correct it.

January 21

Through God's Eyes

(Judges 6:11-27)

An angel visited a man named Gideon one day. This particular angel was the Angel of the Lord *(Jesus Christ)*. He found Gideon hiding and shaking in his sandals. Israel was in bondage to the Midianites, and the people were not even allowed to harvest their grain. Gideon hid in the winepress with the grain. Yet the angel of the Lord called him a *mighty man of valour*. How could Christ look at a poor, scared farmer and call him a man of valor? It was because God had chosen Gideon as the general who would lead the people of Israel to freedom. Everyone else saw just a farmer. But when God looked at him, He saw a warrior.

When everyone else first saw David, they saw just a shepherd boy. But when God looked at him, He saw a king. When the hungry crowd saw a boy, they only looked at a poor child with a small lunch. But when Jesus looked at him, He saw a boy who would be used to feed thousands. God looks at you for what you will become. He sees the particular purpose He placed in you. He sees who you are in Christ. Let Him accomplish His will in your life.

JANUARY 22

A REAL PLACE

(Mark 9:38-50)

There is a little town in Michigan called Hell, a popular place for tourists. At the city limits, a big sign reads, "Welcome to Hell." People stop for photos under that sign. There is a wedding chapel there, and couples actually plan their wedding ceremonies to marry in Hell. The post office is busy with people sending their friends a postcard from Hell. Every year, thousands visit Hell, Michigan. They buy souvenirs, T-shirts, mugs, and plates with catchy little slogans like, "I Survived Hell." All in all, Hell, Michigan, is a "fun" and unique place to stop and visit.

There is another place called Hell that is just as real as the town in Michigan. It is not a happy place of smiling photos, wedding ceremonies, and unique postcards. There are no cute T-shirts or souvenirs sold there. People will not survive this hell. Jesus said that it is a real place of torment where the fire never goes out. When humanity jests and mocks the place of eternal punishment, we diminish its reality and deceive people into disregarding the awful truth of judgment and damnation for those who reject Christ.

BE PATIENT

(Habakkuk 1:1-17)

Walt Disney World attracts seventeen million people per year. That averages out to about 46,500 people per day. With that many people in one theme park, you can stand in line for ninety minutes just to ride Space Mountain. Consequently, in 1999, the executives at Disney World introduced a "fast pass" for people who do not want to wait in long lines. Our world is one of impatient people and instant gratification. There is nothing pleasant or easy about waiting in traffic lines, cashier lines, bank lines, or any other lines. Nobody wants to wait. Often, it is even difficult for Christians to wait on the Lord.

The prophet Habakkuk struggled with patience. He couldn't help asking God, "Why don't You do something?" when facing all the violence and injustice in his day. It seemed as though the wicked prospered, and he didn't understand why. But Habakkuk eventually learned to trust and wait on the Lord. God's lesson for us is simple. Be patient and trust Him. He is in control and His timing is perfect. He sees all, when we only see in part. Patience is putting your trust and confidence in the faithfulness and power of God.

A CITIZEN OF HEAVEN

(Philippians 3:13-21)

According to the United States Citizenship and Immigration Services (USCIS), almost seven million people have become naturalized American citizens within the past decade. In order for an immigrant to become a citizen, some eligibility requirements must be met. For instance, the applicant must be at least eighteen years old and have resided in the U.S. as a green-card holder for five full years. In addition to that, they must be of good moral character, have knowledge of U.S. history, and be willing to be tested and fingerprinted. Finally, they must submit the forms, pay the legal fees, and wait patiently for approval.

Of course, there is another way to become a citizen. The privilege of being born in America is that you became a U.S. citizen instantly. The same is true of a child of God. In Philippians 3:20, Paul declared that our *conversation* (citizenship) is already in heaven. If you are saved, you became a citizen of heaven on the day that you were born again. It is not something you have to qualify for, apply for, or even wait for. It is an instant gift of grace, a spiritual "passport" sealed by the Holy Spirit and the blood of the Lamb.

COUNT THE STARS

(Psalm 147:1-20)

Do you have any idea how many stars are sparkling out there in space? Next time you are restless and can't sleep, don't waste your time counting sheep. Get out of bed, step into your backyard, and try counting the stars. On a clear, dark, starry night, you can see about three thousand stars with the naked eye. But that is just in your neighborhood. Our solar system is in the Milky Way galaxy. Astronomers estimate that it contains over four hundred billion stars. Those same astronomers speculate that there might be over one hundred billion galaxies out there, and some galaxies might contain as many as a trillion stars!

There is somebody who doesn't have to calculate, estimate, or speculate on the number of the stars in the sky. Psalm 147:4 tells us that Almighty God knows the precise number of stars He has placed in the heavens. In fact, God not only knows the number, He also has individual names for them. Praise the Lord. He is the mighty God. The same God who names the countless stars and orders their courses has care of His people. He knows us too by name, and our life and purpose are secure in His hands.

January 26

Hardships In Ministry

(2 Corinthians 11:16-33)

Sometimes ministry can be hard. I am writing today's devotion in an airport in Tennessee, waiting to catch an early morning Delta flight home after a revival meeting. The hotel wakeup call came at 4:00 a.m., after I got to bed last night at around midnight. But for an itinerant evangelist, life is one of pulling suitcases, lonely hotel rooms, weird hours, and constant travel. I confess that there are times that I moan about it. But you don't have to be a traveling evangelist or a missionary in a foreign field to understand the strain of ministry. No ministry is easy.

However, the next time it seems too hard to endure, take a moment and read the eleventh chapter of Second Corinthians. It is amazing what the apostle Paul had to endure. Yet he kept on keeping on and gave God the glory for the privilege of serving Him. You may not be beaten with rods or leather straps today. You may never encounter the same extremes as Paul did, but you will face those moments when it all feels impossible. Those are the times to serve the Lord with gladness, for the joy of the Lord is our strength.

When National
Leaders Pray

(Ezra 9:5-15)

There is a famous painting of George Washington called "The Prayer at Valley Forge." Some believe that it came from tradition or myth, but the painting is based on fact. The hard winter at Valley Forge took its toll on Washington's brave army of citizen patriots. Many of the troops had no extra clothes, shoes, or protection from the adverse weather. Before the winter ended, two thousand soldiers had died. Isaac Potts, a resident farmer who brought grain to the army, recorded in his journal that one day, as he neared a remote section of woods near Valley Forge, he heard a man groaning in prayer. Looking through the trees, Isaac saw Washington on his knees beside his horse, praying for the nation.

Ezra was a leader who prayed earnestly for the survival of Israel. Ezra was filled with shame at the sins of the nation (v. 6). But God heard Ezra's humble prayer and sent a spiritual awakening. How great a revival would come to our churches and our nation if our leaders would bow before God and confess our national sin. Pray today that our leaders would be stirred to fervent repentance and intercession and bear the burden of the nation's sin before God.

ENTER INTO HIS PRESENCE

(Hebrews 10:10-25)

More than ten million visitors take a guided tour of the White House in Washington, D.C. each year. Of course, a person cannot simply stroll through the front door whenever they please. Visitors must plan to tour it well in advance and submit a request through a member of Congress at least twenty-one days in advance. The White House tour includes many beautiful and historical rooms, but one door located in the West Wing is not open to the general public. This door enters directly into the office of the president of the United States. It is the room that is known as the Oval Office.

The average American citizen cannot walk through the secured door into the presence of the president. Our leaders are jealously guarded. But every believer has the privilege of entering straight into the Holy of Holies in heaven and having a personal audience with the God of the universe! We may approach our God and King as members of His own royal family with the assurance that He is also our Father. Free access has been granted only because of the blood that Jesus Christ shed on the cross to purchase our salvation.

Storehouse Tithing

(Malachi 3:1-12)

Most churches have a list of important prayer requests that is given to members of the congregation. A typical prayer list includes those who are hospitalized, infirmed, bedridden, bereaved, or serving in the military – those with special needs that should be prayed over sincerely. But there is one debilitating infirmity that I never see on any sick list. Yet it is a disease that I believe many modern-day Christians suffer from – I call it *Cirrhosis of the Giver.*

Cirrhosis of the Giver is a paralyzing sickness that robs many Christians of the true joy of giving to the Lord and His kingdom work. Over twenty-five hundred times in the Bible, God speaks clearly and candidly about money and possessions. Malachi 3:10 commands us to *Bring ye all the tithes into the storehouse.* Don't dismiss it or ignore it simply because it is an Old Testament passage. A believer should always give more under grace than a Jew gave under the law. It is easy to regard our finances as belonging to us, yet Scripture clearly reminds us that God is the maker and owner of everything.

THE PROMISE

(Matthew 24:36-51)

A father and daughter were swimming when the swift current carried them out into the deeper part of the ocean. The father knew they could not both safely battle the rough sea back to shore, so he said, "Honey, Dad taught you how to float. Now, float on your back while I go for help. I promise you I will be back." It took him one full hour to get to shore, secure a boat, and go back. When he and the help reached her, she was floating serenely on her back. As they pulled her into the boat, one of the crew said, "You are so brave. Weren't you afraid?" The girl replied, "Why should I be afraid? My father promised me he would come back, and he always keeps his promises."

Jesus Christ described the culture of the last days. As we look around at the world we live in, it is apparent that times are turbulent. But Jesus promised that He would come back and take us out of this world. Be brave, be strong, and stand firm. He always keeps His promises. Our eternal security is not governed by the circumstances or the state of this world, but by who God is and what He has promised.

JANUARY 31

TIME TO TAKE A STAND

(1 Samuel 17:17-30)

There is a story about a young soldier whose older brothers were both enlisted in the Civil War. One brother was in the Union army, and the other served for the Confederates. The youngest boy was caught in the middle. So he put on a gray shirt and blue pants, and grabbed his trusty rifle. When he walked out onto the battlefield, both sides shot at him. In this vacillating generation, it's easy – like that poor fellow – to not take a stand. But someone has well said, "People who won't stand for something, will fall for anything."

About three thousand years ago, a teenager named David took a stand. His brothers and the other Israelite soldiers were scared of a menacing bully with a big mouth. But David refused to back up or back down. He simply stood firm and defeated Goliath in the mighty name of the Lord. The brave young man decided to take a stand. Stand up for something today in the name of the Lord. God doesn't need an army to defeat the Goliaths that threaten His people. He simply wants individuals who will courageously stand for Him.

FOR GOD'S GLORY

(1 Corinthians 10:14-33)

Frequently, a middle school or high school student will approach me and ask me whether certain things are right or wrong. On those occasions, I often use an appropriate illustration that the great evangelist Bill Stafford taught me. Bill would hold his coat open and look down at his heart. Then he would literally speak out loud and say, "Jesus, I am thinking about going into that place or I am considering doing that thing. Is it a place that I can take You into? Is that something that I should do with You?" That one simple exercise really helps put things into the proper spiritual perspective. We are to live our lives pleasing and glorifying the One who resides in us.

First Corinthians 10:31 is one of the greatest exhortations in the entire Word of God concerning daily Christian living. On the day that you got saved, you made your last individual decision. Now, we do exactly what He wants us to do, and we go exactly where He wants us to go. The Scripture says that we are to *do all to the glory of God*. If there is even the slightest doubt, walk away. The Holy Spirit leads with certainty, not confusion.

CONFIDENCE

(Job 19:14-29)

It is easy to praise God when the kids are healthy, money is in the bank, our job is secure, and life is prosperous. Someone has said, "Any hummingbird can be happy and sing when the sun is shining. But it takes a special bird to keep singing when the dark clouds roll in." How true that is. During college football season, some Christians are depressed in church on Sunday if their favorite team lost on Saturday. In other words, their praise and worship is affected by their circumstances. Of course, that is human nature. When life gets difficult and demanding, it can take the joy from our heart, the song from our lips, and the fiber from our faith.

Job is in a real mess in the nineteenth chapter. His friends, his wife, and his family have forsaken him. His health is failing, and his money is gone. Yet, in spite of his troubles, Job confidently declares that his Redeemer lives (v. 25) and he would be rescued (v. 26). Our faith and our joy are not dependent on circumstances or on how they affect us physically and emotionally. They are dependent on the eternal love and faithfulness of God and the certainty that our Redeemer lives.

BEAUTIFUL FRUIT

(Galatians 5:16-26)

I have a kumquat tree planted in my backyard. Kumquats are an unusual little fruit. When ripe, you can pick and eat them right off the tree. The skin is actually as sweet as the inside, and you can simply eat the whole fruit without peeling it. One of my little granddaughters loves to pick kumquats and eat them when she is playing in the yard. About seven feet tall, the tree is pretty and green during the spring and summer months. But in the fall and winter, the tree is at its most beautiful. That is when my kumquat tree is festooned from top to bottom with bright orange fruit. After all, the purpose of a fruit tree is to produce fruit.

Galatians 5:22-23 lists the nine visible attributes of a true Christian life. These attributes are called the *fruit of the Spirit*. They are not individual "fruits" but rather one nine-fold fruit that characterizes all who are truly walking in the Holy Spirit. The purpose of a Christian is to produce beautiful fruit. This is the multiplication principle of God at work in us. When Jesus tells the disciples to go and make disciples, He's repeating God's command to creation: "Go forth and multiply."

DON'T FORGET TO
CALL GOD TODAY

(Jeremiah 33:1-14)

There are now almost as many personal cell phones (6.8 billion) as there are people (7 billion) on this planet. One-third of all ten-year-old children and 90 percent of all teenagers in America have their own phone. It seems like everybody is talking at the same time. People make calls on their phones while they walk in crowded airports and drive on busy highways. They talk loudly on phones in restaurants, at ballgames, concerts, and movies, and even in church. It seems that every church that I have the privilege to preach at these days has to display a reminder for people to silence their phones during the service.

Sometimes, we get so busy making calls to others, we forget to make the most important call. God reminded Jeremiah to call Him (Jeremiah 33:3). Literally, the word *call* means to "take the time to cry out." Don't put your schedule ahead of the need to call God. Get off your phone long enough to get on your knees. We are commanded to love God above all, which puts Him before everything else. If we called God as often as we called our family and friends, we would be amazed at the difference in our lives.

BE THANKFUL

(1 Thessalonians 5:1-22)

One day, a small five-year-old boy was having fun visiting at the home of his loving grandparents. After dinner, his grandmother cut a generous slice of chocolate cake and set it down on the table in front of him. The excited child smiled with delight and said, "Thank you, Grandma." Upon hearing those words, the grandmother leaned down, kissed the boy on the forehead, and replied, "You have made me so happy. I just love to hear children be appreciative and say thank-you." The little guy grinned up at his grandmother through chocolate-covered teeth and said, "If you give me some ice cream, I will say it again."

First Thessalonians 5:18 does not read, "In *most* things give thanks." God's holy Word clearly says, *In every thing give thanks.* Of course, we are not thankful for trouble. But we are to be thankful to God even in the midst of trouble. Our thankful response in every difficulty puts our eyes on Him and our faith in Him, and reminds us that His will is perfect and sovereign. Being thankful reminds us of what He has already done, and builds faith for what He will do. Gratitude is not an option, it is an obligation.

FEBRUARY 6

FAITHFUL

(2 Samuel 11:1-17)

Second Samuel 23:39 lists Uriah the Hittite as one of King David's mighty men. That means he was one of the elite soldiers of Israel in the king's special forces. It would be like a soldier of today being a member of SEAL Team Six. As a powerful and skilled warrior, Uriah was often given special ops missions. Yet King David cheated on this faithful soldier and had an affair with his wife, Bathsheba. When the king discovered Bathsheba was pregnant, he brought Uriah home from the battlefield to spend the night with his wife. He hoped Uriah would think the baby was his. But Uriah did an amazing thing. He spent the night guarding the door of the king.

Uriah wasn't being unfaithful to his wife. He was being faithful to his king. There was a war raging, and he was sworn to protect the king of Israel. Uriah's faithfulness cost him his life because David had him killed, but it earned him a lasting reward. His name is found one thousand years later in the very first chapter of the New Testament (Matthew 1:6) in the family tree of Jesus Christ. God never forgets faithfulness, even though the world may scorn it.

DON'T PRACTICE SIN

(1 John 3:1-10)

Although I heard the words about forty years ago, I don't believe that I will ever forget them. I was a young preacher, and I had just preached a revival sermon about the need for Christians to confess sin. After the service, a church leader approached me. The frowning man said sternly, "Young man, you've got a lot to learn. Your message was wrong. Christians don't sin after they are saved. I am Christian, and I haven't sinned in twenty years." I was so stunned that I could not speak. But after the gentleman walked away, I realized that he had unconfessed sin in his life at the moment he spoke. After all, he had a lying problem.

First John 3:9 has often been misinterpreted. The verse says, *Whosoever is born of God doth not commit sin*. However, the powerful tense of the Greek verb *commit* means that this verse is actually saying, "Whosoever is born of God does not *habitually practice* sin." A true believer cannot consistently live in sin. The Holy Spirit will not let that happen. There will be conviction, confession, and repentance. It is the humble and contrite heart that God will not despise, a heart quick to respond to conviction with honesty and repentance.

LEADERSHIP

(Joshua 1:1-18)

Ronald Reagan was the fortieth president of the United States. He is considered one of the most impactful presidents in American history. During his strong administration, President Reagan helped redefine government, strengthen a failing economy, and pressure the Soviet Union to end the fierce thirty-year Cold War. Ronald Reagan was the epitome of a leader. Just two months after his inauguration, he was shot in an assassination attempt. After his surgery, Reagan sat up in the hospital bed, looked at his wife, Nancy, and said, "Honey, I forgot to duck." He was a tough-minded man who led by example.

Joshua was a humble, quiet man who followed a great leader named Moses. Although Joshua had different talents than Moses, he was still used by God to lead Israel. Leaders come in all shapes, sizes, and forms. Some leaders are vocal, and some are silent. But all leaders possess the ability to teach through their godly example, irrespective of their nature or personality. Be a leader to someone today. Let Christ in you be the quality that sets you apart and impacts your generation. The greatest leader of all time taught us that to be a master we must learn to be a servant.

LOOKING WITH EXCITEMENT

(Titus 2:1-15)

My two-year-old granddaughter recently called me her superhero. That's what she thinks I am. In fact, all four of our little granddaughters are still young enough to think Granddaddy and Nana are a big deal. Whenever we arrive at their homes, they wait eagerly at the window with their faces pressed to the glass. Then those precious girls come running outside at full speed with their arms open wide to welcome us. I enjoy it while I can. I am not naïve enough to think it will last. Trust me, the day will come when they won't be that excited to see Nana or me. Of course, they will still love us, but they will have other interests like cell phones, or cars, or some boy!

Are you watching for Jesus Christ today? Titus reminds us that we are all *looking for that blessed hope* (Titus 2:13). The word *looking* means to be "anxious with anticipation and excitement." Truthfully, we sometimes get so boggled with other interests, we don't have our minds on the blessed hope. Get excited – today might be the day that our King returns to take us home. Let's fix our eyes on Him and not be distracted from this wonderful expectation.

SING ... SING ... SING

(2 Chronicles 20:18-30)

The human voice is a precious gift from our Creator, designed and given to us for a purpose – to open our mouths and sing praises to Him. Sadly, I see a lot of professing Christians who never sing during corporate worship in church. Many just stand there looking bored or out of place. Some folks actually use worship time to text on their cell phone. But something is drastically wrong with a Christian who will not lift their voice and sing praise to the Lord. If you are genuinely saved, God has put a song in your mouth (Psalm 40:3). Those close-mouthed believers who have no desire to sing down here on earth will find they cannot help themselves in heaven one day. God wants us to sing. He doesn't hear if we're off-key or out of tune. He hears the songs of our hearts.

The massed armies of the Moabites and Ammonites invaded Judah. God instructed King Jehoshaphat to send the singers out onto the battlefield to praise the Lord in song. That is not exactly conventional warfare. But when the singers opened their mouths and gave glory to God, their enemies were defeated. You might say it was a killer concert!

GOD WANTS EVERYONE TO BE SAVED

(2 Peter 3:1-14)

I had the privilege to preach a revival crusade in a very wonderful church. It was one of those revival weeks with a special and powerful anointing. God blessed the meetings. People were saved, and there was excitement in the air. For the Tuesday evening service, the Lord had convicted me to preach on the sobering subject of hell. Right in the middle of the message, in front of six hundred people, a man yelled out, "What a cruel God!" Then the angry fellow stood up and stormed out of the building. Afterwards, his brokenhearted wife came and told me that her husband believed that God cruelly enjoyed throwing people into hell and watching them burn.

Nothing is further from the truth. In his second epistle, Peter clearly reminds us that God wants everyone to be saved. The Word says that our Lord is *longsuffering* (patient) when it comes to conviction, repentance, and salvation. He is a longsuffering and loving God. He is so committed to making sure everyone has a chance to escape hell that He sent His Son to die and take our eternal punishment. Hell may be real, but it is not God's desire that anyone should go there.

REVIVAL IN A BONEYARD

(Ezekiel 37:1-14)

The word *revival* is a great word, which literally means "to live again." It is a wonderful picture of a refreshing wind blowing on something that is stale, dry, and stagnant, and restoring it to life. People who have never been born again do not need revival – they need regeneration, to be made new. Only those of us who have truly experienced genuine redemption can have revival. As someone has well said, "A person can never have a revival, until they have had 'vival.'" The plain truth is, sometimes those of us that have had "vival" need to have a revival. When our ministry, church work, service, and faith get stagnant and dry, we need the miraculous work of wind-blowing revival.

Ezekiel the prophet witnessed the power of revival in a barren boneyard. God took him to a valley piled up with dry bones and commanded him to prophesy to those bones. When Ezekiel spoke, the bones began to join together. Then he spoke to the wind, and the great army of the nation of Israel experienced revival. But remember, the bones were dead. When we die to self, totally and completely, and surrender ourselves to the purposes of God, restoration is swift and strong.

PEACE

(2 Thessalonians 3:1-18)

My teenage years came in the latter part of the 1960s. There was no decade in the twentieth century quite like the turbulent '60s, the revolutionary decade of Vietnam, civil rights battles, revolution, drugs, demonstrations, upheaval, and the public assassinations of national leaders. During the strife and violence, the American youth adopted a sign that became a national symbol. The "peace sign" was made by holding up the index and middle fingers in the shape of a "V," and it became the emblem of a culture and generation that searched desperately for peace in the midst of chaos.

Christians have a peace sign in the shape of a cross. The only real and lasting peace is found in Jesus Christ. At the end of his second letter to the Thessalonians, Paul said, *Now the Lord of peace himself give you peace always.* The word *peace* means "rest and quiet." Do you need some rest and quiet? Rest in Jesus. As man hungers for peace and strives through meaningless, futile efforts to obtain it, believers have the assurance of a peace that passes all understanding. It is freely available for all at any time. May the peace of our Lord be with you today.

FEBRUARY 14

I LOVE YOU

(Deuteronomy 6:5-19)

Some people woke up this morning in a panic because they suddenly realized that this is Valentine's Day, and they are unprepared. They let the date creep up on them, and they haven't made dinner reservations, purchased a card, or bought candy or flowers to give to the person they love. The drugstores and florists are still open, but it is going to be crazy out there today. Last-minute flowers will be delivered very late, the best cards have all been taken, and the candy on the shelves has been picked over. Whether you have a gift or not, don't forget the most important thing. Take time today to look the person you love in the eyes and say, "I love you."

A fancy gift can never compare to hearing those simple words, "I love you." By the way, those are the words that your heavenly Father enjoys hearing also. Deuteronomy 6:5 instructs us to *love the Lord thy God with all thine heart.* In Matthew 22:38, Jesus called it the *first and great commandment.* Today is a day of love. Tell God how much you love Him today. He's longing to do the same for you.

DON'T GIVE THE DEVIL A ROOM

(Ephesians 4:17-32)

A woman in St. Louis, Missouri, invited a man to move into her house to help her with the bills as a strictly economical arrangement. But he began drinking heavily and being abusive. After several difficult weeks, she asked him to leave. He laughed and said, "You aren't strong enough to throw me out." The woman consulted a lawyer, and a judge issued an injunction. The court ruling declared that the house belonged to the woman, and the man had no legal right to stay. Once more, she told the man to leave her home. Again, he laughed. But when she showed him the legal paper, the trespasser had no choice but to pack his bags and leave.

Some Christians give the Devil a room in their mind or heart, but that residence belongs to God. He bought it and paid for it with the blood of His Son. The Enemy has no legal right to be there. He cannot stay unless you or I allow it. Ephesians 4:27 tells us to *Neither give place [occupancy] to the devil.* Evict him in the name of Jesus. We have the weight of the judge of heaven and our royal priest and advocate on our side.

DESIGNED FROM DIRT

(Genesis 2:7-25)

Twenty-first-century man believes that he is an all-knowing genius because he can create life in a laboratory and a test-tube. But in reality, men only take what God has already created and simply synthesize it. Did you hear the one about the brilliant physicist who got into an argument with God? One day, the arrogant physicist boldly said, "God, you aren't the only creator. I can do what you can do. I can also make a man." God answered, "Let's see you do it." So the physicist walked outside and reached down for a handful of dirt but stopped when He heard God's response: "Hey buddy, get your own dirt."

There is only one Creator. Almighty God formed (designed) a man named Adam from the dust of the ground. Then He took a rib from that man and fashioned a woman called Eve. The first man and woman on earth were the products of a divine designer. We did not come from an ape, or an amphibian, or an alien. God designed us and created us in His own image. Only God holds the spark of life, His own Spirit breathed into us to transform us from dead dust to living creature.

SLEEPING IN CHURCH IS DANGEROUS

(Acts 20:1-12)

Many churches have someone who regularly falls asleep every Sunday during the sermon. During services in the colonial American church of the 1600s, deacons would walk up and down the aisles carrying a long stick with feathers or a foxtail attached to the end of it. If a deacon saw someone dozing, he would reach out with the stick and rub the nose of the sleeper to wake them up. The reason for the public wake-up call was not to embarrass the sleeper. It was strictly a safety precaution. The early pilgrim churches had long, backless log benches. If a sleeper fell backwards, they could end up severely injured.

Paul preached one night in a building that was three stories tall. A young man (probably in his twenties) sat in the top level, listening to the message. As the smoke from the oil lamps rose up and the evening got late, the man fell asleep and dropped three stories to his death. Paul had to stop preaching and raise him from the dead. Sleeping spiritually can be as dangerous as sleeping in the natural. If we sleep and miss receiving the Bread of Life, our spirits starve and spiritual death is inevitable.

LIFE IS IN THE BLOOD

(Leviticus 17:1-16)

It is a little-known fact that George Washington, the first President of the United States, bled to death. One day in his later years, he developed a severe sore throat. Washington's doctor believed that he had dirty blood. So, the doctor performed a medical procedure called bloodletting (phlebotomy), a surgical practice that began in ancient Egypt and lasted well into the 1800s. It was the primitive and painful method of opening veins to drain the bad or dirty blood from the body. George Washington's physician bled him three times in one day. Unfortunately, bloodletting did not cure Washington. It killed him.

Fortunately, doctors no longer prescribe bloodletting for a bad sore throat. By the late nineteenth century, medical science finally understood that blood is essential to life. Fewer people would have died if scientists had only read the Bible. In Leviticus 17:14, God told us that life is in the blood. Everything our body needs to survive and stay strong is circulated by the blood. Proverbs 4:23 tells us to *Keep thy heart with all diligence; for out of it are the issues of life.* Blood flow is directed by the heart. What flows out of our hearts affects us both physically and spiritually.

HOLD ME UNTIL IT
QUITS HURTING

(2 Thessalonians 1:1-12)

One of our little granddaughters, playing in the backyard of our home one gorgeous summer morning, was running, when she suddenly slipped. That sweet child hit the pavement of the patio and badly skinned her knee. Immediately, she screamed, jumped up, and ran into my arms, tears flowing down her face. I carried her inside and held her on the couch. The abrasion was ugly, and I knew she was in great pain. After a few minutes, the crying stopped, and she began to calm down. I looked at her and asked, "Are you okay now? Do you want to get down and go back outside?" That sweetheart looked back at me and said, "Hold me until it quits hurting."

Sometimes, life brings painful suffering. But our Father promised to hold us until it quits hurting. The first chapter of Second Thessalonians is a word for those who suffer. It reminds us that suffering makes us grow, prepares us for glory, and most of all, it glorifies Christ. If you are suffering today, God promised that He will keep holding you, and that what you endure will work not only to your good but also for a purpose that brings glory and honor to Him.

THE LAMB BROKE MY FALL

(Isaiah 53:1-12)

An American tourist was visiting a foreign country when he looked up and saw a magnificent tall building. At the very top, a beautiful sculpture of a lamb was carved into the structure. Curious, he asked a citizen of the country what the lamb represented. The citizen smiled and told him, "When the building was under construction, a worker lost his balance and fell from the top. At the moment he fell, a herd of lambs was being led through the streets to the slaughter. The man fell onto the back of a lamb. Sadly, the lamb was killed, but the man was saved. So, as a memorial, a sculptor carved a picture of a lamb so that no one would forget that a lamb saved a man's life."

Isaiah 53 is one of the most beautiful chapters in the entire Bible. It is a glorious sculpture, a picture of the Lamb of God. The passage is about the cross, written to help you and I to never forget that a Lamb broke our fall, caught us, and saved our lives. Hallelujah! That same Lamb is there whenever we need Him, ready and willing to stand between us and every danger, distraction, temptation, or difficulty.

PRAYING WITH POWER

(1 Timothy 2:1-15)

A bar was being built in a small town in Florida that had previously been a dry town. The local Baptist church was concerned and decided to take action, scheduling a well-publicized meeting to pray that the construction would be shut down. As they prayed, a severe thunderstorm blew in, lightning struck the unfinished building, and it burned to the ground. The owner of the bar blamed the church and decided to sue. Consequently, the church attorney issued a countersuit. At the outset of the trial, the judge made a very profound announcement. He said, "I don't know how this trial will turn out, but one thing is clear. The bar owner believes in the power of prayer, even if the church does not."

In First Timothy 2:1, Paul reminds us of the priority of prayer with the words *first of all.* Prayer is the first thing we should do. Next, he lists four aspects of praying. They include supplications (asking for needs), prayers (worship), intercessions (requests for others), and thanksgiving (appreciation to God). Prayers are the means whereby we have a dialogue with God, and that is the framework for our faith. When we pray using all forms of prayer, we converse with the God of the universe, and we pray with power.

BLESSED BE THE LORD

(1 Chronicles 29:10-21)

I once watched an important NFL playoff game on television. Late in the very tense and close game, a superstar running back broke loose and ran fifty yards for the game-winning touchdown. All of the fans in the lower corner of the end-zone seats immediately fell to their knees in worship and bowed before the runner who had scored the touchdown. Now, I enjoy football, and I will cheer excitedly for my team. But I can promise you that I will never bow down and worship a player. There are also heroes and leaders in this world that I greatly admire, but I will never bow before a head of state, a member of royalty, or a religious leader.

There is only One who deserves that kind of adulation and adoration. At the very end of First Chronicles, King David was worshipping God. David said, *Blessed be thou, LORD God of Israel.* The word *blessed* means "to salute, or bow down and kneel before." Whenever you and I bless the Lord, we are kneeling in His honor. When we give adoration and worship to men or objects, we are guilty of idolatry. God alone deserves all the glory, the honor, and the power, now and .forevermore.

REMEMBER

(Jude 1-25)

A couple, married for sixty years, was eating dinner one night when the husband turned to his wife and asked, "Can I get you something from the kitchen?" She smiled and said, "Yes, I'd like a bowl of vanilla ice cream. But you had better write it down or you'll forget." He huffed and replied, "I won't forget. My mind is good. Is there anything else?" The wife answered, "Yes, strawberries and whipped cream on the ice cream. But you better write it down or you'll forget." He mumbled and shuffled off to the kitchen. After thirty minutes, he brought back a plate of bacon and eggs and set it down in front of his wife. She shook her head and said, "I knew you would forget. Where is my toast?"

Forgetfulness is often the subject of humor and laughter, but Jude reminds us not to be forgetful about the things that are important. He warns us to keep ourselves in the love of God by obeying His Word. In verse 17, Jude says, *remember.* That strong word means to "always keep in mind." We should always remember who and what God is, and all that Christ achieved on the cross.

MILLIONS OF FROGS

(Exodus 8:1-15)

USA Today reported the bizarre story of millions of frogs that caused a huge traffic jam in Northern Greece. Morning commuters on a major thoroughfare couldn't move due to frogs covering the road. Police closed the crowded highway after three cars skidded off the road, trying to dodge the amphibians. There were no injuries to frogs or humans, but traffic came to a standstill for over two long hours. Experts speculated that the frogs had left a nearby lake in search of food. A local traffic authority described the strange sight when he said, "There was a carpet of frogs. It was like a plague of some kind." This is what it must have been like when God sent billions of frogs to cover the land of Egypt.

The Egyptians worshipped frogs. In fact, one of the statues of an Egyptian goddess depicted a frog's head. So, God confronted them by pouring out the plague of frogs on Egypt. There were frogs hopping in houses, beds, closets, shoes, clothes, and food. It's a simple lesson for us all. Whenever we become stiff-necked and obstinate, God will step in and do something to get our attention.

FEBRUARY 25

GOOD CHURCH MEMBERS

(3 John 1-14)

I write this devotion on a Monday morning after a wonderful experience yesterday at a great church where I was privileged to preach. Even before the service started, I was overwhelmed by the gracious hospitality of some of the members. I pulled up to the church, and two excited men greeted me at my car. They unloaded my books and ministry material, brought me water, and made sure that my every need was met. After that, one of them introduced me to the sound tech and ushered me into the pastor's office. When he left, I told the pastor how I much I appreciated the spirit and servanthood of those men. He smiled and replied, "Every church should be blessed to have some members like those brothers."

There are three church members mentioned by name in the book of Third John. Diotrephes (v. 9) wanted to be the boss of the church. But Gaius (v. 1) and Demetrius (v. 12) were the kind of members every church should have. Those two humble men loved the Scriptures, the saints, and the souls of men. Jesus taught us the real meaning of servanthood and of loving our brothers enough to put their needs before ours.

FINISH THE WORK

(Haggai 1:1-15)

Procrastination is a big word. Procrastination. If you use that word the right way on a Scrabble board, you might win. But if it's an accurate description and definition of your life, you are eventually going to lose. For instance, if you have health issues and you procrastinate in seeking medical help, it is only going to get worse. If you procrastinate in repairing your home or car, it is only going to be more costly in the end. Many people routinely procrastinate when it comes to their education, work, daily schedules, and responsibilities. Procrastination is never beneficial, especially when it comes to the work of the Lord.

In the book of Haggai, sixteen years had passed since the laying of the temple foundation. Yet the building was still unfinished. The people had been making excuses and procrastinating. Haggai tells the two leaders of the nation that it is time to get to work and finish the house of God. The busiest day of the week is always tomorrow. Don't procrastinate, and especially when it concerns the work of the Lord. Ask God to stir up your zeal for Him and His work.

THE GATES STAY OPEN

(Revelation 21:15-27)

My grandfather never locked the doors of his house. Whenever he left home or went to sleep at night, the house remained completely unlocked. During the summer months, he often left the windows up. There was never any fear of someone breaking in and taking something. That was a different era. Today, we lock up everything and turn on the home security alarms. After all, crime is all around us. The FBI statistics tell us that there is a burglary or break-in every fifteen seconds. One in every thirty homes in America will be burglarized and robbed this year. The average cost of valuables taken will be $2,230 per home. That computes to $4.7 billion annually.

God has promised that He is preparing us a home that will never need to be locked. There are no security alarms in glory. Revelation 21:25 says that the gates of heaven will not be shut up and closed at all by day. We won't have to worry about the nighttime. It will never get dark. There will be no night, no prowler in the dark, no thief to rob, kill, and destroy. God's gates are always wide open and welcoming.

GOD MEANS WHAT HE SAYS

(Obadiah 1:21)

In Genesis 12:3, God pointedly told Abram that He would bless those who bless the nation of Israel and curse those who curse them. He meant what He said. The little book of Obadiah is the sad account of the judgment of Edom. Israel had sinned against God, and the Lord allowed Jerusalem to be destroyed by the Babylonian armies. As the soldiers of Babylon wrecked the city, the neighboring citizens of Edom cheered (v. 12) in drunken celebration (v. 16). They also took advantage of the situation by looting and pillaging the city (v. 13). However, in the end, God treated Edom the same way Edom treated the Jews.

Obadiah is a short book, but it has a big message. The last sentence says, *the kingdom shall be the LORD's.* Today, in Israel, the King has been rejected, and David's throne is empty in Jerusalem. But when Christ returns, the nation will look on Him whom they pierced. They will be cleansed and forgiven, and His kingdom will be established. Those who mock and ridicule the Jews will face the same fate as Edom. He has covenanted with His people, and God means what He says.

LEAP YEAR

(Psalm 104:1-24)

Today is that rare day that only rolls around on the calendar every 1,461 days. Traditionally, on this day, a woman may extend a marriage proposal to a man. Children born on February 29 can celebrate their real and actual birthday. Ah, leap year. But why do we even have leap year? The answer is found in the heavens. It takes the earth precisely 365 days, 5 hours, 48 minutes, and 46 seconds to revolve around the sun. If the annual calendar were not adjusted for the additional six hours by adding another day every four years, the solar calendar would slowly shift, and the seasons would no longer be aligned with the proper months. Without leap year, the calendar would be off by twenty-four days every one hundred years.

Man created leap year to manage the calendars and seasons. But God doesn't need to make any adjustments to His perfect order. Psalm 104:19 declares that God appointed *(fashioned)* the moon to dictate the seasons of the earth. The sun rises and sets at the command of the Lord. All of creation is in sync because of the Father. He sustains His creation through His perfect will, ordering even the smallest detail according to His sovereign purposes.

MARCH 1

GOD-PLEASING FAITH

(Hebrews 11:1-16)

When my son, Jonathan, was about four years old, we had an adjustable basketball hoop in the driveway. One day, I set the hoop to six feet tall and lifted the little guy up to dunk the ball. As it went through the net, he held onto the iron hoop and joyfully shouted, "I did it!" Then I released him and let him hang high off the ground. Frantically, he screamed, "Daddy, hold me!" I answered, "Just trust me. Let go, and I will catch you." But he wouldn't let go until he felt my arms securely around him again. This went on for many days. He would dunk, I would release, and he would hang there and scream until I grabbed him. Finally, Jonathan trusted me enough to let go of the hoop and fall safely into the arms of the father who'd promised to catch him all along.

Faith is not some emotional "hope-so." It is a firm conviction based on the promises of the Word of God. When we exercise faith, it is pleasing to our Father (Hebrews 11:6). Is there something that you need to trust God for today? Let go and step out. He will be there for you.

THE REMNANT

(Zephaniah 3:8-20)

There is a church in Missouri where I have preached many times. If you visit there today, you will see a dynamic congregation that is on fire for the Lord. Hundreds of excited believers gather every week to passionately worship God and hear His Word. My first experience preaching in that church was over twenty years ago. The congregation only numbered about sixty people at that time, and they didn't worship in a magnificent building or have the powerful ministries that they enjoy today. But they had a remnant of faithful Christians who had a big vision for that church when it was small. They never gave up, and they believed. God has always used a remnant of faithful believers to accomplish His purpose.

In the days of the prophet Zephaniah, there was a small believing remnant that was faithful to the Lord. The third chapter of Zephaniah predicts the battle of Armageddon (v. 8) and the restoration of Israel. God always has a faithful remnant of people in every nation or church whom He uses for His glory. Be part of that faithful remnant. When the Son of Man comes looking for faith on earth, be the one He uses for transformation.

HYPOCRITES

(Matthew 23:13-29)

A man owned a horse that answered questions by stomping his hooves on the ground. One day, he showed off his brilliant animal in front of a large crowd. The owner said, "Ask my horse any math question, and he will answer it." A woman in the crowd asked the horse, "What is two times two?" The horse stomped four times. A man raised his hand and asked, "What is four plus three?" Quickly, the horse stomped his hooves seven times. Another man asked, "What is three times five?" Without hesitation, the horse stomped to fifteen. The amazed crowd applauded. Then a man asked, "How many hypocrites are there in the average church?" Instantly, the intelligent horse started dancing!

Hypocrites in the church are no joking matter. In Matthew 23, Jesus Christ addresses the religious phonies of His day, calling them hypocrites seven times in sixteen verses. The word means "an actor playing a part." God wants His people to be real. The hypocrisy in the church sets Christ up as a laughingstock before humanity. If we, as His representatives on earth, cannot be taken seriously, how will others ever learn to acknowledge His authority and love?

A Savior For Deep Water

(Joshua 3:1-17)

In May of 2015, severe floods swept through Dallas, Texas. News cameras showed video footage of people fleeing their residences and neighborhoods in boats. A woman in a North Dallas suburb watched the flooding rush into her home. She quickly climbed the stairs to avoid the rising water, but while the frantic lady was on her cell phone calling for help, she suddenly looked down and saw a frightening sight. There was a snake and an alligator swimming in her living room. Floods are disastrous and dangerous. But you don't have to be in a literal flood to be overwhelmed by deep water. Floods can rush into our lives in many shapes or forms. Praise God, we have a Savior who can guide us through deep water.

Joshua 3 tells of the crossing of the Jordan River by the children of Israel. In the harvest months, the Jordan can be twelve feet deep with dangerous currents. But the priests bearing the ark of the covenant went first, and as their feet touched the water, the Jordan divided, and the people crossed on dry ground. Our ark is Jesus. When the water is deep, He goes before us to open the way.

FORGIVENESS

(Philemon 1-25)

During World War II, Corrie ten Boom and her family saved many Jews from Nazi concentration camps by hiding them in the attic of their home. However, one day, Corrie's house was raided, and she was sent to a death camp where she was horribly tortured but miraculously survived. After the war, Corrie shared her incredible testimony one night at a church service. Suddenly, a man walked up to her and extended his hand. He was a former German soldier who had brutalized her at a concentration camp. Even though she remembered the inhuman way he had treated her, Corrie forgave him. When asked how she could do it, Corrie said, "When God commands us to forgive, He gives us the love to do it."

Philemon was a Christian who legally owned a slave named Onesimus. Apparently, Onesimus stole some money from Philemon and fled to Rome. The runaway slave came in contact with Paul, who led him to Christ. Paul then wrote to Philemon to tell him Onesimus was saved, and that he needed to forgive him. All of us who are saved have been forgiven, and we must do the same. We will not receive forgiveness from God if we aren't willing to forgive others.

CONFESSION IS GOOD FOR THE SOUL

(Nehemiah 9:1-23)

One night in a revival meeting, the evangelist preached a message about confessing sin. A man heard the Word of God and fell under deep conviction. During the altar call at the end of the service, the man ran down the aisle in humble brokenness and contrition. When he reached the altar, he spoke to the pastor and said, "I want to get right with God." The pastor compassionately replied, "Just get on your knees and confess your sin." Upon hearing those words, the confused man answered, "But I don't know what my sin is." The preacher responded by saying, "Get on your knees and guess." Quickly, the broken man fell on his knees and prayed. After he got up, the man told the pastor, "I guessed right the first time."

In the great revival under Nehemiah, the people of Jerusalem confessed their sins (Nehemiah 9:2). The daily confession of sin is important for victorious Christian living. Our confession needs to be specific and thorough. God knows our sin better than we do, but confessing it sets us free through receiving forgiveness. We only live in bondage when we aren't honest. God sends revival and restoration when we get honest.

SUPERNATURAL WAKE-UP CALL

(Mark 5:21-24, 35-43)

Some people are very difficult to wake up in the morning. They can sleep right through the loudest alarm clock. There are now websites that offer suggestions to frustrated parents on how to wake up deep-sleeping teens. Of course, the advice on the Internet proposes options that range from the practical to the ridiculous. For example, one site simply suggests walking in on the sleeper and crashing loud cymbals over their head. There was one website designed with a surefire tip for waking a slumbering teenager. It is called the "earthquake alarm." Two or more people grab the end corners of the bed, violently shake it up and down, and loudly scream, "Earthquake!" It would be difficult to sleep through an alarm like that.

Nothing can wake someone up quite like Jesus Christ can. In fact, He woke folks up even after they were dead. The gospel of Mark recalls the wonderful story of Jesus raising a twelve-year-old girl from her deathbed. Christ walked into her room, dismissed the scoffers, took the lifeless girl by the hand, and said, "Young girl, rise up." No one can sleep through a supernatural wake-up call like that. If we allow Jesus in, He will make sure we're awake.

REAL FRIENDS

(2 Samuel 13:1-19)

The popularity of Facebook is staggering. It has only existed since 2004, yet one in ten people on the planet have a Facebook page. Fifty percent of people in America who have Facebook boast that they have at least two hundred friends. Fifteen percent claim to have five hundred friends. But the term *friend* on Facebook is a technical term. Most of those friends are acquaintances or contacts, not real friends. If you deleted all of your social media accounts today, how many of those "friends" would be in contact with you next week? A real friend is someone who knows all about you and still loves you. A real friend believes in you when you don't believe in yourself. A real friend loves you enough to tell you the truth.

In Second Samuel 13, Jonadab gave some bad advice to his friend Amnon. In the end, a sister had been defiled, King David was disgraced, Israel was distressed, and Amnon was dead (vv. 28-29). It happened because Amnon listened to a friend who did not give him Godly advice. Choose the right friends and submit everything to Christ before taking action. There is too much at stake to heed foolish or ignorant advice.

CUTE BUT DEADLY

(2 John 1-13)

Pandas are lumbering creatures that look like cuddly stuffed animals drawn by Disney animators. But pandas can be deadly. Gu Gu is a 240-pound giant panda at the Beijing, China, zoo. One day, a twenty-eight-year-old father and his young son admired Gu Gu enclosed in the pen ten feet below them. Suddenly, the child dropped the stuffed panda toy he was holding. When his father tried to catch it, he lost his balance and fell into the pen. Gu Gu immediately attacked him and ripped chunks out of his legs before he was rescued. While recuperating in the hospital, the victim said, "Pandas may look gentle, but they will kill you."

The shortest letter in the New Testament is 2 John. But the thirteen verses say a mouthful. John writes to the elect lady (vs.1), to warn about smooth-talking, syrupy, false teachers. Verse 7 reminds us that the true test of any preacher is what he believes about Jesus Christ. Many preachers look and sound good, but they are deadly. Believers must be constantly in the Word and led by the Spirit, so that we can discern for ourselves and not be seduced by a deadly doctrine.

MARCH 10

RIVER OF REDEMPTION

(2 Kings 5:1-14)

The Ganges River flows 1,569 miles through the nations of India and Bangladesh. It is the sacred river of the Hindus, a lifeline to the multiplied millions of Indians who live near its shores. Named after the goddess of Hinduism named Ganga, the belief is that the waters of the Ganges are supernatural and have healing powers. People bathe there for spiritual purification. But it is the fifth-most-polluted river in the world. Dead bodies are burned and dumped in the water. The waterway is filled with raw sewage, wastes, and deadly toxins. The sad truth is that the Ganges River is not a river of redemption at all. It is a place of disease and death.

It would be hard to find a man lauded more than Naaman in 2 Kings 5:1. But in spite of the accolades, the verse closes with the words *"but he was a leper."* Elisha told him to wash seven times in the muddy Jordan River. Naaman finally did it, and he was healed. If you are saved, it is because you have been washed in a river of redemption. You haven't been washed in the mud, you have been washed in the blood.

SEND DOWN THE HOLY GHOST

(Acts 1:1-11)

One Sunday morning, a pastor preached on the Holy Ghost. He decided to conclude his sermon with a dramatic visual illustration. The pastor placed a young boy and a caged dove in the rafters high above the crowd. He told the boy that, at the climax of his message, he was going to shout, "Holy Ghost, come on down!" When the boy heard those words, he was supposed to release the dove and send him soaring across the congregation. The pastor came to the end of the message and shouted, "Holy Ghost, come on down!" Nothing happened. Twice more, he shouted the same words with no response. Finally, the frustrated preacher looked up and cried, "Holy Ghost, I'm telling you to get down here right now!" The little boy yelled, "A yellow cat ate the Holy Ghost. Do you want me to throw down the cat?"

It is wonderful to know that we don't have to resort to theatrical tricks to encourage the Holy Ghost to show up. In Acts 1:8, the ascending Christ promised His disciples that He would send down the miraculous power (strength) of the Holy Ghost. The Holy Ghost is here today and every day, an eternal, faithful presence.

SALVATION STORY

(Hosea 3:1-5)

The book of Hosea contains one of the most compelling stories of forgiveness and love in the entire Bible. God commanded Hosea to marry a harlot, and He warned Hosea that she would cause him heartbreak. In obedience, Hosea married Gomer, and they were blessed with three children. But she then left her husband and children to live with other men. One day, God commanded the prophet to go and look for his wayward and sinful wife. Hosea found her being sold on the slave market. In an act of unconditional love and mercy, he bought Gomer, forgave her sins, and took her home.

Hosea's Hebrew name means "salvation." The story of Gomer is a picture of Israel's unfaithfulness to God. She committed spiritual adultery and worshipped idols. Like Gomer, Israel went into captivity because of her sin. But God sought, found, forgave, and restored her. He has the same love for His bride, the church. When we sin, we can expect the same response from God. He loved us enough to die for us, and if we go astray, He'll find us. If we confess and repent, believing in Christ, He will forgive us and bring us back into His presence.

THE FINISHED PRODUCT

(James 1:1-17)

There is a picturesque Bible college located in the Midwest. For many years, a magnificent oak tree stood in the middle of the campus. The mighty oak was the focal point of the school, a central location that served as a gathering place for study, eating meals on the lawn, and relaxing under the shade. But during a storm and raging wind, the trunk of the great oak tree began to crack. With a ground-shaking thud, the tree fell. When experts examined it, they discovered that although the outside of the oak looked strong and healthy, the inside had been eaten away by a hidden disease. The mighty oak snapped like a twig because the inside had been destroyed.

God warns us about the destructive disease of sin. James 1:15 says that the finished product of sin is always death. The word *finished* literally means "completed, or run its course." Sometimes, the person eaten up with sin appears strong and healthy. But the day eventually comes when the disease runs its course and life falls apart. But God is our gardener. He knows what's wrong on the inside and will heal and restore us if we come to Him in faith and repentance.

MARCH 14

A GODLY WIFE

(1 Kings 21:1-29)

On the night of March 14, 1975, Judy and I were married. Since 1988, I have been a travelling vocational evangelist. Most weeks of the year, I am on the road, far away from home, for at least five nights. That means that I have now spent well over thirteen years of our married life apart from my wife. She is an amazing person. Judy has managed the home front, raised our three wonderful children, run the office, and kept things going for all these years. She has done it with grace, joy, and style. So on this, our anniversary day, I want to dedicate this devotion to my precious wife. I want her to know how much I love her, and I am so grateful that God gave her to me. Praise the Lord for a wife who is an encourager, prayer warrior, and best friend.

Unfortunately, King Ahab of Israel was not blessed with a godly wife. First Kings 21 is the sad saga of a woman named Jezebel. She manipulated her husband and secretly plotted to destroy the priests and prophets of God. Eventually, both King Ahab (1 Kings 22:34-40) and Queen Jezebel (2 Kings 9:30-37) paid for their crimes.

MARCH 15

THE POWER OF GOD

(Galatians 2:11-21)

I really love classic cars. My three favorite classics are Chevrolet Camaros, SS Chevelles, and Corvettes. While preaching at a revival meeting in Woodstock, Georgia, I met a man who owned seventy classic cars. When he found out that I loved them, he invited me to his garage to look at his magnificent collection. When I walked in, I saw GTOs, Thunderbirds, Corvettes, Monte Carlos, and Oldsmobiles. Unfortunately, he didn't own a Camaro, but he did have a beautiful 1969 SS Chevelle with a four-speed 396 engine. He invited me to drive it, and I could hardly contain my excitement as I climbed in and turned the key. But the battery was dead, and the beautiful car wouldn't start. I must confess that I nearly cried.

That Chevelle looked good, but it had no power. Sadly, there are some believers exactly like that car. They appear shiny and perfect on the outside, but contain nothing of substance within. Paul was a religious man before he was saved. But after he was *crucified with Christ* (v. 20), Paul experienced the risen Lord living in him. Live today in resurrection power. Christ in us is the only power we need to live, work, and praise.

THE CONNECTING PLACE

(Isaiah 6:1-13)

There is a name for the people living with the technology of the twenty-first century. We have been called The Connected Generation. Do you realize how connected we are? In 1998, there were approximately twenty million people connected to the Internet each day. Now, over two billion folks are online every twenty-four hours. People are constantly connecting on Facebook, Twitter, Instagram, and by text messages. Most of us are completely dependent on our many technical devices. We feel lost without them. It is almost impossible to be without a cell phone in the world that we live in. As a matter of fact, psychologists have a clinical term for people who are afraid to be separated from their phones. It is called nomophobia. Everybody wants to be connected.

Isaiah found his connecting place at the altar. When he went to the temple to mourn the death of King Uzziah, he connected with the God of glory. That encounter changed his life and impacted Israel, and later, the church. The altar is still our connecting place. Don't forget to take time to kneel and connect with your Heavenly Father. It's a supernatural, spiritual connection that lifts us beyond the mundane things of this world that we think are important.

ONLY ONE RETURNED

(Luke 17:11-19)

Leprosy was the dreadful disease of biblical times. It was a horrible sickness that began with nodules and ulcerated sores on the skin. As it advanced, body parts and limbs became grotesquely deformed, rotted, and even fell off. People with leprosy were considered disgraced and outcasts. They were secluded and restricted from appearing in public. There was no cure, so those stricken with the disease didn't see a doctor. Instead, they were required to see a priest. But Doctor Luke records the amazing account of ten lepers who came face to face with the great High Priest named Jesus Christ. He simply spoke to the ten dying men, and they were miraculously healed.

It has always been curious to me that only one of those healed lepers returned to thank Jesus. In fact, Christ Himself asked, *"where are the nine?"* (v. 17). He had saved them from leprosy, yet only one returned and gave Him glory. Healings are not simply a blessing for our own benefit. They confirm the gospel and testify that Jesus is the Son of God. Those of us who have been healed from the leprosy of sin should also take time daily to give Him glory for our salvation.

LAUGH OUT LOUD

(Proverbs 17:17-28)

Do you laugh out loud very often? Researchers are now saying that it is healthy to have a dozen good laughs every single day. Medical studies at Vanderbilt University have concluded that twelve big laughs daily will do at least five things to your body: 1) decrease stress hormones; 2) boost immune systems; 3) increase protein; 4) release endorphins, which are natural painkillers; and 5) burn calories. Experts say that ten to fifteen minutes of hearty laughter can burn more than fifty calories a day. The truth is, our bodies physiologically change every time we laugh. Laughter stretches face muscles, makes you breathe faster, sends more oxygen to the muscle tissues, and helps clean out your lungs. The official Vanderbilt study concluded by saying, "Laughter helps people emotionally, physically, and spiritually."

Isn't it amazing that God said that very thing a long time ago? Proverbs 17:22 tells us, *A merry heart doeth good like a medicine: but a broken spirit drieth the bones.* The word "medicine" means "to cure." Nehemiah 8:10 says that the joy of the Lord is our strength. Laughter can cure a lot of things, and it can make us feel better and stronger. Today, don't forget to LOL.

MARCH 19

JESUS KNOWS

(Hebrews 4:1-16)

A man had some purebred puppies for sale, and a father and his small son went to buy one. When the boy saw the pups, his eyes danced with delight as he watched five little balls of fur playing in the pen. Suddenly, another puppy hobbled out of the doghouse. He was clearly inferior to the others, and he walked with a limp. The boy said, "I want him." Quickly, the breeder replied, "No, you don't want him. He was born with a crooked leg. He will never be able to run with you." The young boy reached down and pulled up his pant leg. A steel brace ran down his crippled leg into a special shoe. He said, "I can't run very well either. That is why I want this dog. He needs someone to love him who understands him."

Jesus Christ loves you and knows exactly what you are going through. Hebrews 4:15 tells us, *For we have not an high priest which cannot be touched with the feeling of our infirmities.* That powerful Greek thought means "When you hurt, He feels it." Jesus faced the same worldly trials, pain, and testing that you and I face. You can trust Him with your burden today. He knows what you are going through.

A PROMISE KEPT

(Joel 3:1-21)

Before a big election, politicians will make some huge promises. They go to great expense to buy television airtime so
they can smile and share those promises. Candidates will debate
enthusiastically, and each one will promise Americans that
their election will make our lives better. There will be promises
of tax cuts, peace plans, and answers to the raging crime and
drug problems plaguing our nation. But unfortunately, after
all is said and done, in many cases, more will be said than will
be done. Then, after the election, those in opposition will go to
great lengths to publicize detailed reports listing all the broken
campaign promises. But the real truth is this: A promise is only
as good as the one who makes it.

The prophet Joel describes a future event. He tells us what will
happen to the land of Israel after the Lord returns at the battle
of Armageddon. When Joel preached this, all the people could
see were dry fields and starving cattle. But Joel is telling them
about a land that will exist in the kingdom age when Jesus
Christ sits on Jerusalem's throne. It is a promise that, like all
of His promises, will be kept.

WHAT ARE YOU WORRIED ABOUT?

(Matthew 6:25-34)

A third grade teacher was instructing her students about fractions. She asked, "Billy, what is three-fourths of five-sixteenths?" Billy shrugged and answered, "I don't know, but it's not enough to worry about." A study at the University of Michigan determined that 60 percent of all the things that we worry about are unwarranted. Twenty percent of all our worries involve something in the past that cannot be changed. Eighteen percent of all worries involve something insignificant or petty. In other words, there is nothing fruitful or profitable that comes from worrying. It will put wrinkles on your face, a frown on your lips, and an ulcer in your body.

That is why Jesus Christ commanded us not to worry. Matthew 6:25-34 is a clear command that worry is a sin. It is just as much a sin as idolatry, adultery, hypocrisy, and profanity. When we worry, we are either saying, "God, you can't handle this situation," or "God, we don't believe *you* will handle this situation." Worry denies God's power and promises and is founded in unbelief. Real faith doesn't worry. It trusts God.

TURN OR BURN

(Jonah 3:1-10)

Billy Sunday was a professional baseball player when Jesus Christ saved him and called him into the ministry. He became one of the greatest evangelists of the early twentieth century. Billy preached with fiery boldness and passion. One night, he preached a scorching and convicting sermon on the power of sin. A dignified woman in the congregation was offended by his bluntness. After the conclusion of the service, she approached him and said, "Sir, I want you to know that I didn't like that sermon on sin one bit." Without any hesitation, Billy Sunday replied, "Well, ma'am, the Devil didn't like it either, so classify yourself."

God wants preachers to be bold and speak the truth, just as Jonah did when he walked into the gates of the wicked city of Nineveh. He didn't mince or sugarcoat his words. Jonah had only two points to his sermon. They were "Turn or burn." But after he preached that powerful two-point sermon, revival swept through Nineveh. Today, many preach only what the congregation wants to hear or what won't offend. God's view is simple. It's all of His Word or none of it. We cannot pick out the bits we like and discard the rest.

MARCH 23

MISSING PERSONS

(1 Corinthians 15:38-58)

Hartsfield International Airport in Atlanta is the busiest airport in the world, and around three thousand flights take off and land there each day. I once encountered a small girl about three years old, alone and screaming in a concourse crowded with travelers. People stopped to help, but then a young mom ran out of the smoking area, grabbed the sobbing girl, and said, "Sorry, honey, Mommy needed a cigarette." I was amazed at the irresponsibility of a mother who abandoned her child in a busy airport to have a nicotine fix. I shuddered as I realized how easily that precious little child could have become a missing person.

Imagine the great, eternal separation of families and loved ones when Jesus Christ raptures His church. Paul reminds everyone that this incredible event will occur in a moment. Without warning, millions will be missing persons. It might even happen today. Those left behind will face a terrible future of tribulation and the coming rule of the Antichrist. But they will also endure the indescribable anguish of eternal separation from those they love. We should pray constantly for the salvation of our loved ones so that when the rapture takes place, there will be no missing persons.

AN EYE EXAM

(Psalm 101:1-8)

When I was a boy, we used to sing a song that said, "Be careful little eyes what you see." The words of that old children's tune provide great advice for any generation. It seems that our eyes are constantly under attack. Statistics tell us that the average American home has at least one TV on for eight hours each day. In this generation, 96 percent of all television writers and producers admit that they never attend church. Ninety-one percent believe there is nothing wrong with homosexuality. Eighty-seven percent agree that adultery is not a sin. That explains why much of today's programming is immoral and lacking in Christian ethics. Without a doubt, your mind cannot absorb a steady diet of that kind of constant visual attack and not be impacted by it.

Psalm 101:3 commands, *I will set no wicked thing before mine eyes.* The word *set* literally means "to consider or regard." Matthew 6:22 tells us that the eyes are the lamp for the body. What shines in will affect our hearts. Our eyes should be examined daily by the Holy Spirit. In other words, let's have enough spiritual sense and discernment to change the TV channel if it's an insult to Jesus.

THAT'S HILARIOUS

(2 Corinthians 9:1-15)

A church was raising money to build a multimillion-dollar building. The pastor was frustrated because the wealthiest member of the congregation seldom attended church and had not made a contribution to the building fund. One day, an old, rough, redneck church member stopped by the office and asked the pastor for permission to write a letter to the rich man on behalf of the church. The pastor agreed, and the plea was sent out on church stationary. Five days later, the pastor received a registered letter containing a check for $1 million from the wealthy man. The letter said, *Dear Pastor, I'm very sorry. I promise to be more faithful to the church. Use this money for the building fund. P.S. Please tell your secretary that there is only one "t" in dirty, and no "c" in skunk.*

While we often joke about stinginess, the Bible tells us that God loves a cheerful giver. You will only find the word *cheerful* once in in the New Testament (2 Corinthians 9:7). The Greek word is where we get our English word *hilarious*. Literally, the sentence reads, "for the hilarious giver, God prizes." It is the hilarious giver that receives the prize in heaven.

BEND THE KNEE

(2 Chronicles 7:12-22)

America is known as a Christian nation. After all, there are over three hundred religious cable and satellite television programs that air every single day in this country. Ninety-six percent of all Americans say they believe in God, and seventy million people living in this land claim to be born again. But there are some grim statistics that would suggest that the U.S. is not a Christian nation. Our country has more people in prison than any other country on the face of the earth. For every one hundred thousand people living in America, five hundred are behind bars. Every year in the United States, two million unborn babies are aborted, and $10 billion is spent on pornography. Substance abuse is our number-one health problem, and teenage suicide is the number-two killer of teens.

We are a nation of moral regression, sexual revolution, and spiritual rebellion. Many are concerned about war and terrorism. But I believe that America will not be conquered from without. Instead, we will corrode from within. Second Chronicles 7:14 tells us that awakening comes when God's people are humble (bend the knee) before Him. Pray for our country today. God promises judgment as well as mercy. Our humility and prayer determine which one we get.

SUPER CONQUERORS

(Romans 8:28-39)

An elderly woman was deathly ill. Her faithful doctor had performed multiple medical procedures and run a battery of tests. He had prescribed a dosage of very strong medication to combat her disease. But in spite of all his expertise, ability, and knowledge, nothing helped the sick woman recover. Finally, he walked solemnly into her hospital room one day and gave her the news. "I am sorry to tell you that we have done all that we can. Now you are just going to have to trust the Lord." She looked grimly up at the physician and replied, "Oh, my soul. Has it come to that?"

It's remarkable how often believers have the same attitude. We try everything else and God becomes a last resort. But the last twelve verses of Romans 8 remind us that God can handle anything we go through. Romans 8:37 emphatically and victoriously declares that *we are more than conquerors* (decisive or super conquerors) through our Lord. You can trust Him. He is the perfect provider, perfect Redeemer, and perfect physician. Perhaps if we brought our problems to Him first instead of looking elsewhere, we might find a far quicker and better resolution than the one we try to create for ourselves.

A FEW GOOD MEN

(Judges 7:1-21)

When the United States Marine Corps was founded in 1775, they adopted the words "We're looking for a few good men" as their recruiting slogan. I wonder if the original founders were thinking about the story of Gideon's soldiers. In Judges 7, two mighty massed armies of 135,000 men came against an Israelite army of 32,000 troops. Outnumbered four to one, Gideon didn't think he had enough men. But God knew he had too many. First, Gideon excused the cowards, and ten thousand men left the army. Now the odds were fourteen to one. After a test to see who would drink water and still watch for the enemy, Gideon ended up with only three hundred soldiers. The tiny army was outnumbered 450 to 1. However, no army of God is ever at a disadvantage.

God's minority is greater than the Devil's majority. God does not need quantity. He is looking for quality. In the end, Gideon's soldiers did not throw a spear, thrust a sword, or even hurl a stone. They blew trumpets, broke pitchers, and bared torches (Judges 7:20). When the dust settled, Gideon got the victory, and God got the glory. God is still looking for a few good men.

BRAGGING ON JESUS

(Galatians 6:1-18)

Imagine for a moment that you are a Christian living in the first century, and the church you are attending is having a big revival crusade. The guest evangelist is none other than the apostle Paul. How do you suppose the host pastor might introduce such a preacher? What accolades could he give? He might stand and say, "Ladies and gentlemen, our evangelist is a full-blooded, uncircumcised Jew whose pedigree hails from the tribe of Benjamin. He is a selected Pharisee. This man is the greatest missionary, apologist, and theologian in all of Israel. He has authored almost one-half of the New Testament. Would you welcome Paul the apostle?"

Do you know what Paul would do after such an intro? As the crowd stands in adoring, thunderous applause, he would walk to the podium and immediately boast about Jesus. In Galatians 6:14, Paul said, *But God forbid that I should glory [boast], save in the cross of our Lord Jesus Christ.* Every man, woman, or ministry that is real and anointed will always boast of no one but Jesus. The purpose of every ministry is to lift up Jesus, and Him alone, so that He may fulfill His purpose and draw all men to Him.

OBEYING INSTRUCTIONS

(Genesis 6:1-22)

Has God ever instructed you to do something that you considered too difficult? Consider His monumental request to Noah. He told an old man and his sons to build the very first cruise ship. Noah never said, "God, You're crazy. You want me to build a floating zoo that is four stories high and four hundred and fifty feet long? Why are you asking an old geezer like me? May I remind you that I am five hundred years old?" He did not question God. He never asked, "Why me?" or "Are you sure?" Instead, Noah obeyed the Lord and did precisely what God asked him to do (Genesis 6:22). Not only did Noah build the great ship, he also warned men, and unfailingly preached for one hundred and twenty years that a flood was coming.

It has been calculated that the ark was big enough for 125,000 animals. God gifted Noah with the ability to build the massive boat and gave him the smarts to know the diets of all the animals and stockpile the food necessary for the journey. God will never ask you to do anything He has not equipped you to do. When He commands, obey Him and trust Him to see it through to completion.

A LIVING HOPE

(1 Peter 1:1-12)

Jesus Christ hung lifeless on a cross, high upon Golgotha Hill. A man named Joseph of Arimathaea went to Pontius Pilate and begged for the body. When Pilate granted his request, Joseph took Christ off the rugged timber and wrapped Him in beautiful white linen. Then Joseph laid the Lord's body in his own brand new tomb and sealed it up. Can you imagine some grumbling person walking up to Joseph and saying something like, "Are you out of your mind, Joseph? That is such a beautiful, costly, hand-hewn tomb. Wasn't that for your family? Why in the world did you give it up for someone else to be buried in?" I can see old Joseph just smiling at that person and replying, "Why not? He only needs to use it for a few days. Just wait until you see what happens on Sunday morning."

On Easter Sunday, Jesus Christ rose up and walked out of that tomb. The resurrection of Jesus is what makes Christianity different from every other religion in the world. Unsaved people have no hope. However, we have a living hope (v. 3) because we have a living Savior in us. Christ wants us as a temple, not a tomb.

APRIL 1

DON'T BE FOOLED

(Ecclesiastes 7:1-18)

On April 1, 1976, one of the most famous April Fool's Day pranks of all time occurred in the city of London, England. During his morning radio broadcast on the BBC network, British astronomer Patrick Moore announced a rare alignment of Jupiter and Pluto. Moore told his listeners that at precisely 9:47 a.m., the phenomenon would nullify the effects of gravity for a few seconds, resulting in a once-in-a-lifetime chance for humans to actually float. At 9:48 a.m., the BBC switchboard lit up with hundreds of calls from people who claimed they experienced loss of gravity. One woman reported that she and her friends had risen from their chairs and floated around the room. Finally, Moore told everyone, "April Fool's!"

Those poor people swallowed a lie, and it affected their minds. That is how powerful deception can be. Solomon warns us about listening to foolish talk or advice. Ecclesiastes 7:5 says, *It is better to hear the rebuke [reproof] of the wise, than for a man to hear the [silly] song of fools.* We listen to the foolish preaching of foolish doctrines and are deceived. We cannot believe everything we hear, but should always seek the wisdom of God to discern that which is good.

ETERNAL LIFE

(1 John 5:1-21)

Elizabeth "Ma Pampo" Israel died peacefully at her home in the Dominican Republic on October 14, 2003. In the modern era, Elizabeth has the distinction of being the oldest person who ever lived. She was born on January 27, 1875. That means Elizabeth Israel was 128 years old on the day that she died. Ma Pampo far exceeded the life expectancy of anyone in any country on the face of the earth. In the United States, the average life expectancy for a man is seventy-eight years of age, and for a woman, it is eighty-five years of age. In spite of all the marvelous medical advances and procedures we have achieved today, one important fact remains. Our physical bodies do not last forever. Eventually, your body will break down, wear out, and die.

But don't let it get you down. The most important part of you will never die. God has promised eternal (everlasting) life to those who know Jesus Christ. You can lay your head on your pillow tonight knowing that you have eternal life. There is nothing you can do to lose eternal life. After all, it is not a ten-year life or a hundred-year life. Your life expectancy in Christ is eternal.

April 3

Commitment

(Daniel 1:1-21)

Many years ago, a great revival swept through Mainland China. A seventeen-year-old boy named Watchman Nee was saved and called to preach. During his years of ministry, China was under the iron hand of communism, and there was great persecution. He was brutally beaten, tortured, and imprisoned for preaching Jesus. But in spite of the agony and physical abuse, Watchman would not back down nor shut up. One day, the great preacher was taken to the city square. An ultimatum was given. "Stop preaching or you will pay." When he refused to stop, a soldier violently swung an ax and cut off his hands. Watchman Nee raised two bloody arms to heaven and cried, "Thank you, Lord! I gladly give my hands in Your name!"

Many came to Christ because of the courage and commitment of Watchman Nee. The prophet Daniel too understood a thing or two about commitment. As a teenage boy, he was abducted and taken to Babylon. King Nebuchadnezzar tried to brainwash Daniel and his friends. Daniel 1:8 says that Daniel *purposed in his heart* (made up his mind) to keep his commitment to his God. What a challenge these men are to "comfortable Christianity." The God who gave His all expects our all in return.

April 4

Time To Change Clothes

(Colossians 3:1-15)

W e once lived in a home with a big fireplace in the main living room. During the winter months, that fireplace provided warmth and beauty. But when the springtime rolled around, it needed cleaning badly. One day, I climbed into that dingy fireplace to sweep out the dried ashes and wipe away the dirt that had accumulated during the cold winter. When the ugly task was finally finished, my clothes, face, and arms were covered with black soot. As I put away the trash, I asked, "Is dinner about ready? I am starving." I was hungry and ready to sit down and eat. My wife responded quickly by saying, "Yes, it is ready. But I will keep it warm until you clean up and change. You aren't sitting at my table wearing those filthy clothes."

The Christian life is frequently compared to changing clothes. Colossians chapter 3 uses the words *put off* and *put on*. It is a picture of dressing in different garments. *Put off* literally means "to take off clothing." After we have been washed in the blood of Jesus Christ, we are dressed in the garments of righteousness. These are the only robes we can wear into the presence of God.

TOO BUSY

(Song of Solomon 5:1-16)

Our world is fast and frantic. In spite of all the time-saving technology at our fingertips, most people don't seem to have enough hours in the day to meet the demands of their overloaded schedules. One of the most-used phrases of this hectic and hurried generation is, "My plate is full." Unfortunately, sometimes our plates are so full we miss the most important appointment of the day. We often are too busy to fellowship with God. In Song of Solomon 5, there is an interesting picture of the believer's communion with the Lord. The maiden is asleep when her beloved comes to her door. He wants to spend his time and share his love with her, but she is too comfortable to be bothered.

Then she sees the hand of her beloved (v. 4) and realizes that her sin has wounded him. (Remember, our Lord's hands are nail-scarred.) Sadly, when the maiden gets up to open the door, her beloved is no longer there. She missed the opportunity to fellowship because she was too busy. It's tempting to regard this as an example of those who never commit to Jesus, but it speaks of the beloved – the believer – not the unbeliever.

AUTOPSY OF A DEAD CHURCH

(Revelation 3:1-6)

I was raised out in the country. My Granddaddy and Grandma Coram lived right across the road from my house. They had a pen full of chickens, and it was always an exciting day when Grandma killed a chicken to get it ready for the frying pan. One day, when I was a small boy, I was over at my grandmother's when she took an ax and chopped off a chicken's head. With great amazement, I watched that headless chicken stand up and stagger around. It scared me out of my wits because I thought I was looking at some kind of chicken ghost. Quickly, I screamed, "Grandma, that chicken is still alive!" My granny just laughed and replied, "No, honey. He isn't alive. That chicken is dead and don't know it."

It is possible for something to look alive and yet still be dead. That was the diagnosis that Jesus gave to the church at Sardis. Sardis was a church with a good reputation. There was no false doctrine taught at Sardis, and the church was busy and prosperous. But Christ pronounced the church dead. It is not what a church does, but what a church is, that determines if it is alive.

THE JUICE IS GONE

(Exodus 15:1-27)

One day, my wife, Judy, and I were in my daughter's mini-van with her and two of my precious little granddaughters. The girls sat in their car seats right behind me. Suddenly, the two-year-old threw her juice cup, and it came flying past my head and bounced off the dashboard. My daughter disciplined her, and she started crying. Her sister loudly complained at the noise interrupting the movie playing on her DVD player. There was a complete meltdown in the mini-van. It all started because the younger child ran out of juice. She was unhappy, so she pitched a fit. That is exactly the response of many full-grown Christians when their juice runs out and their cups are empty.

In Exodus 15, the Israelites praised God with the first recorded song in the Bible, because He had saved them from the Egyptian army. By the end of the chapter, however, their juice ran out and their joy cups were empty. When the waters at Marah were bitter, they pitched a fit. When you run out of juice, don't complain. Simply ask Jesus Christ to fill your cup from His endless supply. And, if you stay close to Him, you will never run out again.

APRIL 8

SWEET PERFUME

(Philippians 4:10-23)

What is the most money you have ever paid for a bottle of cologne or perfume? The most extravagant and expensive perfume in the entire world is Clive Christian's Signature No. 1. It comes in a sixteen-ounce bottle made of Baccarat crystal. Hanging on each crystal bottle is a five-carat, pure, white diamond. Signature No. 1 sells for the unbelievably astounding price of $2,150 dollars per ounce. That means that one bottle of Clive Christian's perfume is over $200 thousand. It is no small wonder that there are only ten bottles of Signature No. 1 to be found in the whole wide world.

When Epaphroditus delivered the Philippians' love gift to Paul, he called it *an odour of a sweet smell, ... wellpleasing to God.* The word *odour* means "a sweet smelling fragrance." God is reminding us that our sincere sacrificial gifts and service are a sweet fragrance that is pleasing to His nostrils. That sweet perfume is more valuable than any perfume this world has to offer. In a world that measures desirability by visible and tangible standards, it's often difficult for us to understand that simplicity, humility, and honesty are more pleasing to God than ostentatious and empty gestures.

APRIL 9

THE BIBLE IS RELIABLE

(Zechariah 9:1-17)

In His life, Jesus Christ fulfilled three hundred prophecies that were written long before His birth. Do you know what the odds are of that happening? Here is an analogy that will help you appreciate how staggering that is. If Christ had only fulfilled eight out of three hundred prophecies, it would be comparable to this ... Imagine a fence built around the entire state of Texas and filled two-feet deep by silver dollars, one of which was painted red. If you started blindfolded at the Louisiana border, you would have a better chance of picking up that red silver dollar than one person would have in fulfilling eight prophecies that were written hundreds of years before their birth. Yet Jesus Christ fulfilled all three hundred prophecies down to the smallest detail.

Zechariah prophesied that Jesus would one day ride into the city of Jerusalem on a colt (v. 9). He also predicted Christ would be sold for thirty pieces of silver (Zechariah 11:12) and that His side would be pierced (Zechariah 12:10). The Old Testament prophet made these astounding predictions 450 years before Jesus was born. This is simply another indisputable testimony that the Word of God is alive, powerful, and eternally faithful. You can believe the Bible. It is perfectly reliable.

STAND FAST IN THE LORD

(1 Thessalonians 3:1-13)

A woman in Houston, Texas, was ordered by local police to stop handing out gospel tracts to children who knocked on her door on Halloween. The police told her that it was offensive to those who had other religious beliefs or didn't believe in God at all. Have you noticed that there seems to be an escalating attitude of intolerance, animosity, and hostility toward Christianity in America? Of course, Christians are violently attacked in many foreign countries every single day. Global reports indicate that 150,000 believers are brutally martyred every year. We haven't faced that type of persecution in the U.S. But if our nation continues to abandon biblical standards, Bible-believing Christians will fall under greater attack.

The Thessalonian church experienced many persecutions and afflictions. In First Thessalonians 3, Paul sent Timothy to encourage them to *stand fast in the Lord. Stand fast* means to "remain stationary and don't move." That is a great exhortation for all modern-day saints. Remain firm in your convictions, commitment, and beliefs. Don't back up. Stand fast. Apostasy is already infiltrating the church. If we cannot stand for Christ in our spiritual homes, we can never hope to stand against a concerted attack from outside.

WISDOM

(Proverbs 2:1-22)

An uneducated, hardworking man put up a few advertising signs and opened up a hot dog stand. Before long, his business was booming. He enlarged his stand and put more signs along the highway. Soon, the man was so busy he needed help. One day, he called his college son to come and work for him. The man said, "Son, I am getting rich. I want to share it with you. Come and work for me." His son answered, "Dad, don't you know we are in a recession? The economy is bad. You can't afford to have a business." Foolishly, the man listened. He removed the advertising signs because he thought he couldn't afford them. Sales dropped, and he soon went out of business. He told his wife, "Our son was right. We are in a recession."

Be extremely careful about acting on unwise advice. In Proverbs 2:2, Solomon tells us to *incline* (heed, or give attention) to divine wisdom only. There is a huge difference between the wisdom of the world, and divine wisdom from above. Always seek the wisdom of God. If we obey Him, He will always bless our work. Even a recession has no power against the Word of God.

APRIL 12

WEARING A MASK

(Matthew 26:14-25)

A s a boy, I constantly wore some kind of mask. I had a
Zorro mask and a Lone Ranger mask. But without question, my favorite was my Superman mask. Every afternoon, I
would don my shirt and cape and put on my plastic Superman
mask while I watched those old Superman shows on TV. I would
get so excited, I actually thought I was the superhero. When
the show came on, I'd run around the living room like I was
flying. One day, I ran too close to the end table, knocked the
lamp on the floor, and it shattered. My mother took me to the
room to spank me. However, before the spanking, I removed
my Superman mask. I did it because Superman couldn't get a
whipping.

Judas Iscariot wore a mask. Although he followed Jesus, Judas
was a fake. The other disciples had no clue. Even when Christ
announced that one would betray Him, all of the twelve
responded, *Lord, is it I?* (v. 22). No one suspected Judas. Sadly,
many people who attend church are like Judas. They wear a
Christian mask, but they are not the real deal. Their pretense
betrays the church and the One they profess to serve.

April 13

Divine Dancing

(2 Samuel 6:1-16)

One night, a woman walked up to me after a revival meeting, smiled, and shook my hand and encouraged me. She said she'd been blessed by a message that really touched her heart. Then she quickly informed me that she would not attend the revival the next night because she had to stay home to watch *Dancing with the Stars*. I guess *Dancing with the Stars* was more important to her than worshipping the Bright and Morning Star. It always amazes me that Christians get so worked up and excited about worldly entertainment, yet many of those same believers are so casual when it comes to assembling to praise the name of the Lord together.

In Second Samuel 6, the ark of God was restored to the people. King David was so excited that he spontaneously started dancing before the Lord. Was it undignified for David to act this way? No. His actions were done before the Lord to glorify Him. King David was praising the King of Kings. His dance before the Lord was a divine dance. While we applaud this in worldly circumstances, how many of us are willing to make time to dance in unreserved adoration before our King?

ALWAYS ON TIME

(John 11:1-23)

Do you ever think that God is moving too slowly? We live in a culture that demands instant gratification. We have fast food, instant hair dye, instant laser surgery, instant coffee, and instant messaging. Over two billion instant messages are sent daily. Sixty million photos and five hundred million tweets are sent every twenty-four hours. Now, researchers are designing a computer called the Human Brain Project. It is projected to be a thousand times faster than any computer we have today. Nobody wants to wait on anything, and some Christians get frustrated when God doesn't move when they think He should.

When Jesus heard that His dear friend Lazarus was sick, He purposely waited (v. 6). By the time Christ arrived, Lazarus had been dead for four full days. Martha thought Jesus was late. But she discovered that God doesn't move according to a clock or a calendar. What she thought was a delay ended up with her brother being raised from the dead. Everything God does is part of His eternal purpose, and is not only our blessing but also a testimony to His power and glory. God is always on time.

APRIL 15

GOD'S DEADLINE

(Nahum 1:1-15)

One evening at a pastor's conference, I preached on the subject of revival. At the conclusion of the service, the pastor of a large church approached me and said, "Preacher, we don't have revivals at our church anymore because revivals cost too much." I knew what he meant. It costs to fly in an evangelist, get a hotel, and provide for his meals. It costs to promote, turn on the electricity in the building, and receive money to meet the revival budget. I understood exactly what the pastor was talking about. Revivals cost money. But as he walked away, a thought suddenly occurred to me. *We had better quit asking what it will cost us to have a revival. We had better start asking what it will cost us if we don't have a revival.*

One hundred and fifty years before Nahum, the city of Nineveh had experienced a great revival under Jonah. But they had once again drifted from God. Nahum 1:3 says, *The LORD is slow to anger.* However, when His mercy runs out, judgment falls. We readily accept that certain deadlines in life simply must be kept, but we don't see the danger in not meeting God's deadline. It is time for Christians to wake up.

APRIL 16

THE GREATEST MIRACLE

(Ephesians 2:1-10)

Imagine a man dying from a gunshot wound in his chest who is carried into a miracle-healing service at a revival meeting. The preacher puts his hand on the man's chest and prays. The bleeding stops, the gaping wound closes, and the man is miraculously healed. The people in the crowd would call it the greatest miracle they had ever seen. But suppose the preacher could not perform a healing miracle. Instead, he simply takes the dying man's hand and tells him about the miracle of salvation. Then, in the last minutes of his life, that man prays to receive Jesus Christ and is gloriously saved. Now I ask you, which one of these is the greatest miracle?

There is no greater miracle than the salvation of a lost and dying soul. In the second chapter of Ephesians, the Bible describes what happens when we are saved. Ephesians 2:5 says that a resurrection takes place. We were dead, but we are made alive in Him. The word *saved* in verse 5 means "to be healed." The greatest miracle of all is that of saving grace, yet so many Christians pursue signs and wonders and never share the miracle we can all offer to others.

APRIL 17

ORDER MY STEPS

(Psalm 37:23-40)

Because of a computer glitch, I once lost my reserved seat on an American Airlines flight to Dallas, Texas. I was irritated – after all, the reservation was made months before. My new ticket put me in a middle seat in the last row of the plane. Inwardly, I griped and grumbled over an uncomfortable seat through a long flight. But sitting beside me was a young soldier going to Afghanistan. He was troubled about leaving his new wife for nine long months. I discovered he was a believer. For two hours, I was able to encourage him in the Lord. When we arrived in Dallas, he asked me to pray with him. It was a sweet day. I asked God to forgive me for whining. It was no accident that the computer cancelled my seat. God wanted me in seat 32B to encourage that soldier.

Psalm 37:23 reminds us that our steps are *ordered* (directed) by the Lord. As you start your day, seek His face, and ask God to direct your steps today for His glory. "Order my steps, Lord." If we live our lives for His glory, He has the right to change our plans, change our circumstances, or change our desires.

APRIL 18

A LIFESAVING BOOK

(Acts 8:26-40)

A tough businessman and partner in a successful financial firm was prosperous, but there was deep emptiness in his heart. The depression he felt grew unbearable. One night, in a luxurious hotel in Brisbane, Australia, the desperate man stepped out onto his eighth-floor balcony and looked at the concrete driveway below. About to jump, he glanced back inside the room and saw a Gideon Bible on the nightstand. He later said, "Something told me to read that Bible." He went back inside and reached for the Bible. Before the night was over, Berni Dymet was on his knees, giving his life to Christ. Today, he is a renowned Bible teacher in Australia.

One day, a very important man from Ethiopia sat in his fancy chariot and read from the book of Isaiah about the Lamb of God. God sent a preacher named Philip to talk with him about Jesus. Before the day was over, that Ethiopian man gave his life to Christ and was baptized. When someone opens the Bible, it can save their life. As believers, we must remember that we may be the only "Bible" that some people ever see. Living the Word instead of simply knowing it can save those around us.

APRIL 19

PEACE IS COMING

(Micah 4:1-13)

Planet earth is a violent place. The United Nations defines a *major war* as "a military conflict inflicting one thousand battlefield deaths per year." In 1995, ten major wars were being fought across the globe. By late 2015, there were twenty-seven major wars and 187 military actions taking place at the same time on this troubled planet. Hostile conflicts and battles were actively fought in Syria, Iraq, Afghanistan, Pakistan, Nigeria, Israel, Gaza, Ukraine, Yemen, and South Sudan. Serious armed conflicts raged in India, Uganda, Libya, and Egypt. The entire world seems to have become one big battlefield. Yet there is one place on the globe that has always been a hot spot – the Middle East.

In Micah 4, God's prophet tells of a day when peace and righteousness will reign in the nation of Israel. Mount Zion will be the capital of the world. All armies will be disbanded, and all weapons destroyed. How is peace going to come? It won't occur because of an international peace treaty. Peace is only possible when King Jesus returns and reigns. The rising conflict reveals that His return is near. Look up, and lift up your head, Jesus is coming soon!

FINISH THE RACE

(Hebrews 12:1-13)

In the 1968 Olympics in Mexico City, Tanzanian marathoner John Akhwari finished last. At the twenty-mile mark of the race, John cramped up due to the high altitude. He collided with another runner and fell, badly dislocating his left knee and shoulder when he hit the ground. However, despite his injuries, John Akhwari pressed on and finished the race. By the time he limped into the stadium, John was one hour behind everyone else. There were no longer seventy thousand fans in the stands. Only about two thousand watched as John made his way to the finish line. A reporter asked him why he bothered to finish. John said, "My country did not send me five thousand miles to start the race. They sent me five thousand miles to finish the race."

The Christian life is a race. It's not a sprint, it's a marathon. Many things along the way can weigh us down and even injure us. Hebrews 12:2 reminds us to keep our eyes on Jesus Christ. He finished His race, and He will give you the strength to finish yours.

APRIL 21

WORKING AND WATCHING

(Nehemiah 4:1-23)

It was a beautiful spring Sunday morning, the first day of revival. I was the guest evangelist at an exciting Baptist church. But that day, the pastor stood to make a disappointing announcement. He said, "Folks, we are going to have to cancel Vacation Bible School because we can't get enough workers." His statement stunned me. After all, this was a church with an attendance of well over five hundred people. With all those folks, they couldn't count on enough volunteers to help out with Vacation Bible School. Unfortunately, that's the way it is in many churches today. In the average church, about 10 percent of the folks do 90 percent of the work and service. Many churches struggle today because people won't work.

Nehemiah had the incredible task of rebuilding Jerusalem's walls. In addition to that, he faced great opposition. But the people had a mind to work (v. 6). While one group worked, the others watched, ready for the enemy. The lesson found in Nehemiah 4 should motivate the modern-day church. It is time for God's people to go to work. We are saved for a purpose in His kingdom, not for the pursuit of self-gratification. His work should always come first.

LAST-DAYS LIVING

(2 Timothy 3:1-9)

A storm capsized a sailor's boat, and he was lost at sea. Fortunately, the desperate man was able to cling to a piece of driftwood from his shattered craft. He finally washed ashore on a deserted island. For three long years, he lived on that lonely strip of land in the middle of the ocean. One day, a plane spotted him, and a ship was sent to rescue him. A small boat rowed from the ship to the island. The officer of the rescue party handed the shipwrecked man a newspaper and said, "The captain of the ship wants you to read what's going on in the world and see if you still want to be rescued."

In Second Timothy 3, Paul describes the last days. The word *perilous* is found only once in the whole Bible. It literally means "fierce and dangerous." All you have to do is check the news to realize that we are living in the last days. But God doesn't want us to retreat and hide on an island. He wants His people to be salt and light to a lost world. We are saved not to be removed from the world but to reach it in Christ's name.

GOD'S TEN COMMANDMENTS

(Exodus 20:1-17)

The Freedom From Religion Foundation (FFRF) is a national organization of atheists and agnostics who want public displays of the Ten Commandments taken down from every building in America. For many years, plaques of the Ten Commandments have been prominently displayed in the hallways and classrooms of Muldrow High School in the small town of Muldrow, Oklahoma. But in 2013, the FFRF launched a campaign to remove the plaques from the walls of that school. The organization was met with great resistance. Hundreds of students in the high school rose up in protest and announced that they wanted the Ten Commandments to stay on the walls.

God's Ten Commandments are woven into the fabric of our nation, just as they were for the nation of Israel. They represent the voice of the living God, the very foundation of how to live a life that is pleasing to Him. They define the difference between life and death, and represent the very holiness of God Himself. God's commandments are not obsolete, they are absolute. Americans need to be reminded about the standards that shaped the moral values and principles of this nation. Keep the commandments on the walls. Our world needs them more than ever.

APRIL 24

ANGEL OF LIGHT

(2 Corinthians 11:1-15)

Our student camp theme one year was "Total Makeover." As a visual illustration, I decided to grow a goatee. Now, some men look good with facial hair, but not I. Nevertheless, I kept the goatee for about six months. Several weeks before I shaved it, I preached at a church in Georgia, one I had ministered revival to several times. On Sunday morning, a woman walked up to me and said, "Preacher, shave that thing off. You look like the Devil." I must confess, I am made of flesh, and I responded without restraint. I quickly replied, "How do you know what the Devil looks like? Are you a friend of his?" I doubt if she gave much to the love offering that week.

Truthfully, if you saw the Devil, he wouldn't look scary at all. He doesn't have horns or wear a red suit with a pointed tail. In Second Corinthians 11, Paul talks about false preachers who are slick and deceptive. Then he compares them to our Enemy. Verse 14 says that Satan *is transformed [disguised] into an angel of light,* as something beautiful to deceive and destroy. We should look with our hearts and not our eyes. Appearances alone can deceive us.

BRAVERY

(Esther 7:1-10)

In the book of Esther, we find one of the greatest dramas in the entire Bible. It involves four major characters. First, there was Esther the queen, who was secretly a Jew. Then, there was Persian King Ahasuerus, and Mordecai, Esther's cousin and protector. The last character was the villain, Haman. Satan worked through Haman who convinced the king that the Jews were the enemy. A decree was issued for all Jews to be killed. But Esther boldly revealed Haman's plan to the king (even though it could have cost the Queen's life). Her bravery and her beauty touched the king. He ordered Haman to be hanged on the same gallows that he had erected for Mordecai.

Esther is a beautiful picture of a believer willing to give their all for God. Oriental rulers ruled like gods with an iron hand. Esther realized that entering the king's presence could mean death (Esther 4:16). However, she presented herself as a "living sacrifice" to do God's will. Her selflessness saved her people, exposed the enemy, and ruined Satan's plan. We may not be called into literal danger like Esther, but God still requires us to be a living sacrifice, the living testimony of Christ Himself.

TROUBLE ON THE SEA

(Mark 6:45-56)

The massive cruise ship Triumph is 893 feet long, and was built at a cost of $420 million. It is considered one of the most luxurious jewels of the Carnival fleet. On February 12, 2013, 4,229 vacationers boarded Triumph for a dream cruise, but their dream quickly became a nightmare. A fire broke out in the engine room and stranded the great ship without power and plumbing in the middle of the Gulf of Mexico. For five long days, there was no food, air conditioning, or working toilets. Sewage oozed down the cabin walls, and many people became very ill. After the ship was finally towed back to harbor, news cameras captured the sight of hundreds of passengers falling on their faces and kissing the ground.

As the twelve disciples crossed the Sea of Galilee, their cruise became a nightmare. But before the water took them under, Jesus came walking by. When He stepped into the boat, they were saved. Sometimes, our journey leads us through troubled seas. It's not always easy to look past the thundering waves and roaring winds and see the Savior. But Jesus promised never to leave us nor forsake us. Faith is being sure Jesus is in your boat.

FIRST FRUIT

(Deuteronomy 26:1-11)

A family sat down to dinner one night. Mom brought in the meatloaf and put it at the end of the table. The six-year-old daughter took one look at it and said, "Oh no. Not leftovers again." When the father heard the complaint, he replied sternly, "Young lady, do you know how many people in the world would love a meal like this? Now, before we eat, I want you to say grace. I want you to say thank-you to God for this delicious meatloaf." The little girl looked at her father for a moment. Then, she closed her eyes and prayed, "Thank you, God, for this delicious meatloaf … again tonight." She didn't want leftovers and God doesn't want leftovers either. He doesn't want our leftover time, tithes, or talents. He wants our best.

The Feast of First Fruit was a Jewish feast held in early spring at the beginning of the grain season. No grain could be harvested until the first fruits of the land were brought in and dedicated to the Lord. It is a picture of giving with a grateful heart. As New Testament believers, we should always offer our first fruits. God deserves the best of what He has graciously given us.

A ROYAL RESIDENCE

(Colossians 1:15-29)

Royal residences are places where kings and queens live. There are a number of royal residences occupied by the British royal family. For instance, the Queen of England lives at any one of four different addresses. Her homes are Buckingham Palace, Windsor Castle, Sandringham House, and Balmoral Castle. Passersby can always tell when the queen is in residence. All they have to do is look up at the flagpole on top of the house. The flag known as the Royal Standard of the United Kingdom is always waving over the roof when the queen is inside the house. The same royal flag is also flown on top of the royal yacht when her majesty steps onboard. It signifies that royalty is residing on the property.

Did you know that you are a royal residence? At the moment of salvation, the King of Kings, in all of His sovereign glory and riches, came to live inside you. Colossians 1:27 says, *Christ in you, the hope of glory.* Is His banner flying over your life today? If Jesus Christ is residing in you, people should be able to look at your life and know that the King is at home.

APRIL 29

THE GLORY IS GONE

(Judges 16:4-20)

There is a big church building that was once a powerhouse of praise and glory. Every Lord's Day, hundreds of people flocked there and experienced the mighty, miraculous presence of God. It was an anointed place where the fire of heaven fell and the wind of God blew. But today, that huge building is virtually empty. Just a small group of saints assemble every Sunday. There is no joy, enthusiasm, or passion. Strife, fighting, and pride destroyed that great church. I know the details because I once had the wonderful opportunity to preach there. It was an amazing sight to see the Spirit of God working in that vibrant and exciting congregation. However, that has all changed. The glory is gone.

One of the saddest verses in the Bible is Judges 16:20. Samson thought he still had God's power. But the strength and glory of God was gone. It is a tragedy when God's glory departs from a person, or a church, or a nation. When His glory departs, His anointing goes with it. God will never share His glory. When His people turn inward and focus on themselves, pursuing their own agendas instead of pure worship, He always withdraws His glory and anointing.

DENY YOURSELF

(Luke 9:18-27)

William Borden was the son of the man who founded Borden Dairy. When he finished high school, William's wealthy dad sent him on a world cruise. In China, he met a missionary who led him to Christ and gave him a Bible. William wrote the words "No reservation" inside his Bible. When he graduated college, William turned down the vice presidency of his father's company to be a missionary to China. He wrote the words "No retreat" in his Bible. After one month on the mission field, William died from cerebral meningitis. His body was returned to America. Inside the coffin, William was holding his Bible. When his father opened it, he saw the final entry in the Bible. Before his death, William Borden wrote, "No regrets."

A true disciple of Christ understands the cost of discipleship. In Luke 9:23, Jesus said that a real follower of His must be willing to *deny himself, and take up his cross daily, and follow me.* The Greek word *deny* means "to utterly disown and abstain." William Borden understood what it meant to take up his cross. He served Jesus with no regrets.

THE WRONG WAY

(Proverbs 16:16-25)

On January 1, 1929, the National Football Championship game was played in the Rose Bowl between the California Golden Bears and the Georgia Tech Yellow Jackets. The captain of the Golden Bears was First Team All-American Roy Riegels. During the second quarter of the big game, a Georgia Tech runner fumbled. Roy Riegels scooped up the ball. As he started to run from the pack, Roy somehow got spun around and sprinted the wrong way towards the Golden Bears' own goal line. He ran sixty-nine yards before he was finally tackled by a teammate at the one-yard line. The blunder eventually cost his team a two-point safety. California lost the game and the championship, 8-7. Roy Riegels became known forever as "Wrong Way Roy."

Roy believed he was headed the right way, but was horribly wrong. Proverbs 16:25 says, *There is a way [path] that seemeth right unto a man, but the end thereof are the ways of death.* Many people think they are headed in the right direction in life. But one day, they will discover that the game was lost because they ran the wrong way. Wise counsel and being surrendered to the Holy Spirit will keep us going in the right direction.

KEEP FIGHTING

(1 Timothy 6:11-21)

Aheavyweight boxer was in a championship fight. When the bell ended the first round, the fighter was bleeding profusely under his right eye. His manager tried to encourage him by saying, "He hasn't laid a glove on you." At the end of round two, the boxer's lips and ears were busted wide open. Once more, his manager said, "You're doing great, kid. He hasn't touched you yet." After the third round, the tired fighter staggered to his stool and plopped down. He was a total wreck. His face was bruised and swollen. The optimistic manager blurted, "You are in great shape. He still hasn't hit you." Looking through blurry, bloodshot eyes, the boxer replied, "Then you better watch that referee. Somebody is beating the daylights out of me."

All Christians are commanded to fight, but our fight is not against one another. It is a spiritual battle that is waged daily against the forces of darkness. The word *fight* in verse 12 means "to contend with an adversary." Stand up against the Enemy today and keep on fighting.

STAY AWAY FROM SNAKES

(Genesis 3:1-13)

One evening, I arrived early at the church where I was preaching revival. I decided to walk around outside, enjoy the air, and mentally rehearse my sermon. As I walked down a sidewalk, I saw a snake lying on the pavement right in front of me. Since I was already meditating on my message, I decided to preach to that snake. I looked at the reptile and said, "In the name of Jesus, get off this sidewalk." While I was speaking, a man and his wife walked up behind me. The man asked, "Preacher, what are you doing?" I replied, "I am preaching to this snake." At that moment, the snake slithered off. Without missing a beat, the woman looked at me and quipped, "Brother Rick, I don't think that snake liked your preaching."

You can be sure that one snake out there doesn't like it when the true Word of God is preached, read, and believed. Satan the snake has been attacking God's Word since the Garden of Eden. In Genesis 3, the serpent poisoned Eve's mind by questioning what God had specifically told her (vv. 4-5). His tactics have never changed. Stay in the Book, and stay away from the snake.

MAY 4

JUSTIFICATION

(Romans 5:1-21)

There is a story of a man in England who put his Rolls Royce on a boat and crossed the water to take a vacation on the continent. While driving around Europe, something happened to the motor of his car. He contacted the Rolls Royce factory, and the company flew a mechanic over to fix it. After the vehicle was repaired, the mechanic flew back home. The owner of the vehicle was glad his car was fixed, but he wondered how much it was going to cost. After his vacation, the man waited but never received a bill. Finally, he wrote to Rolls Royce and inquired how much money he owed. He received a brief letter from the office that read, *Dear Sir, there is no record in our files that anything ever went wrong with a Rolls Royce.*

What a fine illustration of justification. Do you know what justification is? It is God's declaration that you are righteous in Christ. Romans 5:9 says that we are *justified by his blood.* Jesus Christ extended His love to us even when we were His enemies (v. 8). If God did that while we were His enemies, how much more will He do for us now that we are saved?

LOOK UP

(Lamentations 3:19-41)

One of the darkest days in American history was September 11, 2001. I met a preacher who has a mission in the inner city of New York. He actually heard the roar and saw the shadow of the second jet fly right over his mission office into the Twin Towers. He testified that all day long, people in the streets looked up at the disaster. It was a great opportunity for ministry. That preacher reminded folks to look up beyond the burning buildings. He told them to look up to the God who is in control. In the book of Lamentations, Jeremiah said those very words to the people of Israel.

Lamentations literally means "funeral poems." The book comprises five funeral songs written by the prophet Jeremiah as he walked around the ruined and burning rubble of Jerusalem. Yet, in the midst of misery, he saw hope. In verses 22-24, Jeremiah tells the people to look up higher than their circumstances. In the midst of shock, grief, and anguish, the helmet of hope offers protection. It is secured by our faith in One who is so much greater than what this world will throw at us. Where do you look when trouble comes?

GETTING WHAT YOU DESERVE

(1 Corinthians 3:11-23)

When I was in the Little League, our teams had animal names. My twelve-year-old team didn't have a cool animal name like the Eagles, Lions, or Tigers. I played for the Possums. All year long, the Eagles made fun of our name. But we were good and ended up playing the Eagles for the championship. The winning team's players would receive individual trophies. I wanted to win so I could shove my trophy into the Eagles' faces. However, we lost the game, 5-4. After the defeat, I was a poor sport, and I refused to shake hands. My father met me at the dugout and asked me why. I slammed my glove in the dirt and yelled, "I want a trophy!" My dad replied sternly, "Get in the car. You are going to get something else when you get home."

When we get home to heaven, we are going to get exactly what we deserve. All who are saved will stand before the judgment seat of Christ. It will be a sobering time for many believers. All who wasted their gifts, abilities, and talents will place the worthless embers of a Christian life (vv. 11-15) at the feet of Jesus. If we give nothing, we will receive nothing.

MAY 7

GREAT GRACE

(Ruth 2:1-19)

Many years ago, evangelist Billy Graham was driving through a small southern town. He was stopped by a local policeman and charged with speeding. Dr. Graham had to go to the city courthouse and pay the fine in person. The judge asked him, "Are you guilty or not guilty?" When he quickly pleaded guilty, the judge fined him. Suddenly, the judge recognized the famous evangelist. He said, "You have violated the law, and the fine must be paid. But I am going to pay it for you." He reached for his wallet, took the ticket, and paid the fine. Later, when Billy Graham told that story at a crusade, he said, "That is exactly how God treats sinners who admit they are guilty. He pays the fine through grace."

Ruth was a Moabite. She was excluded from the temple and was not considered part of God's family. However, she went to work in the fields of a man named Boaz who extended grace to her (v. 10). Eventually, Ruth and Boaz were married. It is a love story of redemption. The same thing happened to you and me at the cross. We – the outsiders – are saved only because of God's great grace.

AN IMPORTANT JOB

(2 Timothy 1:1-18)

A weary executive came home one evening after a grueling day at work. The man was a CEO who managed a firm of two thousand employees. His wife consoled him and said, "You look stressed. Would you like to talk about it?" The man huffed, "You wouldn't understand. I mean, what do you really do?" On hearing those words, the mother of three answered, "Let me tell you about my job, Mister CEO. I am busy all day long socializing three Homo sapiens into the virtues of the Judeo-Christian tradition in order that they might be instruments to help transform the social order into the kind of eschatological utopia that God willed from the beginning of creation. That's my job. Now, tell me one more time, what is it that you really do?"

Being a godly mother might just be the most important job on the planet. In Second Timothy chapter 1, Paul reminds Timothy of his heritage. The young man was raised by a grandmother and a mother who had unfeigned (sincere) faith. Praise God for our mothers. The world measures a woman's worth and success professionally, but being a mother is God's perfect plan to prepare a new generation of righteous, committed believers.

May 9

It's What's Inside That Counts

(1 Samuel 16:1-13)

Who holds the record for the most runs batted in one World Series? The answer is not Babe Ruth or Mickey Mantle. Nor is it some other huge home-run slugger. The answer is Bobby Richardson (who is a Christian). Bobby stood only five feet nine inches tall, and barely weighed 170 pounds. But in the 1960 World Series, the New York Yankees second baseman drove in twelve runs (including six in one game). To this day, that record has never been broken. Bobby was voted the Most Valuable Player of the Series, the only time an MVP was awarded to a player from the losing team. Bobby Richardson's manager called him "the small man with the big heart."

When Samuel went to anoint the next king of Israel, Jesse made the mistake of evaluating his sons by looking at the outside. But the Lord told Samuel that He looks at the inside (v. 7). God chose a small shepherd boy named David to be the king. David was a servant who became a ruler. He was faithful over a few sheep, and God gave him authority over a whole nation. It is the servant-heart the Lord loves, and He will exalt those who humble themselves.

THE PREDATOR

(1 Peter 5:1-14)

One summer day, we took our children and grandchildren to Disney's beautiful Animal Kingdom and the famous animal safari. As we approached the lion compound, I prepared the camera for a picture of those magnificent creatures. But I was greatly disappointed. All the mighty lions were either sleeping lazily under the trees or hiding in the caves. There was nothing menacing or intimidating about them at all. The lions we see in America today are caged, captive, or cartoon characters. They are either locked up at the zoo, trapped behind the bars of a theme park, or animated on a movie screen. It is often hard to imagine how scary they are.

But when Peter wrote his epistle, lions still roamed the Middle East. A wild adult lion is a five-hundred-pound killing machine that can run up to forty miles per hour. It is a predator with thirty razor-sharp teeth that can sever the spine of a bull. In First Peter 5:8, we are reminded that our Enemy prowls about constantly, looking for prey that he can devour (swallow). Familiarity has obscured the real truth of lions, and we're often just as flippant about the Enemy. Spiritual complacency will lead to destruction.

BURDEN FOR REVIVAL

(Amos 2:6-16)

David Brainerd, a missionary to the American Indians in the early 1700s, died of tuberculosis at the young age of twenty-nine. David literally yielded his body to share Christ. The faithful preacher would ride many miles on horseback to preach. He endured freezing weather and slept on the ground, moving from village to village. The power of God rested on him because he was a man of deep prayer. He would kneel in the snow for hours to pray for the Indians. It is reported that David's fervor in prayer for their salvation was so great, the heat from his body would melt the snow within two feet of him. David Brainerd was a preacher with a burden for revival.

Amos the prophet shared this burden. In fact, the name *Amos* means "burden." He was God's man with God's message. In Amos 2, he boldly names the sins of the nation, including greed, adultery, immorality, ingratitude, and drunkenness. Sadly, our nation shares those same sins. We need a burden for revival. We need people willing to weep for the unsaved just as Jesus did, to cry out to God on behalf of the unsaved, and to never stop until they are called home.

MENTAL HEALTH

(2 Corinthians 10:1-11)

A lady said to a psychiatrist, "Doc, please help my husband."
The doctor asked her, "What's wrong with him?" Tearfully,
the woman answered, "I'm afraid that he has lost his mind.
My husband thinks that he is a racehorse." Gently, he took
the wife's hands and said, "What makes you say that?" The
woman replied, "Well, all he desires is to live in a stable. He
walks around on all fours all the time and constantly wants to
eat hay and apples." The esteemed doctor thought for a moment
and said, "Ma'am, I believe that I can cure your husband. But
I'm afraid it is going to take a great deal of time and money."
Quickly, the distraught wife responded, "Money is no object.
He's already won two races."

Sadly, the mind is often food for jest. But it is actually a matter
of life and death. In Second Corinthians 2:3-5, we are reminded
that the mind is a strategic war ground where the Devil desires
to plant his flag. The word *stronghold* literally means "a fortified structure." Our Enemy is fighting to control the spiritual
health of your mind. Even the smallest thought can open the
door to the fort.

GET LOUD

(Psalm 98:1-9)

On the night of September 29, 2014, eighty thousand people assembled at Arrowhead Stadium in Kansas City, Missouri, to watch the Kansas City Chiefs play a football game. But it was highly publicized that they were also there to break the record for crowd noise that had been established at 137 decibels the year before at a football game in another city. During the first quarter of the game, the electronic message board flashed the words "Get Loud." Chief's fans stood and shouted until the volume reached a record level of 142 decibels. Do you have any idea how loud 142 decibels is? That is like standing directly behind a turbo jet when it starts up the engine. In other words, that is earsplitting.

Psalm 98:4 tells us to make a *joyful* and *loud noise* when we open our mouths and sing to the Lord. The word *noise* is a very interesting word. In Hebrew, it means "to sing with an earsplitting sound." God is not telling us to scream and make confusing noises. He is commanding us to sing unto Him with all of our heart and soul. Next time you sing, get loud. It's good practice for when we join with the choir in heaven.

TIME FLIES

(James 4:7-17)

Have you noticed how fast time seems to be flying? Almost anyone you talk to is aware of how rapidly time passes by. People say things like, "Where did the time go?" or "Is it that late already?" Believe it or not, there was an era in American history when things moved at a much slower pace than they do today. For example, in the year 1800, less than 10 percent of all American families even had a clock or a watch in their home. The invention of the alarm clock did not appear until shortly before the beginning of the twentieth century. But today, time has gotten so fast it is measured on computers by something called a nanosecond. Each nanosecond is one billionth of a second. Time is flying faster than ever before.

Scripture gives a sobering look at the brevity and speed of life. In James 4:14, James compares our life to a *vapour* (a mist) that is in the air for a brief moment and then quickly vanishes (disappears) from the scene. You are born for a particular purpose and only put on this planet for a certain length of time. Make it count and fulfill your God-given purpose.

AN UNUSUAL PREACHER

(Numbers 22:20-35)

God's Word tells us that a donkey talked to a man. Many opponents of the Bible laugh at this amazing miracle and say that it is impossible for a donkey to talk. But today, it is possible for a skilled animal surgeon to remove a bark from a chronically barking dog. The medical procedure is called surgical debarking. A veterinarian makes an incision in the dog's throat or enters through the mouth and cuts away the vocal chords, removing the dog's ability to do what God created him to do. But if a man made by God can take away the sound from an animal, can't the same God who made a donkey put words in a donkey's mouth and give the creature the ability to talk? Absolutely.

In the book of Numbers, God told a phony prophet named Balaam that he should not go to a certain place (v. 12). Balaam persisted, and God allowed it, even though Balaam knew he was out of God's will. Along the way, God spoke through an unusual preacher, a talking donkey. Sometimes, God speaks through an unusual mouthpiece. Be sure you are listening. Our preconceived ideas as to how God will speak can mean we miss the message.

MAY 16

JUST ASK

(Matthew 7:1-12)

My granddaughter Jadyn was three years old when she told her parents that her granddaddy was getting her an iPad for Christmas. When she came to my home for Thanksgiving, I asked her what she wanted, and she answered, "I want an iPad." I asked her who was getting it, and she said, "You are." The next afternoon, Jadyn and I were alone. Once more, I asked her who was getting her an iPad. She once again blurted, "You are." I said, "Honey, Granddaddy would love to get that for you. But all you have done is told me that I'm getting you one. You really haven't asked me to get you one." That child smiled sweetly at me, twinkled those beautiful eyes, and said, "Granddaddy, would you please buy me an iPad for Christmas?" I immediately went to Best Buy that night and bought it.

Our gracious and giving heavenly Father wants His children to ask Him. There are three wonderful words found in Matthew 7:7. Those words are *ask*, *seek*, and *knock*. Using the words as an acrostic, the first three letters of each word spell the word *ask* (desire). What do you desire from the Lord today? You are His child. Have a talk with your Father and, as His child, just ask Him.

MAY 17

WHEN THE SUN STOOD STILL

(Joshua 10:6-21)

The sun is the magnificent star at the center of our solar
system. Without it, the temperature of our planet would
be 273 degrees below zero, and earth would be a block of ice.
Without the sun, there would be no photosynthesis, and the
plants that produce life and food would die. There would be no
winds, no flowing rivers, no fossil fuels, and no energy. There
would be no ultraviolet light, which is necessary for the vita-
min D that our bodies need for calcium, stronger bones, and
healthy teeth. Every single day you wake up, the sun is there. It
spins slowly on its axis high above us, providing our life-source.

But there was a day in history when the sun stood still. Five
kings of Canaan joined forces to attack the city of Gibeon for
making an alliance with Israel. As the war raged on, Joshua
asked God to make the sun stand still until Israel vanquished
her enemy (vv. 12-13). That request was honored. The mighty
God, who created the sun, told it to stand still for a day. God
is able to use every part of this universe to accomplish His
purposes or meet our needs if we ask Him.

UNITY

(Ephesians 4:1-16)

Many people don't seem to understand the true definition of the word *unity*. For example, some think that unity means union. But that is not true. The great evangelist Vance Havner once said, "You can tie two cats together by their tails, and throw them over a power line. They will have union, but they won't have unity." How true that is. Some other folks might think that unity means uniformity. However, uniformity is when everyone sounds and thinks exactly alike. Still others may describe unity as unanimity. But none of those three words are adequate. The true definition of unity is best displayed in a Spirit-filled body of believers.

The Greek meaning of the word *unity* found in Ephesians 4 means "all parts combining as one." We have been called into one body, and we are to seek to walk in unity. The unity described here is not organizational uniformity. It is a living organism. Ephesians 4 gives us the grounds of unity (vv. 4-6), the gifts of unity (vv. 7-11), and the goal of unity (vv. 12-16).

LET THE CHURCH SHOUT FOR JOY

(Ezra 3:1-13)

A seventy-year-old woman was worried because her ninety-year-old mother had a date with a ninety-five-year-old man. After all, the senior lady had not been out on a date with a man for a long time, and there was cause for concern. So, the daughter cautioned her mother, "Mama, don't you let him kiss you." The daughter worried all evening, and the next morning, she called to ask how the date went. Her mother replied, "It was awful. I had to slap him three times." When she heard that, the daughter said, "Oh no. Did he try to kiss you?" Her mother answered, "No. I thought he was dead."

Sadly, there are some churches that are like that old fellow. It is difficult to tell whether they are dead or alive. When believers gather, it should be a time of great joy. In the book of Ezra, God's people assembled and shouted with joy even before the temple was built. They celebrated with a time of worship and praise when the foundation was laid. What a great lesson for the blood-bought church. Whenever we are together in God's presence, there should be great joy. The world should see the life of Christ bursting out of us in joyful praise.

LIGHT OF THE WORLD

(John 9:1-25)

Fanny Crosby, a blind woman who wrote some of the most beloved hymns in church history, was not born blind. When she was six weeks old, her eyes became inflamed. A doctor treated her with a poultice that was too strong, and it left her without sight. At the age of thirty-one, Fanny Crosby was saved. During the next sixty-four years of her life, she wrote six thousand hymns. Fanny penned famous songs such as *Blessed Assurance*, *Rescue the Perishing*, and *Near the Cross*. Shortly before her death, she wrote, *I Shall Know Him*. The first verse says, "I shall know my Redeemer when I reach the other side, and His smile will be the first to welcome me." She believed absolutely that the first face she would see would be that of Jesus.

In John 9, Jesus Christ healed a blind man. The Lord did not use conventional medicine. He spat in the clay, put it on his eyes, and bade him wash in the pool of Siloam. The man was cured because he believed Jesus and obeyed. Later, that man boldly told the Pharisees that he had seen the Light of the World. The things of God are seldom seen by the natural eye.

MAY 21

GET UP AND RISE UP

(1 Thessalonians 4:1-18)

One day, every living Christian will audibly hear the voice of Jesus Christ. What a glorious and thrilling prospect. After all, no one has done so for two thousand years. Of course, He speaks to His believers all the time. We hear Him through His Word, His Spirit, and His preachers. We hear His voice through prayer, worship, circumstances, and in the beauty of creation. But for now, He speaks to our hearts. Yet a moment is coming when the saints on the earth and in the grave will audibly hear Him. The same Christ who created the universe, raised the dead, cast out demons, healed the sick, and stilled the storm, is going to shout, and we will hear Him.

First Thessalonians 4:13-18 is a great promise. Verse 16 tells us that the rapture will begin with a shout from the Lord. The word *shout* means "to give a command with great authority." It is a picture of a general ordering his victorious troops to pack up and march out because the battle is over. One day, General Jesus will shout, dead folks will be resurrected, and living saints will rise up to meet Jesus in the clouds. None can resist the voice of God.

MAY 22

SCAPEGOAT

(Leviticus 16:7-22)

A news report mentioned a high school soccer player who became depressed and attempted suicide after the boy's team lost an important tournament game. The winning goal was scored when a ball inadvertently bounced off his leg and into the net. After the match, the young man was so vilified, he tried to take his own life. The truth is, the team lost the game, but they felt they had to blame someone. So the unfortunate player became the scapegoat. A scapegoat is a person who is assigned blame. *Scapegoat* comes from a Hebrew word that means "to remove." The term originated from a ritual found in the book of Leviticus.

On the Jewish Day of Atonement, two goats were chosen for the sin offering. After one goat was killed, the second goat was taken into the wilderness and released. It was a picture of removing sin. Hallelujah! The precious blood of Jesus Christ has removed our sins forever. God Himself testifies to this. The conditions allowing for the Day of Atonement ceased some forty years before the destruction of the temple in Jerusalem, preventing the ritual from taking place again. God would allow no other ritual to replace what Christ did on the cross.

LOVE ONE ANOTHER

(1 John 4:7-21)

One day, a man suffering from a raging fever and severe stomach pains had his doctor run an extensive series of tests. After the last test, the physician entered the examining room with the results. His face somber, the doc addressed the patient. "Sir, I don't know how to tell you this, but you have a rare strand of advanced rabies. I am afraid there is no cure, and your condition is terminal." The man calmly took a pen and a piece of paper and began to write down some names. The doctor placed his hand gently on the man's shoulder and asked, "Are you making out your will?" Never looking up, the man said, "No. I am making a list of all the people I need to bite."

That's a spirit of hatred. But the last fifteen verses of First John 4 remind all Christians that we are to love one another. In fact, some form of the word *love* is found at least twenty-five times in these verses. Christian love does not mean we agree with everything our brothers and sisters think or do. But it means we love them for Jesus' sake and as He did – without reservation.

INFLUENCE FROM THE GRAVE

(2 Kings 13:14-25)

Elisha is one of the greatest heroes of the Bible. The pages of the Old Testament are filled with the exciting exploits and mighty miracles God wrought through His prophet. Elisha was used to raise the dead, cure lepers, restore lost ax heads, capture Syrian invaders, deliver a city, and protect a Shunammite woman. He was also a bold prophet who fearlessly confronted wicked kings, spread the Word, and trained young preachers for the ministry. Even on his deathbed, Elisha counseled the king of Israel and showed him how to fight against the enemies of the Lord (vv. 14-19). Unfortunately, the king's faith was weak, and he didn't claim the victory that would have been his if he had listened to and obeyed the counsel and authority of the prophet of God.

The prophet Elisha was a man so anointed by God that he even had influence from his grave. Second Kings 13 describes pallbearers throwing the body of a dead man into Elisha's grave. The moment the body touched the bones of Elisha, the corpse was revived (made alive). Don't miss the practical application for every believer here. The legacy of a man wholly surrendered to the anointing of God impacts others, even after death.

ONLY BELIEVE

(Acts 4:18-37)

All of us who put our faith in Christ are known as *believers.* The lost world often scoffs and laughs at our faith. But the truth is, everybody puts their faith in something or someone. An atheist will drive a car at high speeds on the expressway, believing that the brakes will work. An agnostic will trust a surgeon they do not know to perform an operation on them. A thirsty person will drink water from a tap, trusting that the water is not poisoned. But there is a difference between that type of faith and Bible faith. After all, those brakes might fail, that surgeon might make a mistake, and that water might be toxic. However, we believe in a God who cannot lie and cannot fail.

In Acts 4:32, the Bible says, *And the multitude of them that believed were of one heart and of one soul. Believe* means "to put your whole trust in." Even in the midst of persecution, the early believers never waffled or wavered. A true believer puts their whole trust in God. The problem faith often presents is that it's so simple. We are taught to question, to reason, and to explain. The Word simply says, *believe.*

THE MOUTHS OF ANIMALS

(Daniel 6:16-28)

It's interesting how many times animals' mouths are mentioned in the Word of God. In the very first book of the Bible, a wicked snake opened his lying mouth and messed up the whole world. After the flood, Noah removed an olive leaf from the open mouth of a dove (Genesis 8:11). Later, a donkey opened his mouth and talked to a disobedient man (Numbers 22:28), a great fish opened his mouth and swallowed a backslidden preacher (Jonah 1:17), and a rooster opened his mouth and crowed after Peter denied Christ (Luke 22:60). Throughout the Bible, there are many examples of animals, birds, or fish opening their mouths.

In Daniel 6, however, the animals' mouths were closed. King Darius had passed a decree banning prayer to anyone other than him for thirty days. This didn't stop Daniel from his daily prayer time. He was arrested and thrown into a den of hungry lions. But God sent His angel to shut (close up) the mouths of the lions. The lions in the den were no match for the Lion of the tribe of Judah. God is in control of everything. God will use His creation for His purposes, in ways both expected and unexpected. He is eternally sovereign.

CHILDREN OF LIBERTY

(Galatians 4:19-31)

A man saw a bratty little boy beating a birdcage with a stick. Inside the cage, a small, terrified bird was frantic. The man asked, "What are you doing?" Grinning, the boy answered, "I'm messing with this bird. Then, I am going to feed him to the cat." The man said, "I want to buy him from you." They agreed on an amount, and quickly, the man took the cage, opened the door, and released the bird. Startled, the boy asked, "Why did you buy that bird and then let him fly away?" The man answered, "I bought the bird so I could save him from you and set him free." That is what happened to me. I was in the Devil's cage. He was going to throw me in hell. But Jesus bought me so He could save me and set me free.

In Galatians 4, Paul uses an allegory of Abraham's two sons, Ishmael and Isaac. Ishmael, a slave's son, pictures the flesh. Isaac was the promised son. The two boys represent the old covenant of law and the new covenant of grace. This means that Christians, under grace, are children of promise (v. 23), and children of the free (v. 31). We have been set free.

GOD'S CALL

(Nehemiah 2:1-20)

When I was in the fourth grade, I wanted to be a baseball broadcaster. All through middle school, that was my heart's desire. I constantly memorized baseball statistics and sports pages. I would sit for hours and call imaginary games on my little reel-to-reel tape recorder. My number-one goal in life was to be a sportscaster for a World Series. In high school, I began to look for colleges that produced outstanding sports journalists. But when I was a junior in high school, everything suddenly changed. That is when God placed a clear, unmistakable call on my life to be a preacher of the gospel. I accepted that call, and I have never looked back.

Nehemiah had a very prominent job. He was the cupbearer for the king of Persia. But 750 miles away, the walls of Jerusalem were torn down. They needed to be rebuilt. God called, and Nehemiah answered. He quit working for the Persian king and went to work for Heaven's King. Our personal dreams and God's purposes do not always line up. A surrendered life means obedience, even when we don't want to. But God's purposes are perfect, abundantly more than we could ever imagine for ourselves.

BEWARE OF DOGS

(Philippians 3:1-12)

O nce, during a revival, I was invited to eat lunch with a sweet family. My host pastor picked me up at the hotel, and we headed to their house out in the country. When we arrived, I exited the car and headed for the front door. I noticed a big, bright sign on the porch that said, "Beware of Dog." Immediately, my head swiveled, and I looked for the killer dog. The man of the house greeted us. I asked, "Is the dog here?" Both he and the pastor laughed. At that moment, a little Chihuahua came running out. The homeowner chuckled, "Preacher, this is the only dog that we own. I only have that warning sign up to keep solicitors and Jehovah's Witnesses out of the yard."

When Paul said, *Beware of dogs* (v. 2), he wasn't kidding. *Dogs* was a derogatory term for those who did not share "pure" faith. His warning to Philippian believers concerned phony teachers who emphasized that Jewish rites and rituals were necessary for salvation. He warned that religion opposes relationship. The great apostle was reminding the church that knowing religion will get you into the church, but knowing Christ will get you into heaven.

SOMETIMES YOU NEED A NAP

(1 Kings 19:1-18)

Sleep experts at the Mayo Clinic say that a power nap of no more than twenty to thirty minutes in the afternoon is beneficial. Studies show that this promotes performance, reduces stress, improves mood, and enhances learning. In the book of First Kings, Elijah needed, amongst other things, a power nap. He had just defeated 450 prophets of Baal when he called fire down on Mount Carmel. But only a few verses after that great victory, the great preacher was running from a woman named Jezebel. She put a contract out on his life, and Elijah was scared, weary, and discouraged. He even asked God to take his life. But God graciously refreshed his servant with food and rest.

After pouring yourself out in ministry, make sure to get proper rest. The truth is, Elijah was flat-out worn out, and he moved his eyes off of God and onto Jezebel. It is wonderful to give everything you have to the Lord. Just remember to take the time to be refreshed so that you can be used again. After his rest, God took Elijah to Mount Horeb and spoke to his heart, then released him to work to prepare for even greater things to come.

MAY 31

ALL-POWERFUL

(Revelation 19:1-10)

B rian Shaw is a muscular mountain of a man who lives in Colorado. He stands six feet eight inches tall and weighs four hundred pounds. On April 26, 2015, Brian Shaw won the international strongman competition in Malaysia. What he accomplished was mind-boggling. Brian became the strongman champion by deadlifting 880 pounds, bench-pressing 850 pounds, and lifting eight Hummer tires on a steel rod that weighed a total of one thousand pounds. The morning after winning the title, his hometown was understandably proud. The local paper had a huge picture and article on the front page. In big letters, the headline read, *BRIAN SHAW, MOST POWERFUL MAN ON EARTH.*

Brian Shaw is a powerful man, but he has neither all power nor the most power in heaven or on earth. Our mighty God holds that distinction. There is one word that describes God's power. It is only found once in the entire Bible (v. 6). That word is *omnipotent* (all-powerful). It's easy to get distracted by those in this world who possess or project visible power, but the Bible reminds us that *greater is he that is in you, than he that is in the world*. Almighty God is omnipotent, and His power is beyond measure.

JUNE 1

AFTER THE FUNERAL

(Deuteronomy 34:1-12)

Three of the largest funerals in history have occurred in this generation. Princess Diana was one of the most famous and most photographed people in the entire world. After her tragic death in 1997, three million mourners lined the streets of London to witness her funeral procession. In 2005, one million people attended the funeral of Pope John Paul II in Rome. The funeral service of pop singer Michael Jackson was broadcast around the globe in 2009. Billions watched on satellite television, thousands attended the invitation-only service in person, and close to one million more stood outside of the Staples Center in Los Angeles in the hot June sun to watch the service broadcast on a big screen.

Only God attended the funeral of Moses. The location of his grave is a mystery to this day (v. 6). He was allowed to see the Promised Land, but never entered it (v. 4). Although no one else was at Moses' funeral, the One who was in attendance made his funeral the greatest ever. It is one thing to be honored with a big funeral, but the real measure of our lives will be found in our heavenly welcome. Our status and identity in Christ is all that matters in eternity.

YOU HAVE BEEN WARNED

(Luke 22:14-34)

Elvis is an eight-foot-long king cobra living in a suburb of Orlando, Florida. In September of 2015, Elvis slithered from his cage and escaped. For one month, the huge venomous snake remained at large. One morning, a woman named Cynthia was drying clothes in her garage when she heard an ominous sound. Each time she put a load of clothes in the dryer, Cynthia noticed a loud hissing sound coming from behind it. The quick-thinking woman called the Orange County Animal Control and they captured Elvis. A spokesman commended Cynthia for not looking behind the dryer to identify the sound. He said, "The woman was smart enough to heed the warning that there was a snake."

At the Passover meal, Jesus told Peter that he would deny Him. Peter arrogantly pledged his allegiance to Jesus, but He warned him that Satan wanted to *sift* (tear) him as wheat. Sifting was the violent process of separating the grain from the husk. Jesus was warning Peter that the Devil wanted to tear him apart. Peter must have learned, in hindsight, the value of this warning. He reminded us that the Enemy is a hungry lion looking to devour us and we must remain alert. Be smart enough to listen.

IT'S JUST GOT TO COME OUT

(1 Samuel 2:1-11)

During an important college football playoff game, the Ohio State Buckeyes beat the Alabama Crimson Tide. After the game, a female wearing a Crimson Tide shirt was leaving the stadium. Suddenly, a woman from Ohio State approached and began to taunt her. The Alabama woman instantly slapped her adversary and started to beat her up. After her arrest, the Crimson Tide fan was questioned about her behavior. She blurted out, "I can't help it. I'm just too full of Alabama, and it's just got to come out." Although we must never be violent and belligerent, all true believers should share the same consuming zeal. If we are full of Jesus, He has just got to come out.

In First Samuel 2, Hannah was full of worship. She prayed for a son and vowed to give him to the Lord. After God blessed her with Samuel, Hannah overflowed with praise. Verse 1 says Hannah *prayed* (praised), *rejoiced* (leaped for joy), *exalted* (lifted high), and *enlarged* her mouth (opened wide and shouted for victory). Hannah was full, and it just had to come out. A life filled with Christ will automatically manifest and reveal Him to the world. He is the living water that must spill out.

OVERWHELMED BUT NOT OVERCOME

(2 Corinthians 4:8-18)

A young country doctor, just starting out in his practice back in the era when doctors made house calls, received a call from a desperate man. "Come quick, my wife is sick." Grabbing his black bag, the doctor hurried to the farmhouse, entered the bedroom, put the husband out, and shut the door. In a moment, the door opened, and the doc said, "Get me a screwdriver." The man obeyed. Two minutes later, the doctor opened the door and cried, "Get me a pair of pliers!" A few minutes later, the frantic doctor said, "Get me a hammer and chisel!" Finally, the farmer screamed, "Wait a minute! What's wrong with my wife?" The doc answered, "I don't know. I can't open my bag."

Sometimes we are overwhelmed, and it often seems like there is no solution. But in Second Corinthians 4, God assures us that although *We are troubled [afflicted] on every side*, we will not be destroyed (vv. 8-9). We walk by faith and not by sight. After all, the suffering of this world is only temporary. You may seem overwhelmed today, but you are not overcome. Turn to God first before trying anything else. He has already provided the perfect solution for everything.

JUNE 5

THE WRONG ALTAR

(2 Chronicles 28:16-27)

One of the most evil kings in Judean history was King
Ahaz. He worshipped a demon god called Moloch. He
sacrificed his own son to Moloch by throwing him alive into
the fire in the Valley of Hinnom (2 Chronicles 28:3). Later,
that same valley was cursed by God and turned into a garbage
dump. It is the place that Jesus pointed to in a New Testament
sermon as a symbol for hell. One of King Ahaz's last acts of
defiance happened when he saw a pagan altar in Damascus. He
made the grave mistake of trying to duplicate that same altar
in the temple at Jerusalem.

The new altar built by the wicked king replaced the God-ordained
altar in the temple. When Ahaz brought the world into the
church, God had enough. King Ahaz ended his sixteen-year
reign in shame, misery, and defeat. His mistake is a great lesson
for the church. Sadly, these are the days when many churches
try to imitate the world by looking and sounding exactly like
it. When the world gets into the church, we are kneeling before
the wrong altar. Compromise is building altars to idols in God's
house. He will not share His glory.

SIN'S D-DAY

(Mark 15:33-47)

Tuesday June 6, 1944, is D-Day. It is the day on which more than 160,000 Allied troops landed along a fifty-mile stretch of heavily fortified French coastline to fight Nazi Germany on the beaches of Normandy. It was the largest seaborne invasion in history. More than five thousand ships supported the amphibious landings on five Normandy beaches given the codenames of Utah, Omaha, Gold, Juno, and Sword. D-Day will forever be known in military history as "The Longest Day." When the fierce battle was finally over, and the sandy beaches were soaked with blood, over ten thousand Allied soldiers, including five thousand Americans, had given their lives. D-Day broke the hold of Hitler on Europe. It was a great day of liberation and victory and an end to the tyranny that had exterminated between five and six million of God's chosen people.

On a bloody hill called Calvary, sin had a D-Day. It was the day that Jesus Christ stormed the gates of hell and invaded the strongholds of Satan. Mark records the solitary agony of Jesus on the cross (v. 34). When the battle was over, sin had been defeated and Christ had won. A single Man, alone, accomplished what even the greatest army cannot.

WHAT ARE YOU LOOKING AT?

(Psalm 121:1-8)

If you put a buzzard in a pen six-feet square and leave the top completely open, the buzzard will not fly away. Although there is a large opening, the big bird will be a prisoner. In order to take flight, a buzzard needs a running start of about ten to twelve feet. Without this, a buzzard won't even attempt to escape. If you drop a bumblebee into an open jar, it will stay there until it dies. It will never make an effort to fly out from the top of the container. Instead, the bumblebee will persist in futilely buzzing around the sides or bottom of the jar, hopelessly looking for a way out. Both the buzzard and the bee will be bound because neither of them will try to escape by looking up.

Very often in the Christian life, we are held captive because we fail to look up. Our circumstances and situations surround us and suffocate us. Many times, we look around us, searching for a way out. Psalm 121:1 says, *I will lift mine eyes unto the hills.* The word *hills* means "mountains, or that which is above us." When you get boxed in, look up and see your Savior.

JUNE 8

THE ANTICHRIST

(2 Thessalonians 2:1-17)

There has always been a fascination with the Antichrist. For many years, people have speculated about his identity. For example, biblical numerologists often take a man's name and use the letters of the alphabet to equal the number 666. The simple equation is done by assigning values, such as 100 to the letter A, 101 to the letter B, and so forth. It all started in the 1930s, when a preacher applied the formula to spell the name *Hitler*. Since then, it has been used on Kennedy, Clinton, and Obama. If you Google "Who is the Antichrist?" you will get about 1.5 million hits. One website insists that the president of the United States must be the Antichrist because the presidential limo is nicknamed "the beast."

Of course, if you keep working the numerology formula, you can make anyone the Antichrist. The truth is, no one knows who he is. Paul reminded the Thessalonians not to be shaken in any way, when writing about the end times (vv. 2-3). Scripture tells us that the coming Antichrist will be the *son of perdition* (destruction). He will wreak havoc in the world. He will be the visible manifestation of Satan through possession. He will be Satan's final, desperate attempt to rule the world.

WATCHMAN

(Ezekiel 3:4-17)

In ancient times, large watchtowers were built into the walls surrounding cities. The man who stood on that tower was called the watchman and fulfilled very important roles. Firstly, he watched for invading enemies. Whenever a threat appeared, he would sound the alarm, and the city would close its gates and prepare for battle. Secondly, as harvest time neared, the watchman watched over the fields as the crops ripened. He stood guard and watched so that animals or thieves could not steal the crops. If a predator appeared, the watchman would raise a loud vocal warning. Finally, a watchman also stood vigil observing the daily business life of the city, looking for cheating or improprieties.

No wonder God used the role of the watchman to illustrate the work of His prophets. In Ezekiel 3:17, God told Ezekiel that he was a watchman over the house of Israel. *Watchman* literally means "to lean forward, observe, and sound the alarm." We need watchmen on the wall today. As disciples and followers of Christ, our task is to identify the danger and sound the alarm against deception and destruction that threaten His people. We are God's mouthpiece, and survival depends on our alertness and willing, faithful commitment.

JUNE 10

HIS WORD WILL STAND

(1 Peter 1:13-25)

I once preached a revival meeting only twenty miles from home. It rained as I left the service on Sunday night. My hands were full as I quickly opened the car door. In my haste to get in, I somehow left my Bible sitting on the roof of the vehicle. When I arrived home, I realized I had lost it. Several days later, a woman called our office. She had found a Bible in the middle of a wet road with my name inside. I feared it was destroyed, but when my Bible was returned, I saw an amazing sight. Although the Word of God had lain on a busy road for twenty-four hours, in a hard rain, not one page was marred or destroyed. Immediately, I thought of a promise that is found in Scripture.

Peter told us that the grass withers and the flower fades away, but the Word of the Lord will endure (remain and stand) forever. If Christians are to walk in holiness (vv. 15-16), we must purify ourselves daily by the Word of God. The instructions, counsel, and advice of this world will navigate you down the wrong path. Saturate yourself with the Word. It will not fail you.

JUNE 11

A NEW WORLD COMING

(Isaiah 65:11-25)

I was eating lunch one day at the airport in Charlotte, North
Carolina, before boarding a flight back to Jacksonville,
Florida. At that moment, a dad and mom and three beautiful
little girls sat down at a table near me. The girls all wore glit-
tering shirts with a Disney princess emblazoned on the front.
On top of their heads were mouse ears. I asked them, "Now,
where are you girls going today?" Almost in perfect unison, the
three precious children beamed, and shouted, "We are going
to Disney World!" I said, "Do you know that I live in Florida?
In fact, I don't live very far from Disney World." Quickly, one
of the girls answered, "You are lucky." Her mother smiled and
replied, "They think that there is no place on earth like Disney
World."

This troubled old world still has some places that are beautiful
for adults and magical for children. However, the most gorgeous places in this world cannot compare to the new world
that is coming. Isaiah writes about the kingdom age when there
will be abundant peace and prosperity. Wild predators will eat
together with animals that were once their prey, and the beautiful presence of the Lord will fill it completely.

HUSBANDS AND WIVES

(Ephesians 5:22-33)

Two men who worked together were talking one morning on a coffee break. One fellow was frustrated because of an argument he had with his wife the evening before. The man asked his friend and co-worker, "Do you and your wife get along well? Do you ever have a difference of opinion?" Without hesitation, the guy sipped his coffee and replied, "Of course, we have differences of opinion all the time. But we always get over them very quickly." Puzzled by his strange answer, the man asked, "How do you do that?" The friend replied, "It's simple. I never tell her about it."

Marriage was not designed to be a battle or a burden. It is a holy covenant established and ordained by God Himself. Wives are to submit (v. 22) to their husbands under the Lordship of Christ. The husband is to love his wife as Christ loves the church. That is a sacrificial and unselfish kind of love (v. 25). A godly marriage is a marriage that is made in heaven. If a husband and wife wholly seek the happiness of the other, self becomes unimportant. Conflict is always created when self comes first. Remove self, and you remove the problems.

WALK IN INTEGRITY

(Proverbs 19:1-11)

At 11:38 a.m. (EST) on the chilly morning of January 28, 1986, the Space Shuttle Challenger lifted off from Cape Canaveral, Florida. There was great excitement and media attention around the historical launch. One of the seven astronauts on board, a New Hampshire social studies teacher named Christa McAuliffe, would be the first citizen in space. Christa would teach lessons to American students from the depths of outer space. However, seventy-three seconds into the flight, the shuttle broke apart and exploded over the Atlantic Ocean, killing everyone onboard. The official NASA report said, "Challenger disintegrated because the integrity of two rubber O-rings in the rocket boosters failed."

When integrity fails, it always leads to disaster. That not only applies to machinery, metal, engines, and equipment, but it is also true in life. In Proverbs 19:1-4, Solomon reminds us that it is far better to be poor and have integrity (moral uprightness, honesty), than to have importance and wealth and be a person with no character. Walk with integrity today. Wealth, possessions, status, and power can all be lost, but integrity is an integral part of who you are. The world cannot take it from you. Yield it up, and you destroy who you really are.

June 14

Keep Growing

(2 Peter 1:1-11)

The sound of my cell phone told me I had a text coming in. I looked and saw a photo from my daughter Jessica of my sweet four-year-old granddaughter modeling clothing. They were buying school clothes because my daughter's firstborn child was about to enter preschool. Underneath the photo, there was a caption from Jessica. My daughter said, "Out shopping for school clothes. I can't believe she is about to go to school. It's kind of sad." I quickly answered, "Yes it is. Get used to it." That is life. Our children grow up quicker than we ever imagined. They get bigger and taller day by day. It would be abnormal if our children were not constantly growing up.

It is the same way for a child of God. Peter starts verse 5 with *And beside this.* There is something beyond salvation. After we are born into God's family, we must be constantly growing into spiritual things (vv. 5-7). When a Christian is not growing, there are three ugly characteristics that reveal themselves. That believer is barren, unfruitful, and blind (vv. 8-9). Our spiritual life must follow the same path as our physical life. We are born, we mature, and we reproduce. Our purpose is to produce fruit – other believers.

JUNE 15

TURN! TURN! TURN!

(Ecclesiastes 3:1-15)

In late October of 1965, an American folk rock band called The Byrds released a popular song called *Turn! Turn! Turn!* The group wrote the musical chords and tune for the song. But the lyrics were adapted almost word for word from the first nine verses of the third chapter of the book of Ecclesiastes. The song very quickly became a mega international hit, and on December 4, 1965, it climbed the charts and hit number one. In fact, the song still holds the distinction as the number-one hit with the oldest lyrics ever written. *Turn! Turn! Turn!* was not really written in 1965. The words have been around for thousands of years. They were first authored by King Solomon and inspired by Almighty God.

Although The Byrds' song became a catchy tune, they failed to mention something very important. Verse 15 reminds us that *God requireth that which is past.* In other words, we are accountable for the time that God gives us. Use the time wisely that God has granted to you. Like the servants with the talents, we will all be judged by what we have done or not done with the gifts God has given us for use in His kingdom purposes.

THE PASTOR'S OFFICE

(Titus 1:1-16)

I once preached revival in a rural church. One night, a man asked if some of the men could pray with me before the service. I immediately noticed that there were ten or twelve men in the room, but not the pastor. One of the men spoke up. "Preacher, we want you to give us some advice on the best way to fire our pastor." I was appalled, and I quickly did two things. First, I told those men sternly that their action was unbiblical and I would have no part in it. Next, I informed the pastor. Obviously, we didn't have much of a revival that week. Those misguided men didn't respect or understand the office of the pastor.

Paul left Titus in Crete to organize the church there. In verse 5, he uses the words *set in order,* a medical phrase that describes a physician setting a broken bone. The church is a body, and sometimes the pastor (bishop) must be a spiritual physician and set some bones. He may offend some people by doing what is required of him by God, but the office of the pastor is a holy and God-given office. Pray for your pastor today.

WRESTLING WITH THE LORD

(Genesis 32:22-32)

Wrestling has been around since the dawn of time. The first signs that wrestling existed since the earliest days of the earth were verified when archaeologists found primitive drawings of wrestlers on the walls of caves in France. In the beginning, wrestling was often used as a means of settling disputes without using weapons. However, somewhere along the way, wrestling became a sport. In fact, some wrestling holds that are still used today were thought to have originated as far back as ancient Babylon and Egypt. When the Olympic Games began, the sport of wrestling was the number-one event. The first recorded wrestling match in the Olympics took place in ancient Greece around 708 BC.

But the real first documented wrestling match took place in Genesis. Jacob was journeying to meet with his estranged brother, Esau. While he camped, a man wrestled with him. However, the man was not an assailant. He was an Old Testament appearance of Jesus Christ. Jacob wrestled with the Lord, and received a blessing. That night, his name was changed to Israel. Wrestling is an intense, physical, contact sport. Wrestling in prayer is something all believers are called to do. It challenges us to an all-encompassing, transforming encounter with God.

JUNE 18

IT IS FINISHED

(John 19:28-42)

General Jonathan Wainwright commanded the Allied forces in the Philippines during World War II. He received the Medal of Honor for his courageous leadership. During a battle near the war's end, Japanese soldiers captured General Wainwright. He was taken to a prison camp and endured unspeakable torture. Every single day, he was beaten and interrogated by his captors. One day, a plane landed in the camp with the news that the war was over. General Wainwright heard the announcement. The next day, by sheer habit, the Japanese came to his cell to beat him. Jonathan Wainwright boldly said, "I know that the war is over, and we have won. Put down your weapons. You are now my prisoners."

On the cross, Christ said, *It is finished.* In the Greek, this phrase was just one word. Merchants used that word to mean "the price is paid in full." On the cross, Jesus finished the battle and won the victory. You don't have to remain defeated by the Enemy. Too many Christians haven't grasped the full meaning of the good news. The Devil would love to deceive them into remaining in bondage and defeat. Jesus won the war, so tell Satan you have won. It is finished.

THE GRACIOUS KING

(2 Samuel 9:1-13)

The ninth chapter of Second Samuel is one of the greatest stories in the Word, a magnificent Old Testament picture of New Testament salvation. King David had made a covenant with Jonathan years before (1 Samuel 20:11-23), so the king was committed to show kindness to Jonathan's family (v. 3). Jonathan had a crippled son named Mephibosheth, who lived in poverty. King David sent the royal chariot to fetch him. Much to the young man's confusion and astonishment, he was moved into the palace and treated like royalty. From that day forth, Mephibosheth ate all of his meals at the king's table (v. 10). It happened only because David had made a covenant with Jonathan.

Think about the parallels. Mephibosheth was born into a rejected family. He was lame and dying. David reached out to him personally, took him into his royal family, and provided for his every need. That is New Testament Christianity. The only reason you are sitting at the King's table today is because the Father made a covenant with His Son on your behalf. To God, covenants are sacred, unbreakable agreements. If we could live in the certainty of every single promise, we would live in the power of God.

FAITHFUL FATHERS

(Colossians 3:16-25)

After a revival service, I overheard a rather loud conversation in the church lobby between a father and his son. The boy, who appeared to be about twelve or thirteen, asked his dad for permission to go somewhere with some guys. When the father said no, the angry son immediately and publicly retorted, "Why not? I hate you." The dad just smiled at his boy and answered, "Because I love you, that's why." What a great response from that wise father. He understood the true meaning of Colossians 3:21. Sadly, some fathers have misinterpreted that verse to mean "Never do anything to make your children angry." That is not what that verse means. Sometimes children will get angry at their parents.

A father doesn't provoke his children to anger when he corrects them, tells them no, or forces them to do something they don't want to do. But a father can provoke a child to anger when he does things such as showing favoritism, belittling them, insulting them, or taking no interest in their life. Faithful fathers love children enough to raise them in the nurture of the Lord. We are to treat our children as God treats us, with fairness, wisdom, and godly authority.

JUNE 21

TEARING DOWN OBSTACLES

(Joshua 6:1-20)

A man teaching a Sunday school class of young boys suddenly said, "I want you boys to tell me who tore down the walls of Jericho." The boys shrugged and looked around at each other. Adamantly, the teacher said it again. Once again, the pupils shrugged their shoulders. Finally, one brave boy stood and said, "We don't know who tore down the walls. But don't blame us. We didn't do it." After class, the discouraged teacher saw a deacon in the hallway. He said, "I feel like quitting. Did you know my class didn't even know who tore down the walls of Jericho?" The deacon put a sympathetic arm around him and replied, "That's no reason to quit. I don't know who tore down those walls either."

The walls of Jericho were impenetrable and imposing. But Joshua's army learned that when they used spiritual weapons, their faith could overcome any obstacle (v. 20). The walls fell because God tore them down. We miss out on so much critical truth when we don't study the Word. It reveals God, and it reveals what He can and will do. How big is your wall? It is not too high for God to bring it down.

NEVER-CHANGING

(Hebrews 13:1-8)

I have frequently had the privilege to preach at one particular church, but my schedule, at one time, did not allow me to return there for three full years. At the first service of the revival, a sweet woman walked up to me and said, "Brother Rick, you never change." Of course, I assured her that I had changed, and I joked with her that she just might need some new glasses. People change every single day. For example, I hate to break it to you, but you will lose about seventy hairs on your head today. Also, you will be taller in the morning than you will be at night. On top of that, every three to five days, you will grow a brand new stomach lining. From birth until death, you are in the process of constantly changing.

Jesus Christ never changes. Hebrews 13:8 promises us that our great Savior is the *same yesterday, and to day, and for ever.* Our Lord has no bad days, mood swings, or personality changes. He never gets tired, fatigued, or has too much on His plate. The King of Kings does not need a vacation, nap, or weekend getaway to be refreshed. He is perfect and He is eternal.

JUNE 23

GOD'S HOUSE

(1 Chronicles 22:1-19)

There are some luxurious and costly buildings in this world. The two most expensive structures on the planet are both located in Singapore. Those magnificent five-star hotels are the Marina Bay Sands, constructed at a staggering cost of $6 billion, and the Resorts World, which was completed at a price of $5.4 billion. Next on the list is the Emirates Palace Hotel in Abu Dhabi. It was built at a cost of $4.46 billion. The fourth most expensive building is the $4.16-billion Cosmopolitan Resort located on the Las Vegas strip. Rounding out the top five is the $4-billion skyscraper known as The Shard in London. Altogether, the five most expensive buildings in the world were built at a total cost of around $24 billion.

It has been estimated that if Solomon's temple were built today, it would cost in excess of $400 billion. David could not build it. So, in First Chronicles 22, the king commissions his son Solomon to construct the temple. Verses 14-16 describe some of the building materials. God intended for His house to be magnificent (v. 5) and to exceed anything man could ever build on his own. It's a reminder that He is sovereign.

JUNE 24

EXCUSES, EXCUSES, EXCUSES

(Luke 14:15-24)

I heard about a pastor who was troubled because church attendance was declining. It seemed that many of the folks were excusing themselves from church because of sports schedules. Consequently, the pastor sent out a letter to every member of the congregation. The headline of the letter read, "I Quit Sports." Then, the pastor listed the reasons he was quitting. (1) The sound system is too loud. (2) Every time I go, they want money. (3) The people who sat near me weren't friendly. (4) The coach never came to visit me. (5) The referee made a decision I didn't like. (6) All the games are too long. (7) The band played some songs I didn't like. (8) I recently read a book on sports, and I believe I know more than the coach.

Jesus knows all about excuses. Luke describes three specific men who made excuses why they couldn't accept an invitation to a great supper. Ultimately, all those who made excuses were excluded. It is a dangerous thing to let other things keep you away from Jesus. The Bible is filled with phrases like *seek ye first, deny yourself, and love Him with all of your heart.* We cannot serve God only when it's convenient.

GIFTED CHILDREN

(Exodus 4:1-17)

Can you imagine the look on Moses' face after he threw the rod on the ground and instantly it turned into a snake? Then God told Moses to *Put forth thine hand, and take it by the tail.* Are you kidding me? Some scholars believe that Moses had a stuttering problem. This could be where his stutter started. Moses took one look at that big snake and said, "W-w-what d-d-did y-y-you s-s-say?" But Moses did pick that snake up, and it once more became a wooden rod. Next, God performed the miracle of turning Moses' hand leprous and then restoring it. After all that, Moses still did not believe that God could use him for the great task at hand.

Moses didn't seem to fully understand that he was a gifted child. All that he could say was, "I can't." He looked at his own flaws and failures instead of at God's power. The same God who made a man's mouth can use that man's mouth for His glory. If God tells you to do something, He has gifted you to do it. Use your gift today for His purpose and trust Him to empower, enable, and equip. His strength is made perfect in our weakness.

A STANDING OVATION

(Acts 7:51-60)

The standing ovation is considered to be one of the highest forms of honor and tribute that can be paid. Standing ovations are routinely given for great theatrical productions, concerts, and sporting achievements. Reportedly, the longest recorded standing ovation ever occurred on June 30, 1991, at an opera house in Vienna. That night, people stood and enthusiastically applauded Spanish opera singer Placido Domingo during a performance of *Othello*. The standing ovation lasted for eighty minutes and 101 curtain calls. In the summer of 1995, when baseball star Cal Ripken Jr. broke Lou Gehrig's record for the most consecutive games played at 2,131, the crowd at Camden Yards in Baltimore stood and cheered for twenty-two straight minutes.

Jesus Christ stood in honor of a man. In the book of Acts, a preacher named Stephen boldly confronted the religious leaders of his day. In anger, they stoned God's man to death. As Stephen was being attacked, he looked up and saw Jesus standing up. Hebrews 10:12 says that Jesus *sat down* after He got to heaven. Acts 7:55 says that Stephen looked up into heaven and saw Jesus *standing*. Whether others recognize our achievements or not, the only accolade that has any real, eternal value is Christ's gracious approval.

BLESSED BE THE NAME OF THE LORD

(Job 1:1-22)

An Alabama pastor told me about a man in his congregation. One night, a raging fire destroyed the man's house and belongings. When the pastor received the call and arrived at the house, it was engulfed in flames. The man stood on the front lawn with his arms around his wife and children. As the pastor approached his church member, he put a sympathetic hand on the man's shoulder and said, "Brother, I am so very sorry." Without hesitating, the fellow looked at his pastor and replied, "Oh, preacher, those are just things. My family is all safe and sound. Would you offer a prayer of thanksgiving for us?" The pastor was moved that a man who had lost all of his material, earthly belongings could still stop and praise the Lord.

In verses 13-19, a man named Job gets an incredible series of bad-news reports. When it was all over, Job had lost his livestock, his servants, his children, and his house. How did he respond? He mourned the dead and worshipped the Lord. Job 1:21 says *the Lord gave [that is easy to say], and the Lord hath taken away [that is hard to say]; blessed be the name of the Lord.*

HOW TO BE SAVED

(Romans 10:1-13)

One night after a revival meeting, a little six-year-old boy approached me and said, "I want to ask Jesus into my heart." I knelt down and asked, "You mean that you want to be saved? Why do you want to be saved?" He looked quizzically at me and shrugged his shoulders. So, I asked him if he had ever sinned. Once more, he stared at me, dumbfounded, and answered, "No." Tenderly, I smiled and asked him if he had ever done anything wrong. He quickly said, "Well, I slapped my sister yesterday." I told him, "Well, young man, that is a sin." The stunned little guy glared at me and loudly said, "That is not a sin! My sister is a brat!" He did not understand that he had sinned.

Romans chapter 10 is about righteousness. The Jews tried to get righteousness by their works. Righteousness comes after salvation. Paul reminded them that salvation comes when a person confesses that Jesus is Lord, and believes in their heart that He was raised from the dead (v. 9). Whoever calls on the name of the Lord will be saved (v. 13). But we have to acknowledge first that we are sinners and cannot save ourselves.

JUMPING FOR JOY

(Habakkuk 3:1-19)

Inflatable rentals are all the rage today. Those huge blowup slides and bounce houses are frequently rented for birthday parties, church events, and everything in between. Children sure do love to jump and play on those great big air mattresses. One day, driving down the road not far from my home in Jacksonville, I saw an inflatable rental company with the greatest name. It was called Jump For Joy Inflatables. Then it suddenly hit me. What an appropriate way to describe the Spirit-filled life. As Christians, we really should be jumping for joy. After all, Jesus Himself commanded us to *leap for joy* (Luke 6:23), and Paul said that *the fruit of the Spirit is ... joy* (Galatians 5:22). New Testament saints have a reason to jump for joy.

The Old Testament prophet Habakkuk begins his book by asking why there is so much suffering. But by the last chapter, a great change takes place. Habakkuk prays and praises the Lord. Verses 17-19 are a great confession of faith. He declares that God will give him strength to run like a deer and jump over the mountains. He is so full, he jumps for joy. Life in Christ is a life of abundant, supernatural, irrepressible joy.

HUMILITY

(1 Corinthians 1:18-31)

A young lawyer had just passed the bar exam and opened up his own private practice. He rented a prominent office with his name embossed in gold on the glass door. He was still awaiting his first client when he started to unload his boxes. As he stacked books on the shelf, he heard the door open. Quickly, he picked up his phone. The lawyer wanted to look busy for his approaching visitor. Putting the phone to his ear, he said, "Yes, I would love to take your case. But I am just swamped right now. Can you hold one second? Someone has just come into my office." Looking up at the fellow standing in the doorway, he asked, "May I help you?" The visitor replied, "I'm from the phone company. I'm here to hook up your phone."

That attorney tried to impress someone. So many believers deceive themselves and others, pretending to be something they are not, in order to impress others. But God always knows the truth. Unfortunately, there are also too many ministries and churches that are more impressed with themselves than they should be. Paul reminds us all that *no flesh should glory in his presence* (v. 29). God uses those who are humble.

SUMMER IN THE PSALMS

It is hard to believe that we are halfway through the year. Six months have come and gone. It is my deepest prayer that the simple devotions found in *Good Morning God* have been a blessing and a help to you. Through the first 182 days of the year, you have spent time in all sixty-six books of the Bible. Six of those days have been in the book of Psalms. Now, as we come to the middle of the year, let's spend the remainder of the summer in the Psalms. After all, there are 365 days in a year, and there are 150 psalms. So each Scripture and devotion for the next sixty-two days will be taken from this one wonderful book that is found right in the center of your Bible.

Psalms is a devotional book, a prayer book, and a great hymn-book. In fact, the Hebrew word for *Psalms* means "the book of praises." King David wrote seventy-three of the Psalms. How appropriate that Israel's singer of songs (2 Samuel 23:1), and the man who organized temple ministry (1 Chronicles 16:7), would write almost half of this great book of worship and praise. Psalms is a book of devotions in itself. Let's spend July praising Him in Psalms. Be blessed.

JULY 1

WATCH WHERE YOU WALK

(Psalm 1:1-6)

Dad said, "Watch where you walk." I heard what he said very clearly, but I didn't listen. I was about ten years old, and we were on our annual vacation at a lake in Lake Wales, Florida. One night, I left our cabin with some change melting a hole in my pocket, and I wanted a bottle of Dr. Pepper from the vending machine by the boat dock. I was barefooted, and instead of taking the circular, smooth, dirt path, I decided to take the dark shortcut across the grass. Halfway across, I stepped on a twisted, jagged aluminum can and cut my foot badly. I learned that my wise dad knew what he was talking about when he said, "Watch where you walk."

When you read Psalm 1:1, you can almost visualize a young man walking near sin, standing to consider it, and sitting down to enjoy it. This is contrary to the wise believer who is saturated with God's Word and is compared to a tree planted by fresh water with deep spiritual roots (v. 3). That is the type of wise person who listens to the Father and watches where they walk. They avoid sin and spiritual danger and receive blessing.

SHIELD OF DEFENSE

(Psalm 3:1-8)

The nation of Israel has spent $560 million developing a defense system that has one purpose. It locates and intercepts missiles fired at Israeli communities. The name of the elaborate system is called the Iron Dome Missile Shield. Israel's Defense Department began developing the Iron Dome after the Lebanese militant group, Hezbollah, fired thousands of rockets at northern Israeli towns in 2006. The Iron Dome's first real test came in November of 2012 when Gaza militants attacked. After the dust settled, the Israeli military said that the Iron Dome intercepted 389 (80 percent) of the rockets that had been launched. The shield is equipped with a radar detector, a unit that predicts where the rocket will land, and a missile interceptor.

The Iron Dome is impressive. But David had a shield that was better than that. In Psalm 3, King David is running for his life. His rebel son, Absalom, sent a mighty army to stalk and kill him. In the middle of the danger, David declared, *But thou, O LORD, art a shield [defense] for me.* Our battles are first won in the spiritual realm. We have a powerful shield, the blood of Jesus, and a God who has vowed to protect, defend, and avenge us.

JULY 3

DON'T LOSE THE WONDER

(Psalm 8:1-9)

Little children are filled with wonder. Their eyes dance with delight, their minds are always in awe, and their mouths laugh with excitement as they experience the magical world around them. But as children become teenagers, they can quickly get bored with life. It seems that it is much harder for them to be thrilled and impressed. Finally, when they reach adulthood, many of them become jaded, bitter, and passionless. Those same eyes that once danced with delight are too often filled with emptiness or tears. The mind that was open, creative, imaginative, and amazed by everything is now suddenly closed. The mouth that used to laugh out loud and shout for joy is, in many cases, filled with pessimism, criticism, questions, and anger.

As God's children, we must never lose the wonder. How tragic it is when our lives get so frantic or so mundane and cynical that we fail to recognize the glory of God. This psalm of David is especially exciting because it is a messianic psalm. Several times in the New Testament, Psalm 8 is applied to Christ (Matthew 21:16; Ephesians 1:22; Hebrews 2:6-8). When you lose the wonder, just think about Jesus and the abundant life He offers.

CRUMBLING FOUNDATIONS

(Psalm 11:1-7)

The Saint Anthony Falls Bridge is part of Interstate 35 in Minneapolis, Minnesota. It spans the mighty Mississippi River. On August 1, 2007, the bridge collapsed at 6:05 p.m. (CST), and many vehicles plunged into the river. Thirteen people died and 145 were injured. The engineer's report stated that the bridge fell because the foundation had a crumbling infrastructure. It is believed that there are hundreds of bridges in our country with the same problem. Experts estimate that it will cost about $225 billion a year for the next fifty years to repair all the crumbling foundations. But as frightening as that is, there are some other crumbling foundations in America that need to be repaired.

I refer to the crumbling foundations of faith, wisdom, and moral character. Today is Independence Day. As we celebrate this day and honor America, let's not forget why this nation has been blessed. Our forefathers built this land on biblical standards. Psalm 11:3 poses a great question. A house is only as good as its foundations. Unless we restore and repair the crumbling foundations of our nation, we cannot expect to stand strong. It's up to the people of God to step forward and start the work.

GOD IS REAL

(Psalm 14:1-7)

A young college freshman sat in philosophy class when his agnostic professor said, "If you believe there is a God, raise your hand." The freshman, a believer who loved the Lord, raised his hand boldly. Laughing, the professor said, "There is no God, and I can prove it. Let me ask you, have you ever seen God or touched God?" The student replied, "No." Arrogantly, the professor continued, "Well, what makes you think there is a God?" The student answered, "Professor, I have some questions for you. Have you ever seen your brain, or touched your brain?" When the philosophy professor responded by saying no, the freshman said, "What makes you think that you have a brain?"

It is foolish to believe that there is no God and live as if there is no judgment or accountability. Without God, men are fools (v. 1). They are depraved and corrupt (v. 3). Salvation has *come out of Zion* (v. 7) in Jesus Christ. Though many laugh and mock Him, God's Word promises that every knee will bow and every tongue confess that Jesus Christ is Lord. Belief is, first and foremost, a choice. If we choose to believe, He will give us the faith to believe.

JULY 6

BEING CERTAIN IN AN UNCERTAIN CULTURE

(Psalm 16:1-11)

Someone has said, "There is only one thing in life that is certain, and that is uncertainty." We live in a culture of great uncertainty. Perhaps no generation in American history is facing the political, financial, moral, and military uncertainties that our generation confronts on a daily basis. The housing market and the stock market are uncertain. The fluctuating economy and the frail environment are uncertain. The next targets of violence and terror are uncertain. Yet, in this fearful and uncertain world, you can be certain about one thing – God is still in control. You can put your refuge, hope, and trust in the Lord.

Psalm 16 is a personal hymn of joy sung by King David. The personal pronoun *my* is used over a dozen times in the eleven verses. Verse 1 says, *Preserve me, O God: for in thee do I put my trust.* David lived in an uncertain world, and declared that he put his trust (confidence) in the Lord. The world that we live in is constantly changing. Change is a natural and expected part of life. But if you stay in God's presence, you will have fullness of joy (v. 11) despite uncertainty. You can be certain of that.

JULY 7

THE GLORY OF GOD

(Psalm 19:1-14)

A world-famous biologist named Edward O. Wilson has released some amazing facts and statistics about the creatures and plants of this world. Dr. Wilson claims that there might be as many as 1.6 million species of fungi on the planet today, ten thousand species of ants, ten thousand species of birds, three hundred thousand species of flowering plants, and five thousand species of mammals. Those are amazing numbers, but they pale in comparison to the unfathomable number of heavenly bodies in the universe. When David looked into the heavens, he didn't have scientific data or telescopes. All he knew was that, as he looked at the spectacular creation of God, David was overwhelmed by His glory.

When it comes to learning about God, Psalm 19 is often considered the greatest psalm. David tells us that we can know God by what we see (v. 1), by what we read (vv. 7-8), and by what we feel (vv. 12-13). When we see God, read about God, and feel God, we can truly praise God. Mankind devotes billions of hours and dollars to studying our universe, yet so many people refuse to use this knowledge to get to know the God who made it or acknowledge His glory.

TELLING THE FUTURE

(Psalm 22:1-18)

In 1984, some computer analysts looked sixteen years into the future and predicted chaos. They determined that a computer calculation error would cause a massive, worldwide technology collapse on January 1, 2000. As the 1990s began to wind down, those predictions sparked fear and hysteria. Some people planned for apocalyptic scenarios and rushed to buy computer software and hardware that would fix the coming problem. Conspiracy theories abounded, and websites were created to help the population prepare for the disastrous event known as Y2K. But as we all know, the predictions were wrong, and the world did not come to an end.

Acts 2:30 calls David a prophet. Indeed, in Psalm 22, David writes about the death and resurrection of Christ one thousand years before Jesus was even born in Bethlehem. This is another one of those messianic psalms. In David's day, death by crucifixion was not common. But verses 16-18 specifically describe the horrors of the cross. Psalm 22 is telling the future, but with the full authority of God Himself. Biblical prophecies are never simply foretelling. They are God speaking things into being and instructing us accordingly. False predictions bring chaos. Biblical prophecy reveals God's truth and power.

JULY 9

OUR SHEPHERD

(Psalm 23:1-6)

I consider Dr. John Phillips to be one of the best writers and Bible commentators of my lifetime. I am happy to say that a number of his works have a special place on the shelves of my own personal library. In his book *Exploring Psalms,* Dr. Phillips talks about the death of his dear mother. After her death, he found her Bible on the table beside the bed, opened to the twenty-third psalm. Dr. Phillips noticed that there were some words penned in the margin beside the passage. His mother had written the words *The secret of a happy life, a happy death, and a happy eternity.*

That is a powerful, beautiful description of the psalm known as "The Shepherd's Psalm." He watches, guards, and cares for His sheep in every phase of life. The Good Shepherd cares for our frailties (vv. 1-3), He takes care of our foes (vv. 4-5), and He will take care of our future (v. 6). Our Shepherd is the only shepherd who ever died for His sheep. He knows each of us individually, intimately, and by name. He has already made provision for every conceivable human need, and His constant presence brings us to the place of grace.

JULY 10

OPEN THE GATES

(Psalm 24:1-10)

In high school, I attended a basketball game in which our team played our archrivals, one of the best teams in the state, while ours wasn't very good. Before the game, our cheerleaders excited the huge crowd. They shouted, "We've got spirit, yes we do! We've got spirit, how 'bout you?" The fans would respond antiphonally with those same words. It was very thrilling, as the volume shook the building. By the third quarter, our team was getting beaten pretty badly. Once again, our cheerleaders shouted, "We've got spirit, yes we do! We've got spirit, how 'bout you?" About half of the crowd chanted back halfheartedly, and one guy yelled, "Shut up! We ain't got any spirit!"

The crowd was too defeated to respond. In Psalm 24, two choirs antiphonally share a song of victory. One sings in verses 7 and 9, and the other in verses 8 and 10. For the past three days, we have read Psalms 22-24, a trilogy of Christ the Shepherd. In Psalm 22, the Good Shepherd dies for the sheep. In Psalm 23, the Great Shepherd cares for the sheep. In Psalm 24, the Chief Shepherd returns with His sheep. Open the gates. The Shepherd always brings His sheep home.

JULY 11

DON'T FEAR THE DARK

(Psalm 27:1-14)

A grieving father and his six-year-old daughter returned home after a funeral service for their precious wife and mother. Later that night, the dad heard his frightened girl crying. He ran to her room and as he held his child in the darkness, she whimpered, "Daddy, it is real dark and I can't see you. Is your face towards me?" The loving dad consoled her and said, "Yes, sweetheart, I'm looking at you right now." After she finally went to sleep, he slipped down on his knees beside his bed and prayed, "Father, it is dark and I can't see You. Is Your face towards me?" Gently, the heavenly Father spoke to his heart and said, "Yes, my child. I am looking at you right now."

Sometimes, life gets so dark it is difficult to see the Father's face. But David reminds us that we do not have to be afraid. The Lord is your light and your salvation. He is the strength (rock and fortress) of your life (v. 1). In His grace, He sent the Light of the World to dwell within us, ever present, ever constant, ever shining to comfort and empower us in the darkest night.

JULY 12

THE VOICE

(Psalm 29:1-11)

*T*he *Voice* debuted on April 26, 2011, and became one of television's most-watched reality shows. The concept is to find new singing talent from aspiring singers across America, chosen at public auditions. Those picked for the show display their talent in front of a panel of four coaches and a national television audience who votes for the champion. The season's eventual winner receives $100 thousand dollars and a recording deal with Universal Music Group. Without question, *The Voice* is one of America's most-popular TV shows. Yet something baffles its producers. Even though there have been some very talented singers, none of them have gone on to achieve great national success or fame.

There are gifted people in this world who possess amazing voices. But the most-powerful voice on the planet pales in comparison to the voice of God. Psalm 29 declares that God's voice is so powerful, it can break trees (v. 5), shake the wilderness like an earthquake (v. 8), and make the angels shout, "Glory!" (v. 9). The voice of the Lord is truly *the* voice because it contains the power of God Himself.

ZERO BALANCE

(Psalm 32:1-11)

It is always a sweet day whenever any type of debt or loan is paid in full. One morning, I stopped by the drive-through window at the bank to make a car payment – not just any routine payment, but the last one. This meant that both of our vehicles were completely paid for. Shortly after I dropped the check into the plastic cylinder, the teller's voice came over the speaker. She said, "Congratulations, sir." With a smile I replied, "Thank you. It sure does feel good." Then the lady sent me the receipt back through that air-powered tube. As I opened it and read it, I felt even better. The statement read, "Balance – $0."

David starts Psalm 32 by excitedly declaring *Blessed [happy] is he whose transgression is forgiven.* The word *transgression* means "crossing over the line." David had rebelled and sinned against God but rejoices because he has been forgiven (v. 5). He closes the psalm by reminding us that we should shout for joy (v. 11) because our debt is paid in full. This is the incredible grace of God at work. The blood of Jesus has wiped the slate clean, and there is no longer any claim against us.

Setting Up The Tent

(Psalm 34:1-22)

When my son Jonathan was about five years old, he wanted to camp out in the backyard. But the tough guy wanted a tent all to himself. So I set up tents side by side about fifty feet from the back porch. We had a wonderful father-and-son night of roasting hotdogs and marshmallows by the fire. Finally, it came time for us to go to sleep. After a few quiet minutes, the nighttime chorus began. Crickets chirped, neighborhood dogs barked, and the screeching sound of an owl pierced the night. My son asked nervously, "Dad, are you still there?" I answered, "Yes, I am here. Do you want me to come over there in your tent?" The little guy answered, "No. I just wanted to be sure that you are still there."

Every time I read Psalm 34:7, I think about that sweet memory of my son. The Hebrew word for *encamp* means "to pitch a tent." God constantly guards your life. In fact, He has given a perfect promise that His mighty angel camps right beside you at this very moment. The name *Lord* is found sixteen times in twenty-two verses, reminding us that He is always near us.

A SLOW BURN

(Psalm 37:1-8)

Many years ago in Pennsylvania, a mining town was built right over a large coal mine. One day, a spark started a small fire in one of the deepest shafts. The fire was so deep there was no way to put it out. So the mine owners closed the shaft, hoping that the fire would eventually burn itself out. Weeks went by, then suddenly, a crack opened in one of the streets and raging fire billowed through. The town had to be completely abandoned. What had happened? The fire had slow-burned, building in intensity, until it found a weakness in the surface. That which was hidden underneath erupted and became a danger to everyone.

Surely you have heard or even used the expression, "That just burns me up." In Psalm 37:1 God says, *Fret not.* The word *fret* means "to get heated up and burn." It is a picture of a smoldering fire that builds in intensity until there is an explosion. God gives four instructions for putting out the inner fires. He tells us to *trust* in the Lord (v. 3), *delight* in the Lord (v. 4), *commit* yourself to the Lord (v. 5), and *rest* in the Lord (v. 7).

JULY 16

SOLID ROCK

(Psalm 40:1-17)

On February 28, 2013, a man in Tampa, Florida, tragically disappeared when a deadly sinkhole opened up underneath his bedroom floor while he slept. Sinkholes are a geological hazard that can instantly swallow up houses, cars, highways, and apartment buildings. They are very common in Florida because the state sits on top of several thousand feet of very porous limestone. Limestone holds large amounts of water in underground aquifers. As the surging groundwater flows through the limestone, it slowly dissolves and eats away the foundation. When the limestone is completely eroded, the ground will simply cave in because there is no solid rock underneath it.

Those who are lost in sin are sliding, slipping, and sinking into the pit of hell. Often, they cannot even see or recognize the danger, which only makes it more deadly. But when Jesus Christ saves a soul, He lifts them up and sets their feet on solid rock. An old country preacher once preached a powerful sermon on Psalm 40:2-3. His points were: 1) God brought me up; 2) God stood me up; 3) God tuned me up. After a soul is saved, that person has a rock to dance on and a new song to sing.

THIRSTING FOR GOD

(Psalm 42:1-11)

I am a recovering Coca-Cola addict. I confess that I used to drink it way too much. It was my beverage of choice at meals, snacks, and even before bedtime. In fact, I always felt it was kind of patriotic. After all, it is very much an all-American beverage. All right, I know that's a stretch, but whatever it takes to justify it, right? At any rate, I've cut down my Coca-Cola consumption considerably. With the encouragement of my wife and the counsel of my doctor, I drink water almost exclusively now. I discovered, fortunately, that I have developed a taste for water. There is nothing better for quenching thirst than a bottle of water. It is not only good, it is also healthy.

The writer of Psalm 42 sees a deer desiring water, and it reminds him of how much he thirsts for God. Notice the essentials for physical life in Psalm 42. There is air (v. 1), water (v. 1), and food (v. 3). But without worship (v. 4), life is nothing. Be thirsty for God today. It is healthy. The analogy is powerful. The psalmist is reminding us that, just as water is essential to our physical life, God is essential to our spiritual life.

A MIGHTY FORTRESS

(Psalm 46:1-11)

One of the most famous and beloved hymns ever written is called *A Mighty Fortress Is Our God*. A preacher named Martin Luther wrote it almost five hundred years ago. Many historians feel the inspiration for the hymn was taken straight from the forty-sixth psalm. After all, it's a song of victorious celebration sung after a great battle. Scholars believe the historical context of the psalm refers to the day that God delivered the city of Jerusalem from the Assyrian army. They also believe that King Hezekiah of Israel is the one who joyfully wrote this magnificent psalm. Verse 1 declares, *God is our refuge [fortress] and strength [security], a very present help in trouble.*

The same God who was Hezekiah's fortress is also your fortress. Psalm 46:10 commands us all to *Be still, and know that I am God.* The words *be still* literally mean "take your hands off the situation and relax." I'm afraid that each one of us often tries to be "hands-on" and manage our own lives. But God is our mighty fortress. He is our refuge and strength. When we let go and let God, He is able to accomplish so much more than we ever could.

PLAY YOUR INSTRUMENTS

(Psalm 47:1-9)

A great-grandmother visited her grandchildren's church one Sunday. The sweet, elderly woman loved to worship God. Unfortunately, her grandkids attended a dry, cold, liturgical church. As the choir sang about the blood of Jesus, the granny couldn't help clapping her hands loudly in praise to the Lord. An usher walked over to her and said, "Ma'am, I need to ask you to calm down and quit clapping your hands. We are a dignified church." The precious lady responded, "I can't help it, sir, I've got the joy of the Lord." Frowning, the somber usher replied, "Well, you didn't get it here, so you need to be quiet." That sweet woman simply obeyed God and did what He commanded us to do.

You have been given the ability to play an instrument. In fact, God has equipped your body with two musical instruments – your hands and your mouth. We are commanded to clap our hands, and *shout unto God* (v. 1). There is a time to be quiet before the Lord (Psalm 46:10), and there is a time to loudly praise Him. Praise the Lord with your instruments today. We are created to praise and worship Him. Don't let the world stifle your divine purpose.

DON'T PUT YOUR TRUST IN MONEY

(Psalm 49:1-20)

Alexander the Great was the Greek king who conquered the world and was the most successful military leader in history. Alexander's mighty armies never lost a battle. After the last country had been vanquished, he made the long trip home. On the way, the great leader became ill. In the last moments of his life, Alexander gave two orders that were to be carried out at his funeral. He wanted his gold and silver to be scattered along the path to his grave, and he asked for his open hands to be extended outside his coffin. What were the reasons? He wanted everyone to learn two lessons. First, all the wealth that you earn in life will be scattered after you die. Second, you came into the world empty-handed, and you will leave the same way.

It is not a sin for you to have money, but it is a sin for money to have you. Sadly, far too many people confuse price with value. Psalm 49 is a reminder that wealth does not purchase salvation (vv. 6-8) or buy a destiny (vv. 15-17). Put your trust in God, not in money. What we have belongs to Him, to be used for His kingdom.

JULY 21

THE MIGHTY JUDGE

(Psalm 50:1-10)

Judith Sheindlin is an American lawyer, judge, TV personality, and author best known to the public by the name of her internationally popular daytime television program *Judge Judy*. The long-running series has aired for two decades. Judge Judy is known for her no-nonsense wit and her judgments based on the Ten Commandments. One of her most famous quotes came on the day that a big football player stood before her. The young man, wearing a shirt that said, "Beer Equals Fun," addressed her most disrespectfully. Judge Judy studied the football star and said, "Young man, when you address me, you call me 'Your Honor.' You've never been tackled worse than I am about to tackle you."

The respectful term in addressing any human judge is "Your Honor." But the supreme judge of heaven is mighty (v. 1) and righteous (v. 6). Twice in Psalm 50, we are reminded that God is our judge (vv. 4, 6). One day, when the Mighty Judge enters the courtroom, we will not stand in His honor; we will fall down and bow to His glory. We are so used to the superficial authority of the world that we forget the might and power of our holy God.

CLEAN

(Psalm 51:1-19)

My grandchildren are perfect. They just have mean parents who punish them. One day, one of them visited our home. She did something that her mother had forbidden. Suddenly, my daughter took her to the bedroom and spanked her. But let me tell you what my daughter didn't do. She didn't take her little girl by the hand, put her outside the door, and say, "You are no longer my daughter. You can find a new family because you have sinned your way out of this family." Truthfully, there is nothing that a child can do to be put out of the family, because she was birthed into it by blood.

Christians are born into God's family by the precious blood of Jesus, and we are in God's family forever. But sometimes, Christians get dirty and need to get right. Psalm 51 is David's prayer after Nathan the prophet confronted him about his sin with Bathsheba. David says, *cleanse me* (vv. 1-7), *Restore unto me* (vv. 8-12), and "use me" (vv. 13-19). If you are a child of God, you feel dirty when you sin. But God will wash you in the perfect blood of Jesus that cleanses from all sin if you ask Him.

MAKE ME AN OLIVE TREE

(Psalm 52:1-9)

Psalm 52 is a past record of events found in First Samuel 21-22. It tells of a difficult time in the life of David. King Saul was after him, and David was running in fear. He went to a place called Nob, and the priest Ahimelech fed him and ministered to him. But Saul put a contract on Ahimelech's head. A man named Doeg killed the priest and used his lying tongue to attack David. But even when David was facing these human obstacles, he continued to trust the Lord to fight his battles. What a lesson for the New Testament Christian. Even when men come against us and evil seems to be triumphing, we must continue to obey the Lord and trust Him.

Perhaps David was enjoying the shade of an olive tree when he wrote this psalm. He declares that he is an *olive tree in the house of God* (v. 8). An olive tree lives for many years and continues to bear fruit for generations. The wicked are eventually uprooted and destroyed. But the olive tree, a symbol of righteousness, peace, and godly anointing, keeps on standing tall. Ask God to make you an olive tree, a vessel for His glory.

UNDER HIS WINGS

(Psalm 57:1-11)

Thousands of feet above the ground in Afghanistan, a special aircraft is flown, undetected, by the soldiers of an elite unit known as Bravo Company. The plane is filled to the brim with high-tech equipment, computer monitors, and a sophisticated surveillance and reconnaissance system. The crew is able to provide troops on the ground with lifesaving protection and information. From high above, insurgent forces can determine enemy locations and also be instructed where they can safely avoid enemy attacks. United States Army Major Matthew Moore says, "Our aircrews and operators in the sky are responsible for saving the lives of the troops on the ground. We are guarded under their wings."

David gives us another look at his conflict with Saul. Moving as a fugitive, he hid in a cave but was always under the protective hand of the Lord. Psalm 57:1 paints a beautiful picture of safety and security underneath the massive, majestic, and mighty wings of God. These words call to mind Jesus' imagery of a mother hen gathering her chicks to safety, and the Holy Spirit hovering over the waters at creation. What a joy to know that as you walk out in the world today, you are guarded under His wings.

JULY 25

ONLY GOD CAN GROW GRASS

(Psalm 65:1-13)

When the Astrodome opened in April 1965, it was the first completely domed sports stadium in history. Never had baseball been played indoors, and the futuristic Astrodome was hailed as the eighth wonder of the world. During that first season, real grass was used on the playing surface and cared for under synthetic lighting and a high-tech sprinkler system. But by early summer, the grass under the fancy roof had died. For the remainder of the baseball season, the dead grass was sprayed with green spray paint. That is when Astroturf (synthetic grass) was invented. When the season opened in 1966, the Astrodome was covered with Astroturf. The head of the grounds crew said, "We finally realized that only God can grow grass."

They could have saved themselves a lot of frustration, work, and money if they had just taken time to read the Bible. Psalm 65 reminds us that God waters and grows the earth (vv. 9-10). God sends the rains to fill the rivers and streams, produce the harvest, and nurture what He has made. He sets all things in the places where they will grow best. The perfection of nature shouts for joy, and sings praises to the God of creation.

LOADED WITH BENEFITS

(Psalm 68:19-35)

You hear people say it all the time. Frequently, when you ask somebody how their day has been, they will reply in exasperation, "Whew! It's been one of those days." Maybe today has been "one of those days" in your life and family. The alarm didn't go off, and you overslept. Everybody in the whole house woke up with an attitude. You forgot to iron a shirt last night before you went to bed. While you search frantically for something decent to wear, you trip over the dog. The kids miss the bus. There is no milk in the fridge. When you finally rush out the door, ready to jump in the car, you have a flat tire. And all of that happens before eight o'clock in the morning.

Before you go any further, you owe it to yourself to stop for a moment and focus on the God who loads you down with benefits every single day (v. 19). Even during a time of burdens, David saw the blessings that God had given Israel. Harassment, difficulties, and things going wrong so often distract us from our abundant blessings and the God who loves us. Just like Israel, you are loaded daily with benefits.

GROWING OLD BUT NOT GETTING COLD

(Psalm 71:9-24)

I met an old preacher named Emmett Roper one night while preaching in Alabama. For many years, he had been an anointed traveling evangelist. Age, surgeries, and physical afflictions had taken his strength. Now in his eighties, he could no longer travel and preach. In fact, a church member had given him a ride that night. But he sat in the front row, holding his Bible, lifting his hands to the Lord, and cheering me on while I preached. After the service, Brother Emmett hugged my neck. With the glow of Jesus on his face, he told me three times, "Get some rest tonight, and keep on keeping on." As that sweet soldier of the Lord left, I saw a man who had lost his strength but had never lost his joy.

The author of Psalm 71 is anonymous. Many believe an aging man who felt the burdens of age wrote this psalm. But through it all, one thing is clear. The writer may be growing old, but he is not getting cold. He knows that his hope (v. 14) and strength (v. 16) are in the Lord. He promises to sing and praise God all the days of his life (vv. 19-24).

GOOD NEWS

(Psalm 74:1-23)

Whether at home or in a hotel, at some point during the day, I sit down for a few minutes of a Fox News broadcast. One day, at home, I was on the couch listening to the news, and my three-year-old granddaughter asked if she could watch *Doc McStuffins.* I quickly put on a video of her favorite cartoon and got so immersed in her program I didn't realize that she had left the couch and gone back to the playroom. My daughter noticed, and said, "Dad, she isn't even in here anymore. You can turn *Doc* off and go back to the news." I thought about it for a moment and said, "No, I think I will keep watching this. This is a lot better that the news."

In Psalm 74, the news report was bad. The Babylonians had attacked Jerusalem and destroyed the temple. However, the psalmist, Asaph, decides to focus on the good news. He realizes that God reigns (vv. 12-17) and remembers His people (vv. 18-23). There is a lot of bad news in the world we live in and it can bring us down. Just keep your heart and Bible open, and focus on the good news.

JULY 29

LISTEN UP

(Psalm 78:1-16)

On every airline flight, attendants will say, "Please direct your attention to the front of the aircraft for some important safety tips." Nobody ever listens. While the attendant speaks, folks are sleeping, thumbing through magazines, reading books, or listening to music. Of course, frequent fliers have heard the same speech numerous times. But I recall once sitting beside a man who was flying for the very first time. While the safety tips were being given, he was reading. As soon as the attendant finished, she walked down the aisle. When she passed the man, he asked her a question about something she had just covered. The sweet lady was gracious, but I just know she wanted to say, "I just told you that. Listen up next time."

God begins Psalm 78 by telling the people to listen. He says, *Give ear* and *incline your ears to words of my mouth.* This is an historical psalm reminding Israel about the dangers of their forefathers' rebellion. When God gives safety instructions, they are there to ensure our safety. Too often, we ignore them or are too busy to listen until it's too late. If we listen up and hear what God says, it keeps us out of trouble.

JULY 30

PRAYING FOR AWAKENING

(Psalm 85:1-13)

Many Christians spend a lot of time and energy talking about how bad the world is. They moan about how it needs to wake up and get right. Believers say things like, "If only we could elect Godly people," or "If only abortion could be outlawed," or "If only the liquor industry went out of business." Sometimes, we talk as though we expect the world to suddenly get right. But I want to remind you that the church cannot depend on America to get right. America must depend on the church to get right. Revival is not for sinners but for the saints. It is not the baby-killing abortionist, loose-living prostitute, or liquor-selling bartender who needs revival. It is the lazy, lethargic, lukewarm church that needs a revival. Our revival will impact the unsaved.

The writer of Psalm 85 is praying for revival and spiritual awakening. In verse 4, the psalmist says, *Turn [restore] us.* Establishing the nation, rebuilding the temple, and following the law was not enough. The people needed to be revived in heart and spirit. That word *revive* in verse 6 means "to be renewed in life." It should be the prayer burden and heart's cry of every church: Revive us again.

JULY 31

FOREVER FAITHFUL

(Psalm 89:1-18)

On the afternoon of September 18, 1870, the members of the Washburn-Langford-Doane Expedition team were traveling through Wyoming. Suddenly, a geyser erupted and sparkling water was shot high into the air. They marveled at the magnificent spectacle and decided to camp near it. For the next twenty-four hours, the team recorded that the geyser erupted almost every hour on the hour. The men called the phenomenon Old Faithful. Today, the Old Faithful geyser is the most-popular attraction of Yellowstone National Park. For almost 150 years, every single day, every sixty-five to ninety minutes, Old Faithful can be counted on to erupt and shoot thousands of gallons of boiling water almost two hundred feet into the sky.

When the explorers saw the amazing sight, the only word they could think of to describe it was *faithful*. The dictionary defines *faithfulness* as "reliable and consistent in duty." That is how the psalmist defines our God. Four times in the first eighteen verses of Psalm 89, God is praised for His faithfulness. His great grace saves, sustains, and secures. As He was in the beginning, so He will be at the end. All that He is, says, and does will endure forever. God is forever faithful.

AUGUST 1

GOD IS IN CONTROL

(Psalm 90:1-17)

In the fall of 2014, the horrific Ebola virus was spreading across America. At the very same time, ISIS terrorists and Russian aggression were causing global concern. Also during that time, the president of the United States was in New York City, speaking at a Democratic National Convention fundraiser. When someone asked the president about the world situation, he replied, "This world is spinning so fast, it appears that no one can control it." Indeed, you and I are living in a world that appears to be spiraling into complete chaos. But you can rest assured, in a world that is out of control, we have a sovereign God who is in total control.

Moses wrote Psalm 90, and it is the oldest recorded psalm. He begins the psalm by calling God the Hebrew name of *Adonai*. It means that God is the "master who is in total control of everything." Nothing ever takes God by surprise. He rules over everything, even death. Though we return to *destruction* (dust) (v. 3), God has promised us that we will return from the dust. Remember, our God created this infinitely complex, challenging, perfect, complete, and detailed universe out of chaos, and He is still in absolute control.

AUGUST 2

A JOYFUL NOISE

(Psalm 95:1-11)

God called me to preach. I am definitely not a singer. If I tried to make a living as a music evangelist or a gospel singer, I would starve to death. While I would not publicly sing a solo, that won't stop me from singing praise to the Lord. I once attended a revival meeting with a dear pastor friend of mine. During an evening service, the congregation began a great song of worship that lifted up the name of the Lord. I sang with all of my heart and voice. In the middle of the song, my friend leaned over and whispered in my ear. He said, "Brother, you are a terrible singer." I just looked back at him and replied, "Mind your own business. I'm not singing to you."

Twice in Psalm 95, we are commanded us to make *a joyful noise* to our God (vv. 1-2). It has occurred to me that the word *noise* adequately describes my singing ability. It is noisy when I try to sing. But I am assured that my God loves it. He is delighted when the *people of his pasture, and the sheep of his hand* (v. 7) *bow down … kneel before the Lord* (v. 6), and make a joyful noise. Don't forget to praise Him today.

AUGUST 3

HE IS HOLY

(Psalm 99:1-9)

Have you ever had a conversation with someone who casually referred to God as "the man upstairs"? I have seen athletes interviewed on television after they starred in a sporting contest say things like, "The man upstairs was with me today," or "The big man helped me." There have even been popular gospel songs written that have lyrics such as, "When I get to heaven, I am going to walk right up and shake God's hand." Actually, nothing could be further from the truth. Nobody is going to stroll up to God and shake His hand. When we see God, we will be awestruck and overwhelmed. People will instantly fall on their faces at His feet and worship Him. God is not the big man upstairs or our good buddy. He is holy.

That's how the psalmist referred to God three times in the ninety-ninth psalm. If you had to come up with one word to describe God, what would it be? Some folks would immediately say a word such as *love*, *truth*, or *powerful*. However, the word the Bible uses the most is *holy*. God is worthy to be worshipped because He is totally pure and set apart. He is perfectly, inexpressively holy.

THANK YOU, LORD

(Psalm 100:1-5)

As a young boy, I couldn't resist it. Even as a grown man, I confess it is difficult to avoid. Whenever I stand before a still body of water such as a pond or a lake, I have a desire to pick up a rock and throw it into the water. Of course, the objective is to see how many times it will skip rapidly across the water. The farther the rock skips, the more ripples appear. Do you realize that is exactly how the word *thanks* or *thankful* is used in the Word of God? The Hebrew word for *thanks* actually paints a picture of the act of throwing or casting something out across the water.

When you pray, start thanking God for your blessings. Each blessing you name will be like skipping a rock across a pond. As you begin to give thanks for the things we often take for granted, the ripples will grow. Suddenly, you will be amazed to see how many blessings the Lord has given you. Not only that, but the ripples extend to the future too. When we remind ourselves of past blessings, our faith for future blessings increases. Fall on your knees today and say, "Thank you, Lord."

SPEAK UP

(Psalm 107:1-16)

You see it every football season. Flags fly from car windows, magnets are all over the doors, and colorful stickers are proudly stuck on back bumpers. College football fans will unashamedly let you know who their favorite team is. I was driving around Jacksonville, Florida, one day when I saw a vehicle that was impossible to miss. It was a truck completely covered with paraphernalia boasting the University of Alabama Crimson Tide. There were multiple flags flying from all four doors, decals on the rear windows, and a huge "A" magnet that totally swallowed the hood of the big truck. When we stopped at a red light, I had the greatest urge to roll down my window and ask the guy, "Who is your favorite team?"

That man was shouting that his allegiance, love, and support belonged to Alabama. Don't you wish all Christians would be that publicly excited about Jesus Christ? In Psalm 107:2, the psalmist is speaking of God's great redemptive power. The verse says, *Let the redeemed [next of kin] of the LORD say so.* Too often, we even avoid simply mentioning Christ in casual conversation, thus denying our purpose in Christ. Those who are saved should always speak up.

BE CONFIDENT

(Psalm 108:1-13)

Do you look forward to the opportunities that each day holds for you? Sadly, there are a multitude of dreary folks who do not. They wake up each morning expecting the very worst to happen. Believe it or not, there is actually a national organization in this country known as Despair, Inc. The group has an Internet journal called *The Pessimist*, featuring all the bad news, views, and information of the days we live in. Depressed people visit it to wallow in negativity and purchase T-shirts and gifts. One of the most-popular shopping items available on *The Pessimist* is the daily tear-off calendar that features despairing news for each day of the year. The calendar is called *A 365-day journey into darkness.*

Pessimism has no place in the life of a Christian. In Psalm 108, David writes from a position of supreme confidence. He begins the psalm in verse 1 by declaring, *O God, my heart is fixed* (sure, certain, and firm). David enthusiastically exalts the Lord (v. 5), and puts his whole trust in Him. Whatever life throws at you today, be confident in your God. We are to be salt and light, to show the world there is a better, happier way.

THE PRAYER WARRIOR

(Psalm 109:14-31)

One night, a little girl got angry with her mother because she was told to go to bed early. After the child put her pajamas on, the mother walked into the girl's bedroom and said, "Young lady, be sure to say your prayers and ask God to forgive you for your attitude towards me." The little girl got out of bed and down on her knees. She prayed for God to bless everything and everyone in her life. The child sweetly and specifically prayed for all of her brothers, sisters, aunts, uncles, grandparents, her daddy, and even her dog. She finished her prayer, said "Amen," and climbed into bed. As her mother tucked her in, and kissed her on the cheek, the child looked at her mom and said, "I guess you noticed that you weren't in my prayer."

That little child prayed with the wrong attitude. In Psalm 109, David prays with the right attitude. David was a warrior, a king, and a great leader, but he recognized that he needed God's strength to fight against his enemies. He knew God had the real authority and power for victory in every situation and that he should always obey. When you pray, do it like a warrior.

AUGUST 8

HAPPY, HEALTHY FEAR

(Psalm 112:1-10)

The word *phobia*, derived from the mythological Greek god of terror called Phobos, is used often in our generation. Of course, a phobia is an anxiety or disorder defined by a persistent fear of something or someone. Psychologists tell us there are well over five hundred different types of phobias in the world today. For example, 74 percent of all Americans suffer from glossophobia, the fear of public speaking. About 68 percent of the populace is smitten with the phobia known as necrophobia (the fear of death). I will admit that there is a phobia or two that I suffer from. For instance, I know I have ophidiophobia (the fear of snakes). On the other hand, I can gladly testify that I have been set free from phalacrophobia (the fear of baldness).

Actually, phobias are nothing to joke about. Fear and fearfulness can be very debilitating and destructive, which is why the Bible encourages us not to fear. The fear the psalmist speaks of in Psalm 112:1 is not the paralyzing fear the world knows. Instead, it is a healthy respect and awe for the great majesty and power of our God. The Bible says, *Blessed [happy] is the man that feareth the LORD*. It is a healthy fear.

GOD'S PERSPECTIVE ON DEATH

(Psalm 116:1-19)

Many years ago, I pastored a wonderful church with a cemetery beside it. My family and I lived in a beautiful home next to the church. One Friday, I worked late into the evening. At about ten o'clock, I turned out the lights and walked home. As I passed the very dark cemetery, I heard loud voices. One voice hollered, "Hey, how do we get out of here?" Another voice yelled, "I don't even know where we are!" I wasted no time getting inside my house and calling the police. As it turned out, two guys had gotten drunk and somehow staggered into the cemetery. I admit, it was a little freaky hearing voices coming from deep in the graveyard.

Death, funerals, and graveyards are often ominous and forbidding subjects for many folks. But God has a far different perspective on death. Psalm 116:15 is one of the greatest promises in the Bible. It informs us that the death of a saint is precious (valuable) to our Lord. In the eyes of God, death is beautiful because it means a saint is going home to be with Him forever. He has already prepared our mansion and waits to welcome us home for eternity.

AUGUST 10

OPEN THE GATES

(Psalm 118:15-29)

I once had the opportunity to attend the NCAA National Championship football game in Miami, Florida. It was the game for all the marbles, and my friends and I arrived at the stadium early. There was a festive atmosphere as thousands of fans gathered around the entrance, waiting for the gates to open. As the clock neared the appointed time, the crowd began to chant, "Open the gates!" Finally, the locks were removed and the gates were swung wide to the cheering people. Directly in front of me was a poor fellow who was refused admittance. In fact, the man was detained, and the police took him away. It seems that he had a counterfeit ticket. Even though the gates were open, he couldn't walk through them.

Heaven's gates are open for everyone. But you cannot enter without the proper pass. In Psalm 118:19-20, David is praising God for the *gate of the Lord* that is open to the righteous. The word *open* in verse 19 means "loose, unlock, and throw open." "Open the gates" is the command of the King of heaven. But, though the gates are open to all, only those who come with their "ticket" – salvation – may enter.

HIDDEN IN THE HEART

(Psalm 119:1-16)

A busy minister was running late for a very important appointment one morning. Unable to find a parking space, the frantic pastor finally parked in a restricted, no-parking zone. Feeling guilty, he left a note on the windshield. "I am extremely sorry. I am a preacher, and I hate to break the law. But I have circled this block ten times looking for a place to park. I must park now, or I will be late. Forgive us our trespasses." Later, he returned and found a parking ticket under the wiper. Underneath the ticket was a note from a police officer. The note said, "I am sorry for your difficulty. But I have circled this block for ten years. If I don't write you a ticket, I will lose my job. Lead us not into temptation."

Those two fellows knew how to use the Word. Psalm 119 is the longest chapter in the Bible. It is like a daily journal that David kept. Within the first sixteen verses of this great psalm, David speaks of the enduring power of Scripture. Verse 11 has been called the key to spiritual warfare. When God's Word is hidden in your heart, you can use it for living or for battle.

HE REMEMBERS HIS PROMISES

(Psalm 119:49-64)

I have been blessed with two wonderful sons-in-law. Bryan is a preacher of the gospel, and Patrick is a high school football coach in Saint Augustine, Florida. During football season, my wife and I attend as many games as my schedule will allow. Of course, one of the great perks of going to the games is spending time with two of my precious granddaughters. One Friday night, we sat in the bleachers with those girls. Early in the first quarter, I promised them a candy snack before the game was over. During the evening, I got really interested in football and forgot all about the promise. Finally, in the fourth quarter, my four-year-old granddaughter jarred my memory and said, "It's about time for my snack that you promised."

In Psalm 119:49, David asked God to *Remember the word unto thy servant.* The Hebrew translation reads *Remember your promise to me.* It is wonderful to know that our God never forgets His promises. Anytime you need to be reminded of His promises, just open the Book. When we pray using the promises God has given, we are not asking Him to remember because He never forgets, but rather to fulfill His Word in us.

HEARING VOICES

(Psalm 119:81-96)

I f someone were to tell you that they "hear voices," you would quickly raise your eyebrows and come to one of two conclusions. You would diagnose that they were either totally insane or suffering from schizophrenia. Yet, it's estimated that at least 10 percent of the American population "hears voices." The truth is, every single one of us hear voices daily. Our world is filled with noisy voices clamoring for our personal attention. Those voices surround us from every direction imaginable. They scream and blare at us from social media, Madison Avenue, peers, family, colleagues, and classrooms. Some of the voices we hear despise God's truth and even deny His very existence. The Enemy delights in distractions, and who we listen to will determine what decisions we make and what we end up believing.

There is one voice that will never give you wrong advice or guidance. Long after the voices of this world have been silenced, God's truth will still remain. Psalm 119:89 emphatically declares, *For ever, O LORD, thy word is settled [standing like a strong pillar] in heaven.* Since God's Word is settled in heaven, it should be settled in your heart. Listen to His voice and hold it tightly.

AUGUST 14

A LAMP AND A LIGHT

(Psalm 119:105-120)

Judy and I own two little female dachshunds. Those dogs have been a part of our lives for a long time. The oldest dachshund is Gracie. One day, I reached down to hand her a doggie treat, and I noticed that she could not see my hand. After a series of tests, our veterinarian sadly informed us that she was blind. His exact words to us were, "She has no light."

Whenever Gracie is in the backyard, she must have constant supervision. One day, I took my eyes off of her for a brief second and she walked right into our swimming pool. She swam courageously for a moment. But if I had not lifted her out, she would have eventually tired and drowned. Without light to guide her, Gracie walked right into danger.

One of the very first Bible verses little children learn is Psalm 119:105. But it is a verse that should be remembered even by the oldest of us. David says that God's Word is a lamp (candle on a dark night), and a light (bright as the sun). Without God's truth to light our path, we can all walk blindly and stumble into something dangerous that will eventually overwhelm us.

Next Of Kin

(Psalm 119:145-160)

During the turbulent 1960s, America was starting on its moral downslide. Church attendance ebbed, the drug culture thrived, and modern science was eliminating and explaining away the existence of God. Finally, on April 8, 1966, the cover of *Time* magazine asked the question, "Is God Dead?" The great evangelist Vance Havner immediately preached a famous sermon that refuted the premise of the magazine article. In his message, Dr. Havner eloquently said, "I have a few simple questions for those who believe that God is dead. (1) Who identified the body? (2) What was the fatal disease that killed God? (3) When was the funeral held, and where is God buried? (4) Why wasn't I notified? I'm next of kin."

If you are saved, you are in God's immediate family. You are His child, His heir, adopted into a privileged place. His covenant, sealed in the blood of Jesus, has named you His eternal beneficiary, His next of kin. That is what the psalmist shouted in Psalm 119:151. That great verse says, *Thou art near, O Lord.* The word *near* literally means "next of kin." God is as close as your next breath, thought, and heartbeat. He is your next of kin, and you are His.

AUGUST 16

FINDING TREASURE

(Psalm 119:161-176)

Treasure hunters estimate that there is more than $4 billion in lost treasure scattered throughout the United States. For example, in the Black Hills of South Dakota, it is believed that an old prospector hid well over $1 million in gold nuggets that has never been found. Civil War experts say that Confederate soldiers buried $120 thousand in gold currency after they robbed a Union bank in 1864. To this day, that precious gold has never been recovered. Other reports state that there is over $200 in small bills that was buried by John Dillinger in the woods of Wisconsin three months before he was killed. Treasure hunters from all over the world are constantly looking for these and other hidden treasures.

It would be incredible to find treasure from a shipwreck, a buried chest, or some priceless artifact. But did you realize that there is a treasure that is more valuable than any gold or silver on this earth? In Psalm 119:162, the psalmist rejoiced and declared that opening God's Word is like finding a great treasure. Worldly treasures can be found and lost and perhaps never recovered. The Bible says that the Word is the only treasure that will endure forever.

LYING LIPS

(Psalm 120:1-7)

There is a very familiar rhyme and phrase that has been used in the American lexicon for two hundred years. During the 1800s, slaves uttered the words while overseers brutally beat them. In the year 1894, the rhyme first appeared in print in a bestselling book entitled, *Folk Phrases of Four Counties*. Children taunted and pushed around by bullies have used the phrase for generations. "Sticks and stones may break my bones, but words will never hurt me." Although it is a popular phrase that has stood the test of time, there is one problem with the rhyme. It is just not true. The words that we use can and will hurt, tear down, and destroy the life and reputation of someone else.

Undoubtedly, the psalmist knew the deep pain of being hurt because someone told lies about him. Psalm 120:4 uses two vivid word pictures to describe lying lips. Lies are compared to sharp arrows that can pierce, and hot coals that can burn. As believers, we should be people of truth who seek to live in peace (friendly and healthy) with all men (v. 7). The Bible is full of reminders to watch our words and be aware of their potentially damaging implications.

WHEN YOU NEED HELP

(Psalm 121:1-8)

On October 23, 2015, Hurricane Patricia became the strongest storm ever measured in the Western Hemisphere, as she rapidly churned through the Pacific Ocean. Patricia was a lethal Category-5 hurricane with maximum sustained winds of two hundred miles per hour. As she headed for the coast of Mexico, over seven million residents were warned to prepare for the worst-case scenario. But when the monster storm made landfall, Patricia was immediately sheered by the tall, rugged mountain range on the Mexican coastline. The mountains became a safety barrier. Patricia was quickly reduced to a tropical storm, and no casualties were reported. So often, we assume the worst when God has already provided the perfect protection and put everything in place.

When the storms of life come raging in, we should *lift up [our] eyes unto the hills.* That is what the psalmist wrote in Psalm 121:1. The word *hills* literally means "a mountain range." What a wonderful picture of our God the Rock who is our firm foundation and our stronghold. Our help comes from the God who surrounds us and sustains us. He never tires or goes to sleep (v. 4). You can rest tonight knowing that God is your keeper (v. 5) and preserver (vv. 7-8).

WE GET TO GO TO CHURCH

(Psalm 122:1-9)

It seems that attending church has lost importance. A Christian man once informed me said that he doesn't bother to go to church every week because he can download a service on the Internet or turn on the TV. I cautioned him that forsaking church means missing the *joy of the gathering*. There is something spiritually healthy about sitting in a community of brothers and sisters and worshipping God corporately. There is something contagious about praying together with other believers and listening with other saints as the Word of God is preached. It is not that we have "got to go to church." It is that we "get to go to church."

In Bible times, for a Jew to go to church often took days to journey the many arduous miles to Jerusalem to visit the temple. They had to camp out, and endure rugged terrain, weather, and even predators, in order to attend a service. Yet the psalmist was always *glad* (cheerful) when he had the opportunity to *go into the house of the LORD* (v. 1). If the hands, feet, or any other part are missing, the body of Christ is incomplete and the joy is also incomplete. We are created to be one in Him.

GIFTS FROM THE LORD

(Psalm 127:1-5 and Psalm 128:1-6)

My oldest daughter sent me a wonderful video on my smartphone of my three-year-old granddaughter, Brooklyn, naming every book of the Old Testament. As that sweet child pronounced and recited all thirty-nine books, I watched that video with a smile on my face and tears in my eyes. Immediately, I thought of the powerful and glorious promise found in the pages of the 128th psalm. In verse 6, God promised us that if we raise our children to love God, we would also live to see our grandchildren serving Him. What a joy it is for me to know that all of my children and my grandchildren love Jesus Christ, read His Word, are faithful to His church, and serve Him in ministry.

Psalms 127 and 128 are considered beautiful bookend psalms about the family. Whenever God *builds* (sets up) the house, it will be strong. Psalm 127:3 is a reminder to us that our children are God's *heritage* (gifts) to us. They are gifts that grow as *olive plants* (Psalm 128:3), and then mature to produce fruit and shade for the next generation. The gift of children raised in Christ is a lasting legacy. Praise God for His great gifts.

A PATIENCE PROBLEM

(Psalm 130:1-8)

A man pushed a shopping cart through the aisles of a busy grocery store one day. Inside the cart, a baby boy screamed at the top of his little lungs. The haggard man put food into the cart, and said repeatedly, "Be patient, Billy. Calm down, Billy. It will be all right, Billy." An elderly woman observed the man for a few minutes. She admired his great patience in an extremely stressful situation. Finally, she walked over to him and said sweetly, "Sir, I have been watching you. I want you to know that I think it is wonderful how patient you are being with little Billy." The frustrated man looked at her and replied, "Thank you, ma'am. But my baby's name is Tommy. I am Billy."

Most of us probably have some type of patience problem. I heard about the woman who prayed, "God, give me patience, and give it to me right now." One of life's most difficult challenges is waiting. It stirs up self-focus, along with irritation, frustration, resentment, and confusion. Psalm 130 is about waiting on the Lord. But the waiting psalmist reminds us that our *hope* (patience) is in the Lord. Be patient. God knows what time it is.

WORLDWIDE WORSHIP

(Psalm 135:1-21)

Did you realize that all of us are born with the desire to worship? Every person that is living on this planet worships something or someone. Some people worship athletes or celebrities. Others worship money, material possessions, hobbies, sports teams, relationships, or a way of life. In fact, there are some people that are so narcissistic, they even worship themselves. After all, this is the generation that invented something called the "selfie." As I said before, all of us must worship something. The Bible tells us that we were created to worship God. But if we don't guard our lives, something or someone will take the place of God. So, here is the big question – who in the world do you worship?

Psalm 135 is a song of adoring praise and worship of the Lord. The psalmist is praising God for His goodness (v. 3), His greatness (v. 5), His creation (vv. 6-7), His power (vv. 8-12), and His endurance (v. 13). God has commanded that we love Him with all of our heart, mind, soul, and strength. This is the picture of true worship – God is first in all things. Bless the Lord. He is the only one who is worthy to be worshipped.

AUGUST 23

WHAT DO YOU SAY?

(Psalm 136:1-26)

My three children were greatly blessed while growing up. Benevolent grandparents and relatives surrounded them. Christmas and birthdays always seemed to provide an abundance of gifts. From their earliest ages, my wife, Judy, and I constantly tried to teach our kids to be thankful. We never wanted them to take for granted or be unappreciative of the gifts that they were given. So, immediately after they excitedly ripped the colorful wrapping off the packages, we would ask them that familiar question, "What do you say?" Of course, as they got older and matured, we no longer had to tell them to say thank-you. It simply became the natural thing to do.

In Psalm 136, the writer is pouring out his thanksgiving to God. In all twenty-six verses of the 136th psalm, he gives thanks to God because *his mercy [favor and kindness] endureth for ever.* So let me ask you a personal question. In light of all that God has done for you and all the blessings that God has given you, what do you have to say to Him today? We must never assume that just because He knows what is in our heart we don't need to say it. Thank you, Lord.

AUGUST 24

DON'T HANG IT UP

(Psalm 137:1-9)

Harps were very important instruments of praise in the Old Testament. Even today, the harp has been called the national instrument of Israel. In Bible days, it was really considered a lyre. It was a small stringed instrument that could be carried easily. Singers would often walk the hills, paths, and roads of Israel, singing praises to God. In Psalm 137, the singers were not at home in the beautiful city of Jerusalem. Instead, the enemy had invaded, and the Israelites had been taken captive to Babylon. As they gathered sadly on the banks of the Tigris and Euphrates rivers, they mourned. Instead of playing and praising, the singers hung their harps dejectedly on the flowing branches of the willow trees (v. 2).

Sometimes, the very same thing can happen to New Testament believers. When difficulty comes, we let the Enemy rob us of our song. Rather than walking through life praising God, we just stop and hang it up. Don't dwell on where you are today. Focus on who He is. God is still on the throne. Don't hang your harp on the weeping willow tree and stop singing. So many passages in the Bible remind us that God's power is released through joyful praise.

AUGUST 25

BODY MADE BY GOD

(Psalm 139:1-24)

The human body is the most amazing machine ever built. Do you know how complex and magnificent your body is? Here are a few amazing facts about the body God has created. For example, you have seven octillion atoms in your body. That is seven with twenty-seven zeros behind it. In addition, you also have 300 trillion cells. The lungs in your body contain 300,000 million capillaries. If they were laid end to end, they would stretch fifteen hundred miles. If all the blood vessels in your circulatory system were stretched out, they would cover sixty thousand miles. There are five hundred thousand sweat glands on your feet and nine thousand taste buds on your tongue.

David used two words to describe God's amazing design. In Psalm 139:14, the psalmist said we are *fearfully* (reverently, awesomely) *and wonderfully* (marvelously) *made.* Verse 13 declares that God knits a body inside the mother's womb. At conception, the baby's sex, hair, and eye color are present. That is why abortion is murder. Life begins at conception. But one of the most awesome things about us is that God knew from the very foundation of the world who we are and what our purpose is. He made us according to His eternal blueprint.

AUGUST 26

A CALL OF DISTRESS

(Psalm 140:1-13)

There are few things in sports more compelling than the seventh game of a championship series. The 2014 World Series between the San Francisco Giants and the Kansas City Royals went the full seven games. I watched the seventh and deciding game on television. As the home team Royals batted in the bottom of the ninth, they were trailing the Giants by one run. With two outs, a Royals batter got a big hit and reached third base. The Kansas City crowd was frenzied. They had the tying run on third and the potential winning run at the plate. At that moment, the TV cameras panned the stadium and focused on one guy. He had his hands clasped and his eyes closed. The broadcaster said, "That man is praying for a miracle."

Obviously, that guy felt like he needed to make a distress call. Now, although I can promise you that God doesn't necessarily help a team win a game, He does want us to call on Him in stressful times. Many scholars believe that David wrote Psalm 140 when he served in King Saul's court and enemies were stalking him. David, in humble faith, made a distress call to the Lord to cover for him (v. 7).

THE GREATEST

(Psalm 145:1-21)

*W*ebster's definition of the word *greatest* is "highest in importance, significance, and achievement." The title has been given to world rulers such as Cyrus II of Persia, Alexander of Greece, Frederick II of Prussia, Wilhelm I of Germany, and Czar Peter of Russia, just to name a few. Historians name Renaissance painter Leonardo da Vinci the greatest artist, and William Shakespeare the greatest author. In the sporting world, heavyweight champion Muhammad Ali once declared that he was "The Greatest." There is even an entire generation of people referred to as the greatest. The Americans who fought during World War II, as well as those who kept the home front intact, are affectionately called "The Greatest Generation."

There is nothing wrong with recognizing and rewarding outstanding people. Indeed, they should be honored and applauded. But even believers sometimes seem to give men and women the same praise that should be reserved only for the Lord. Describing people with the words we should use to describe God is stealing His glory. In the true sense of the word, there can only be One who is truly "The Greatest." In Psalm 145:3, David said, *Great is the Lord*. In Hebrew, the word *great* means "higher than anyone." That describes our God. He is "The Greatest."

THE PRIORITY OF PRAISE

(Psalm 146:1-10)

As you come to the end of this hymnbook known as the book of Psalms, you will discover that the last part of the book is almost entirely filled with exhortations of praise. In the last five chapters of Psalms, the word *praise* is written almost forty times in fifty-nine verses. So, we are going to spend the final four days of this month praising the Lord. Today, we discuss the priority of praise. Sadly, some saints act like they never received that important memo. They wake up feeling lousy and spend their entire day making everyone around them feel miserable. When God tells us to praise Him, it is not a request, it is a requirement. Whatever your schedule is today, take some time to praise God. Praise is a priority.

Psalm 146:2 says, *While I live [have life in my body], will I praise the LORD.* You might be facing some huge obstacles and pressures today. But when you stop for a moment and praise Him, it fills you with joy and happiness (v. 5). Praise Him today because you're alive. If we're breathing, we should be praising.

THE PARTICIPANTS OF PRAISE

(Psalm 148:1-14)

An old farmer's wife was out of town one weekend. On Sunday, the old fellow decided to visit a new church. When his wife got home on Monday, she asked him about the service. He said, "Martha, you wouldn't believe it. They sang praise choruses instead of hymns." She looked at him, rather confused, and asked, "What in this world is a praise chorus?" The farmer answered, "Well, let me explain it like this. If I sang, 'Martha, the cows are in the corn,' you would call that a hymn. But if I sang, 'Martha, Martha, Martha, oh dear, Martha, the cows, cows, cows are in the corn, corn, corn,' you would call that a praise chorus."

In the 148th psalm, all of creation is joining together to participate in a great chorus of praise to God. The word *praise* is found in this psalm thirteen times in fourteen verses. Notice the universal participants of praise. First, the angels in heaven praise Him (v. 2). Then, the heavenly bodies praise him (vv. 3-5). Next, He is praised by all of creation and the created beings of the earth (vv. 7-13). Finally, in verse 14, His saints, and the children of Israel are praising God.

AUGUST 30

THE PLACE OF PRAISE

(Psalm 149:1-9)

S uppose that I ask a man how he is doing, and he quickly says, "I feel just awful all the time. I don't even feel like getting out of bed each day. I am very weak." So I ask him, "Have you been to the doctor?" He tells me he hasn't. Finally, I ask him about his diet. The sick fellow answers, "I go to this restaurant about one Sunday a month. I snack on junk food occasionally. But I only get one good meal a month." Of course, with that kind of nutrition schedule, he would stay weak, anemic, and sick. Yet that is how some professing believers treat the church. They only gather with other saints once in a while. No wonder they are spiritually weak.

Earlier this month (August 19), we discussed the importance of attending church. Psalm 149:1 reminds us that there is a corporate place for God's children to sing ... *his praise in the congregation [assembly] of saints.* It is good to worship privately. But God also wants us to worship Him publicly in the place of praise. God inhabits the praises of His people and blesses unity. Corporate praise is powerful praise.

THE PASSION OF PRAISE

(Psalm 150:1-6)

It was the first service of the revival. As the pastor and I walked to the sanctuary, an angry church member approached us. It did not matter that the pastor was with the guest preacher. The disgruntled member said, "Pastor, I am not staying for the service, and I won't be back until those drums are removed from the sanctuary." With those blunt words, he spun on his heels and left. The embarrassed pastor apologized and confided to me that the church was in a hostile "worship war" over instruments in the church. Sadly, some churches across the land are still fighting worship wars over styles of music and choices of musical instruments.

Psalm 150 tells us that God enjoys musical instruments. This psalm is a psalm of passion. Worship is used too much as a noun and not enough as a verb. For two months, we have examined the songbook of the Bible. For the past four days, it has reminded us about the *priority, participants, place, and passion of praise.* The earth, the heavens, the whole of creation, and all the angels of heaven continually offer passionate and undistracted praise to God. We should do so with every means available to us. *Let everything that hath breath praise the Lord!*

DECISIONS THAT DETERMINE DESTINY

(Genesis 13:1-18)

School was out for the summer, and a teenage boy was looking for a job. Driving down the road, he saw a huge watermelon farm. There was a big sign on the fence that said, "Help Wanted." Quickly, he applied and was hired. His first day on the job, the farmer took him to a huge barn filled with melons that had been harvested. The farmer said, "I want you to separate these watermelons into piles. Put the little melons in one pile, the medium-size melons in one pile, and the big ones in another pile." The boy diligently went to work. Two short hours later, the young man told the farmer, "I quit." Shocked, the farmer inquired, "Was the work too hard?" The frustrated teenager replied, "No, but these decisions are killing me."

Life is filled with important decisions. A man named Lot chose to *pitch his tent toward Sodom* (v. 12), a wicked city. It wasn't long before Lot left his tent and *sat in the gate of Sodom* (Genesis 19:1). His unwise decision cost him his family. It all began when he left his uncle Abraham and looked in the wrong direction. Our decisions, right or wrong, determine our destiny.

FOLLOW THE LIGHT

(Romans 12:1-21)

An automobile is equipped with headlights for driving in the dark. The bright beams shine four hundred and fifty feet in front of the vehicle, and the low beams one hundred and fifty feet ahead. Let's suppose it is nighttime, and you are about fifteen miles from your home. You realize that the headlights won't shine fifteen miles in front of you. So you turn them off and say, "Since my lights don't shine all the way home, I am not going to move." Of course, that would be ridiculous. You simply move out, following the light you do have. When it goes left, you go left. When the light goes in a valley, you go in a valley. When it turns a corner, you turn a corner. You keep following that light until it leads you home.

In Romans 12:3, Paul says that God has given every single believer a *measure [portion] of faith*. Although you can't see the end of the road, God expects you to step out and follow the light He has given in faith. Some believers never fulfill God's will and plan for their life because they are afraid to take a step of faith. Follow the light. His light will lead you home.

THE RIVERBOAT OF REDEMPTION

(Exodus 2:1-10)

Pharaoh of Egypt was wicked. As the number of his Jewish prisoners multiplied, Pharaoh was concerned that they would one day overthrow him. So he concocted a plan to start drowning the Hebrews' newborn male babies in the Nile River (Exodus 1:22). But the Jews were praying for a leader to be raised up to lead them from bondage. One day, a baby boy named Moses was born. When Moses was three months old, his mother built a little ark – a riverboat of redemption – and set the baby afloat in the river. Pharaoh's daughter heard the child crying, and Moses' sister (who was standing nearby) suggested that a Hebrew woman raise the baby. In a brilliant plan, she called Moses' own mother (Jochebed). His mom, in the very palace of Pharaoh, raised her son Moses.

Satan inspired Pharaoh to kill the Hebrew baby boys in an attempt to stop the Jewish Messiah from being born. Has it occurred to you that Moses was saved in the very river where the babies were being killed? God so often works in and through the very circumstances Satan designed for evil. All things work to the good for those who love Him. Only God can do that.

SEPTEMBER 4

IT'S PERSONAL

(John 14:15-31)

One of the most famous and popular quotes in motion picture history is from the *Star Wars* movies. Of course, that familiar line is, "May the force with you." A believer once told me that anytime he hears that phrase, "the force," it always makes him think of the Holy Spirit. But that is not a very accurate comparison. The precious Holy Spirit is not some sort of invisible energy or force field. Nor is the Holy Spirit an "it" or a "thing." Instead, the third person of the Trinity is just that. He is a person. The Holy Spirit has emotional feelings (Ephesians 4:30), intellect (1 Corinthians 2:10-11), and a will (1 Corinthians 12:11). There is a real person guarding and guiding your life. He is the person of the Holy Ghost.

When Christ refers to the Holy Ghost in God's Word, He always uses the personal pronouns *he* or *him* (vv. 16-17, 26). In John 14:26, Christ calls Him our *Comforter*. The word *Comforter* literally means "consoler, advocate, and intercessor." As you leave home today, you are protected and secure. You are wrapped up with your own personal Comforter, a personal gift from the Father and Son to you.

THE TROUBLE WITH ALCOHOL

(Proverbs 20:1-5; 23:29-35)

We live in an alcohol-drinking culture. Breweries and distilleries spend over $1 billion a year trying to entice Americans to drink. Every seven minutes, there is a television commercial about beer or alcohol. However, it seems that most people in our country don't need much encouragement, because there sure is a whole lot of drinking going on. Statistics tell us that 75 percent of all Americans drink alcohol. Over 80 percent of the people in the U.S. between the ages of eighteen and thirty drink socially. During the course of the year, Americans will consume thirty-three gallons of alcohol per person. Last year, somebody must have drank more than that, because I didn't drink any. At any rate, alcoholism is the third-highest health problem in our country.

Scripture repeatedly warns us about the dangers of alcohol. Proverbs 20:1 says, *strong drink is raging* (trouble.) In Proverbs 23:29, Solomon tells us that alcohol will bring tears to your eyes. Within the next twenty-four hours, 50 percent of all the murders, highway fatalities, domestic violence incidents, arrests, and children born with birth defects will be a direct result of alcohol. What we put into us will come out and manifest its real fruit in our lives.

KEEPER OF THE KEYS

(Revelation 1:9-20)

When my children were small, we took a family vacation to Gatlinburg, Tennessee. One gorgeous morning, I drove our trusty minivan to a public park and we went hiking and exploring. After several hours, our tired group came trudging back to the parking lot, excited about heading back to the hotel for an afternoon of napping and swimming. But when I looked in the window of the locked van, I saw the keys still in the ignition. We didn't own a cell phone back in 1988. So I had to hike to find a phone and call a locksmith to come and unlock the van. My kids were whining, my wife was tired, and I must confess that I briefly thought about picking up a rock and breaking the window.

It is frustrating whenever you are locked out without the right key. However, when it comes to eternity, I am glad that I know the keeper of the keys. Revelation 1:18 reminds us that our risen Lord has *the keys of hell and of death* in His nail-pierced hands. His keys have opened the prison doors and set me free, and in Him, I'm free indeed.

BELIEVING IS SEEING

(2 Kings 6:8-23)

Do you know what a stereogram is? It is a 2-D picture or painting that has a 3-D image hidden inside of it. You have to focus and stare intently at the stereogram until the hidden image appears. I was once in pastor's study, looking at a painting that appeared to be an abstract mass of colorful dots. The pastor asked me, "Do you see the face of Jesus?" Smiling skeptically at him, I answered, "All that I can see is a jumbled mess." He said, "Just focus on the center of the picture." I stared closely at it for a few moments. Suddenly, the face of Christ leapt out from the middle of all those colors. Excitedly I shouted, "Yes! I can see Jesus!" The pastor laughed and said, "Everybody has the same reaction when they finally see Jesus."

The world says that seeing is believing. But for Christians, believing is seeing. That is what the servant of Elisha discovered in 2 Kings 6. The Syrian army surrounded him and he was fearful (vv. 14-15). However, Elisha asked God to open the servant's eyes so he could see the angels surrounding and outnumbering the Syrians (v. 17). What do your eyes of faith see today?

CONFESSION IS GOOD FOR THE SOUL

(1 John 1:1-10)

A conceited woman attended a revival service one night. When the evangelist preached passionately on the sin of pride, a deep conviction came to her soul. During the altar call, the broken lady walked quickly down the aisle to pray with the pastor. She said, "Pastor, I need to confess my sin." Gently, the pastor asked, "What sin do you need to confess, sister?" The lady answered contritely, "I can't quit looking at myself. Every time I pass by a mirror, I have got to stop and gaze at how beautiful I am. I can't help it. I think that I am the most beautiful woman in the world." When the woman finished her confession, the pastor said, "I've got good news for you. That's not a sin, that's a mistake."

True confession is good for the soul. First John 1:9 is one of the most familiar passages in the Bible. God tells us to *confess* (agree with Him). When we genuinely confess, God forgives. It would be tragic if there were conviction of sin but no cleansing. Humility is pleasing to God, but it involves absolute honesty. We must tell it as God sees it, not how we see it. When we confess, He cleanses.

September 9

His Ways Are Higher

(Isaiah 55:1-13)

On January 8, 1956, Jim Elliot and four other missionaries were brutally speared and murdered by Auca Indians on a beach beside the Curaray River in the Ecuadoran jungle. The horrible news shocked the world, and many considered the deaths of the five young men to be a tragic waste. But after Jim's death, his wife, Elisabeth, did not come home. Instead, she chose to stay and work with the people who had killed her husband. The love of Christ that was shown through Elisabeth's forgiveness allowed her to have amazing success with the Aucas. Some of those who killed Jim were saved because of Elisabeth Elliot's witness. Jim's life was not a waste. God has used his story as an encouragement and inspiration to thousands all over the world.

The prophet Isaiah declared to us that God's thoughts and actions are nothing like ours. In fact, Isaiah reminds us that God's ways and thoughts cannot be compared to ours because they are much higher. That word *higher* means "lofty, great, and exalted." None of us can explain the reason things happen, but the essence of faith is believing without knowing or understanding. All that we can do is put our trust in Him. His ways are higher.

MIDNIGHT GLADNESS

(Acts 16:25-40)

College basketball has a popular tradition called Midnight Madness. Every fall, teams from around the country hold a public practice that officially begins at the hour of midnight. Students and fans eagerly stand in line for hours just to get a ticket so they can watch their team practice and have dunk contests. In 2015, the University of Kentucky reported that twenty-four thousand tickets were snatched up in just thirty-five minutes. The concept of Midnight Madness has become a massive media spectacle. ESPN broadcasts Midnight Madness nationally from multiple college campuses as fans scream and shout until the wee hours of the morning.

One night in a prison cell, Paul and Silas were involved in "midnight gladness." At midnight (v. 25), the two jailed preachers started to sing and praise the Lord. God rocked the jail with an earthquake (v. 26). The Roman guard thought he had lost the prisoners and was going to commit suicide. But he and his family received eternal life. It was midnight gladness. So often, we think of the midnight hour as something that belongs to the Devil. But God's light and power bring infinite joy in even the darkest hours if we hold on to the gladness we have in Christ.

HEAVEN'S HERO

(Zechariah 12:1-14)

September 11, 2001, was a horrific day of hurt and heartbreak in America. But it was also a day for heroes. Firefighters, policemen, and first responders risked their lives so that people could be saved. A decoration known as the 9/11 Heroes Medal of Valor was created in memory of the 442 public safety officials who were killed in the line of duty on that grim September morning. In September 2005, President George W. Bush posthumously presented the beautiful medals to families of the fallen officers at a moving ceremony on the White House lawn. The medals have no pins or ribbons, so they cannot be worn. They are to be displayed in recognition of heroes who laid down their lives.

The greatest hero of all is Jesus Christ. He laid down His life so that we could be saved. One day in heaven, we will see the wounds in our Lord's hands. Zechariah reminds Israel that they will look upon the *pierced* One (v. 10). At that moment, they will mourn and repent. The hands of Jesus will forever be nail scarred. They are the medals of valor of heaven's hero. He displays them as a testimony to the love He has for us all.

WHAT DOES YOUR NAME MEAN?

(Luke 6:12-26)

The name of Benedict Arnold will always be associated with treason and betrayal. He was a general in the American Continental Army who fought the British during the Revolutionary War. But in 1780, Benedict Arnold defected and turned his back on George Washington. Arnold became a spy for the British and plotted a siege against West Point. Down through history, when people hear the name Benedict Arnold, the first word that comes to mind is the word *traitor*. That is how folks remember Judas Iscariot. Although he was a follower, friend, and disciple of Jesus Christ, Judas committed an act of high treason and became a traitor.

That is what Judas is called in Luke 6:16. The Greek word for *traitor* means "to give over or surrender to the enemy." Although the name of Judas will forever be associated with treason, this is not what his name originally meant. The Hebrew name for Judas is from the word *Judah*, and it means "to praise." But no one will ever remember that, because Judas blew it. Your name is very important. When people think of your name, what does it mean to them? What does it mean to God, who knows each of us by name?

GOD RUNS THE UNIVERSE

(Job 38:22-41)

Snow fascinates people from Florida. One January, in snowy Ohio, my wife asked me to build an Olaf snowman and take a picture for the grandkids. So, being an indulgent granddad, I trudged out in minus-ten-degree weather. When the snowman was finished, I removed my gloves because smartphones aren't smart enough to take a picture through them. In doing so, I dropped both my gloves and phone in the snow. After I retrieved my phone, I knocked Olaf's head off with my shoulder. Since my gloves were full of snow, I had to fix it with my bare hands. By the time I got inside, I was sure I had frostbite. Snow can be both beautiful and fun. But on that frigid day, I decided the best way to look at snow was from my heated hotel room!

In Job 38, God reminds Job of who runs the universe. The great Creator is the only one who controls the snow, hail, rain, and ice (vv. 22-30). Job 38:22 speaks of *the treasures of the snow*. The word *treasures* is translated "treasuries." In other words, Almighty God stores up the snow and tells it exactly where to fall. He is the supernatural CEO who runs the universe.

Fellowship

(Philippians 1:1-11)

W e live in a digitalized and de-personalized world. Ours has become a cold and automated society where people are known and classified by zip code, area code, and social security number. In our culture, it is hard to call a number and not get an automated and computerized voice. Is it just me, or does anyone else ever get frustrated trying to make a phone call and having to deal with all the recorded voices? There are times when you want to shout, "Please let me talk to a real, live, warm-blooded human being!" There has never been a generation in American history with a greater need for the personal touch of fellowship than the one we live in today.

Nowhere is fellowship more important than in the blood-bought church. Paul starts chapter 1 of Philippians by telling the servants of God that he thankfully and fondly remembers them (v. 3). Then Paul encourages all of us, when he reminds them that believers are in *fellowship* (partnership) together. Christians are in partnership with one other. We are created to come together as one body, sharing our strengths and helping each other's weaknesses. We need fellowship. It is a unity designed by God for our every need.

OBEDIENCE BRINGS BLESSINGS

(Deuteronomy 28:1-10)

Two teenagers named Chad and Eric were driving around together one Friday night. Chad suggested to Eric that they do something that was wrong. Eric immediately said, "My father wouldn't want me to do that." Chad asked, "What's the matter, man? Are you afraid your dad might find out and he will hurt you?" Eric quickly replied, "No. I am afraid my dad might find out and it will hurt him." That is the spirit and attitude that every believer should have toward our heavenly Father. Our rebellion and sin hurts the heart of God. But on the other side of the coin, God is pleased when we walk in obedience. In fact, obedience brings blessings.

That is the theme of God's Word. In Deuteronomy 28, God promised material blessings to Israel if they obeyed Him. God told them He would bless their cities, farms, fruit, and cattle. He said that He would stop their enemies and fill their barns, and that everyone would know their reputation (vv. 3-10). Nothing has changed. God still blesses and prospers those who obey Him. The omnipotent God of the universe is also our Father. Our disobedience wounds Him and our obedience pleases Him because He loves us as our Father.

WATCH AND PRAY

(Colossians 4:1-18)

As a young boy, I was constantly amazed by my father's ability to watch and pray at the same time. When I was small, I would often become preoccupied and restless at the family dinner table. On more than one occasion, my dear dad would be praying to bless the food, and right in the middle of the prayer, he would say things like, "Rick, sit up and bow your head right now." I would look at him, and his eyes were completely shut when he spoke to me. I always wondered how he did that. Many years later, I realized my father was just practicing what Paul preached in the book of Colossians, chapter 1. He was watching and praying.

The word *watch* in verse 2 carries with it the idea of "being alert or praying with your eyes open." There is an Old Testament picture of watching and praying found in the book of Nehemiah. As the people rebuilt the walls, the enemy threatened. Nehemiah had the people pray and watch (Nehemiah 4:9). Christ told us to watch and pray so we would have victory over temptation (Mark 14:38). Keep praying, but keep watch also. It's a spiritual ability that comes from the Holy Spirit who lives in us.

THE POTTER AND THE CLAY

(Jeremiah 18:1-10)

One day, God spoke to Jeremiah and told him to take a field trip. God instructed His preacher to visit the local potter's house and observe him working on the clay. Jeremiah intently watched the potter spin the clay on the wheel. At one point in the project, God's prophet noticed that the man was not satisfied with the vessel he was shaping. But the potter didn't throw the clay away. Jeremiah realized that he had his own design and plan for the clay. So he watched while the potter patiently started over and worked until he had fashioned the perfect vessel. It was the one that the potter had in mind from the beginning.

Jeremiah clearly understood the lesson that God was teaching him. God is the Potter, and man is the clay (v. 6). Clay cannot mold itself. The only person that can shape the clay is the one who knows what he wants the clay to become. You are the clay. The Potter has a perfect plan for your life. It's a plan and a purpose He had in mind for you from the beginning of creation. Let Him mold you into the vessel that He wants you to be.

RADICAL EVANGELISM

(Mark 2:1-12)

I remember when I first heard the words "We've never done it that way before." In the early 1970s, while in Bible college, I preached a student-led revival in Florida. Each night before the services, the students would meet at church. We prayed, got in our cars, and scattered throughout the community, picking up teens to bring them to church. Many of the people we picked up were not part of the typical churchgoing crowd. God used that unconventional method of evangelism to save souls that week. Sadly, some of the members of the church were uncomfortable with it, and they complained, "We've never done it that way before." Over the years, I have come to realize that those are the seven words of a dying church.

Our message never changes. But we must always be open to using new and often radical methods to bring people to Jesus. In Mark 2, four guys got pretty creative with their evangelistic outreach. They climbed on the roof of a crowded building (v. 2), tore it open, and lowered a palsied man down to meet Jesus and be healed. That is radical evangelism.

SINS OF THE FATHER

(Joshua 7:13-26)

Late one night, a father got a dreadful telephone call from the police department. He was told that his eighteen-year-old daughter had been killed in an automobile accident. Brokenhearted, he and his wife went to identify her. When he saw her scarred and mutilated body, he sobbed. "How did this happen?" An officer said they had found an empty liquor bottle in the car she was driving. Enraged, the dad exclaimed, "If I ever find the man who sold it to her, I will tear him apart." Back home, the shaken father wanted a drink. When he opened his liquor cabinet, he found a note from his daughter. It said, *Dear Dad, I borrowed a bottle from your cabinet to celebrate my eighteenth birthday. Don't worry ... I will pay you back. I love you.*

The Bible warns that a father's sins affect his children (Numbers 14:18; Ezekiel 18:2). A dad named Achan discovered that God means what He says. God had made it clear that the spoils of Jericho would be placed in the treasury of the Lord (Joshua 6:19). But Achan stole some things and hid them in his tent. Achan's family paid dearly for his careless sin (Joshua 7:24-25).

THE DESIRE OF THE EYES

(1 John 2:15-23)

Much of my life is spent on the road. Consequently, it is a constant battle to eat healthy. Late one evening, I faced a long drive home after concluding a revival. Hungry from preaching, I decided to pick up something for the trip. I had already settled my mind on a 280-calorie wheat and tuna Subway sandwich. But suddenly, a Whopper hamburger popped into my head. A Whopper is seven hundred calories of savory grilled beef topped with juicy tomatoes, fresh-cut lettuce, creamy mustard, crunchy pickles, and sliced onions on a sesame seed bun. Quickly, I rebuked the thought and looked for a Subway. But my eyes fell on a bright Burger King sign. I think you know the rest of the story.

In First John 2:15, God commands us to *Love not the world, neither the things that are in the world.* The word *world* is speaking about Satan's system. As we travel life's road, the bright, tempting lights of the world always shine in our eyes. John warns us against *the lust [desires] of the eyes* (v. 16). Lust frequently enters through the eye gate. Keep your eyes on Jesus. If our eyes are filled with Him, there won't be space for anything else to slip in.

A LIFE WORTH LIVING

(Ecclesiastes 1:1-18)

You are probably not familiar with the name of William Claude Dukenfield. He was better known as W. C. Fields, a famous American comedian, actor, writer, and juggler. Fields was one of Hollywood's most-popular stars of the 1920s and '30s. Sadly, as gifted and multi-talented as he was, Fields was an agnostic who spent his whole life denouncing the Bible and denying the existence of God. On Christmas Day 1946, he died from an alcohol-related stomach hemorrhage. Several days before his death, a friend visited and said that he caught the actor lying in bed, reading a Bible. When asked what he was doing, Fields simply said, "I'm looking for a loophole."

Solomon was the wisest man on earth. Yet, in Ecclesiastes 1, the king is asking, "Is life worth living?" In verse 2, he declares, *all is vanity* (emptiness). Fortunately, after a long journey, Solomon concludes that life is not worth living unless you live it for God (Ecclesiastes 12:13). He was also the wealthiest man in the world. There was nothing he desired that he couldn't acquire. If the man who had everything tells us nothing has value without God, shouldn't we learn from him and seek God before seeking other things?

STAND STRONG

(Ephesians 6:10-20)

Two young boys burst suddenly and breathlessly into a dentist's office one morning. Catching his breath, one of the boys blurted, "Mister dentist, I've got to have a bad tooth pulled, and I want it pulled right now!" The dentist put his firm hand on the boy's shoulder and said, "Now, just calm down, son. Take your time and tell me all about it." Quickly, the boy answered, "I don't have time. My friend and I need to get to the ballgame. I want you to pull the tooth right this second. We don't even have time for you to numb it with a needle. Just yank it out." The dentist replied, "Well, I must say, you are a courageous young man. Which tooth is it?" Turning to his friend, the boy said, "Show him which tooth it is, Johnny."

It isn't always easy being courageous, especially when you face spiritual warfare. But God has promised us that we do not fight alone. In fact, you will experience great pain and defeat if you attempt to fight the Enemy alone. Ephesians 6:10 admonishes us to *be strong [enabled and empowered] in the Lord*. Stand in God's armor today, and you will stand strong.

LISTEN AND LEARN

(Judges 2:11-23)

Judy and I have been blessed with three great children, two girls and a boy. When my two daughters were growing up, they were totally different. If we told our oldest child, Rachel, that something was dangerous, she would stay away from it. But our girl Jessica was a different story. One day after I finished mowing the grass, I told her not to touch the exhaust of a hot lawnmower. She immediately grabbed it and burned her hand badly. On another occasion, Judy told her not to touch a hot stove. Of course, she instantly touched it. Jessica spent many childhood hours in doctor's offices getting stitched or bandaged up. It was always because she wouldn't listen when Dad and Mom warned her that something was dangerous to her health.

In Judges 2, God the Father had the same trouble with His children. Even though the Lord graciously gave Israel righteous judges to lead them, the people continually rebelled (vv. 18-19). They would not listen or learn. It doesn't matter what generation we are living in. Our Father tells us how to stay out of harm's way because He loves us. Those who refuse to listen to His warnings will always get burned.

True Love

(1 Corinthians 13:1-13)

Have you ever had a drummer in your home? When my son was a teenager, he wanted to play the drums. One Christmas, I bought him his very first drum set. He put the drums in his bedroom and immediately started practicing. There is something about constantly hearing the noisy clanging of cymbals every day that cannot be described. When January rolled around, it was time for me to resume my schedule and get back on the road. One night after a revival service, I called home to speak with my wife. She said sweetly, "By the way, I want to thank you for getting Jonathan those drums. Maybe he could take them and travel with you." What our young drummer heard as sweet music sounded very different to my wife.

Paul begins the love chapter of the Bible with a very powerful analogy. It doesn't matter how flowery or eloquent the words are. If real *charity* (agape love) is not in the heart, it is like the loud and noisy clanging of brass cymbals. True biblical agape love is essential (vv. 1-3), effectual (vv. 4-7), and eternal (vv. 8-13). Like Jesus, we must learn to listen to the heart, not to what we think we hear.

SMART ENOUGH TO KNOW

(Daniel 12:1-13)

We live in an amazing age of technological and scientific achievement. When I became a traveling evangelist in the late 1980s, I left my wife and children each week and missed them terribly. I would speak to them by calling them on our house landline phone. Today, I can both speak to my grandchildren and also look right into their smiling faces on the smartphone that I carry in my pocket. Just over a century ago, the amount of knowledge had been doubling every one hundred years. In the twenty-first century, knowledge doubles every twelve months. It is believed that 80 percent of the world's knowledge has been brought forth in the last decade. This is the smart generation. We are surrounded with smartphones, smart TVs, smart cars, and even smart homes.

This explosion of knowledge was prophesied thousands of years ago. Daniel 12:4 tells us that in the last days, *knowledge shall be increased* (greatly and rapidly enlarged). There are many brilliant, gifted, and smart people in the world today. But the really smart people are the ones who are smart enough to recognize that Jesus Christ is coming soon. All man's knowledge avails nothing if we ignore the biblical truth that Christ will return as King of Glory.

CHRISTIAN EVIDENCE

(1 Thessalonians 1:1-10)

Outstanding speaker, author, and apologist Josh McDowell once asked, "If you were arrested for being a Christian, would there be enough evidence to convict you?" Think about this very compelling question for a moment. In gospel-hardened America, many people are under the delusion that being a Christian simply means to be a baptized church member, or at least attend church faithfully. Others interpret being a Christian as being a good, moral, religious person who lives rigidly by a strict set of rules and requirements. However, the evidences of real Christianity go much deeper than that.

In First Thessalonians 1, Paul reminds all of us that the *church* (called-out ones) bears some undeniable marks of authenticity. The Thessalonian saints were workers (v. 3), witnesses (v. 8), and waiters on the Lord's return (v. 10). Verse 6 describes them as followers of the Lord. The word *followers* means "imitators of Jesus." That is the evidence of a real Christian. We are called to live like Christ, not simply speak as though we do.

WHEN A NATION WAKES UP

(1 Samuel 7:1-17)

Over one hundred years ago, a young Bible student named Evan Roberts received a burden for revival to come to the country of Wales. He organized a prayer meeting one Wednesday night, and seventeen students gathered to pray. The next night, they met for a revival service, and the rest is history. Within five months, over one hundred thousand people were saved. The local police station had seventeen policemen, and twelve of them made up gospel quartets. The crime rate dropped so radically that there were more calls for the quartets than there were for the police. Bars closed all over town, and illegitimate births dropped by 50 percent. The revival in Wales swept through Britain, Germany, Africa, and America. It began with seventeen burdened people on their knees.

Samuel got a burden for Israel and called the nation to wake up and seek God. First Samuel 7 is a record of the awakening. Initially, Samuel poured out water before the Lord as a symbol of the nation's repentance (v. 6). Next, the prophet called the nation to the altar of sacrifice (vv. 9-10). God gloriously delivered Israel from the iron hand of the Philistines and revival fell. The prayer burden always comes first, obedience second, and then revival.

HOME WITH THE LORD

(2 Corinthians 5:1-10)

Samuel Morrison spent twenty-five years on the mission field of Africa. When he left Africa, he boarded an ocean liner and returned to the U.S. President Theodore Roosevelt, returning from a hunting expedition in Africa, was also aboard. As the ship steamed into New York Harbor, massive crowds lined the docks to cheer for the president. No one was there to greet Samuel Morrison, and it hurt him. He complained to God and said, "The president was in Africa for three weeks killing animals, and when he comes home, he is greeted as a hero. I have given twenty-five years for the gospel, and no one is here to greet me." At that moment, the Father spoke to Samuel's heart and said, "You're not home yet."

While Christians are at home in this body, *we are absent from the Lord* (v. 6). Second Corinthians 5:8 says that it is better to be *absent from the body, and to be present [home] with the Lord.* The *building* in verse 1 is not our mansion. It is the glorified body we will receive after our temporary tent is taken down. Keep on serving, Christian, you're not home yet. Great rejoicing awaits when you come home to heaven.

PRAYER FROM THE PIT

(Jonah 2:1-10)

Some folks aren't really serious about praying until they land in the pit of trouble. In the book of Jonah, a backslidden preacher didn't pray and seek God's will when he was told to go to Nineveh. He didn't pray when the ship of rebellion he was on was overwhelmed in the storm. Jonah waited until he was way down inside the belly of a fish. His prayer was not a prayer of affection, it was a prayer of affliction. Did you notice the very first word found in Jonah chapter 2? It is the word *Then*. After Jonah was tossed overboard into the sea, after he was gulped down, after the preacher became fish food … *then* he prayed.

I believe I would have prayed then too. Jonah was literally down in the pit. Read chapter 2 carefully and notice how descriptive the language is. Verses 2-3 use the words *hell* and *deep*. In verse 5, Jonah says that he has seaweed wrapped around his head. No doubt the big fish had a little salad with his entrée. Jonah was deep in the pit, and he needed divine intervention. Are you in the pit? If you are, this is the time to pray.

OPEN YOUR GIFT

(1 Peter 4:1-11)

I spend a great deal of my life on the road. Many times over the years, I have returned from a revival trip and brought a gift home to my wife, Judy. Of course, she is always gracious and grateful to receive any gift. But let's suppose that I came home one week with a very special gift for her. Imagine that I gave it to her, she thanked me, and then put it, unopened, on the kitchen counter. Now, just suppose for the next two or three days, my wife still didn't take time to open that special gift. Finally, it is time for me to go out of town again. As I walk past the kitchen counter to head for the door, I notice that the wonderful gift I chose just for her is still wrapped up and has never been opened. How do you think I would feel?

How do you think your heavenly Father feels when His children never open the spiritual gifts that He has given? First Peter 4:10 reminds us that every Christian has received at least one spiritual gift. If you are saved, you are a gifted child. Open your gift and use it for the Lord.

HOLY HATRED

(Proverbs 6:12-19)

One of the very first songs I ever learned to sing as a small child was about the love of God. That old chorus said, "Praise Him, praise Him, all ye little children; God is love, God is love." The first Bible verse I ever memorized as a child was John 3:16. That wonderful verse begins with the words *For God so loved the world.* Indeed, God is love. Yet Solomon tells us that there are seven things that God hates. In fact, Proverbs 6:16 reminds us that God hates these seven things so much, they are an *abomination* (disgusting) to Him. Yes, God's love is great. It cannot be measured or fathomed. However, God is also holy, and He has a holy hatred for sin. Specifically, there are seven things on God's hate list.

When you read the sins listed in Proverbs 6:16-19, there are some obvious ones. After all, God mentions pride (the sin of the Devil that began the whole mess), murder, and wicked minds. But God also names lying and *he that soweth discord [strife] among brethren.* Make no mistake about it. God hates it when people, often with lies or deception, cause strife, division, and discord in churches.

OCTOBER 2

HEAR THE BELLS

(Matthew 12:22-37)

As a boy left home for his freshman year in college, his father said, "Promise me you will go to church next Sunday." During the first week of classes, he met some guys who invited him to a party at the lake on Sunday. Forgetting his promise, the young man agreed. Early Sunday morning, as they drove to the lake, the car passed a country church. The steeple bells were ringing, and he remembered the promise. As the car sped past the church, the bells got fainter. Finally, under deep conviction, the boy said, "Stop the car. I need to get out. Those bells reminded me that I promised my dad that I would go to church. I can barely hear them now. I need to go back while I can still hear the bells."

In Matthew 12:31-32, Jesus Christ speaks about blaspheming the Holy Ghost. This is the sin of refusing God for the final time. Our great God is loving, patient, and longsuffering. However, He will not repeat His invitation forever if we keep rejecting Him. Isn't it wonderful to know that there was a moment when you heard the bells of conviction, opened your heart to Jesus Christ, and avoided blaspheming the Spirit?

SON-SHINE

(Numbers 6:22-27)

As I write this day's devotion, I am at home, sitting at my desk, and looking out the window at a dreary day. Jacksonville is in the middle of a second-straight North Florida weather event known as a Nor'easter. The back-to-back Nor'easters have brought six days of continuous strong winds, clouds, and steady rains in from off the coast. Much of North Florida is under a flood watch. Trees have fallen because the ground is so saturated with water. This morning on television, our local meteorologist said, "The sun hasn't broken through and shined in Jacksonville for almost a week. But I have good news. Tomorrow, the sun will be shining."

Numbers 6:22-27 reveals the blessing that Aaron and the family of priests pronounced on the children of Israel. Verse 25 is a declaration that the *face of the Lord shine upon them.* The word *shine* means "to break through and glow." No matter what storms or dark, dismal circumstances we face, Jesus is the light that will always shine through. He is the bright and morning star that heralds the break of day and the end of darkness. His light transcends our situation and our emotional response. Today, may you experience God's *Son*-shine.

OCTOBER 4

WARNING LIGHTS

(John 16:1-16)

I magine that you are driving down the road, and a bright red light suddenly appears on your dashboard panel. The light is the little oilcan symbol. Now, you don't have to be a neurosurgeon to understand that the red light is a warning. It means that you are low on oil in the crankcase. If you ignore it and continue to drive without checking it, you are eventually going to seize up the engine. But let's suppose the light is interfering with your day. It is bothersome to you. Eventually, you just decide to pick up a hammer and break it so you won't have to look at it anymore. Of course, that would be ridiculous. If anyone did that, sooner or later, it is going to cost them dearly.

God has given His followers a wonderful warning light called the precious Holy Spirit. In John 16, Jesus Christ describes the work of the Comforter. The eighth verse tells us that the Holy Spirit *reproves* (convicts or convinces of sin). When He warns you of sin, it is for your own good. You never react in anger or complain about the warning light. Instead, you just let Him fix the problem then and there.

OCTOBER 5

HE UNDERSTANDS

(Isaiah 40:18-31)

Early one evening, a busy mother had finished cleaning the kitchen after dinner. Just as the weary woman sat down for a few relaxing minutes on the soft couch, she heard her five-year-old son screaming. The mom rushed upstairs and asked, "What's the matter?" Her crying son pointed to his one-year-old sister and answered, "She pulled my hair." Sweetly, the mother consoled him and replied, "I'm sorry, honey. She doesn't understand that pulling hair hurts." The mom hugged them both and headed back downstairs. When she returned to the couch, the woman heard the little girl scream. Running back up to the room, she saw her son holding a clump of his sister's hair. The boy looked at his mother and said, "She understands now."

There will always be things we do not understand, but Isaiah reminds us there is no one like our great and glorious God. The God who created you understands everything about you. Isaiah 40:28 says, *there is no searching of his understanding* (wisdom or intelligence). God knows how high your joy is and also how deep your pain is. If you are weary today, wait on the Lord. He will renew your strength (v. 31).

OCTOBER 6

GET TO WORK

(James 2:14-26)

It has been my privilege to preach in hundreds of churches down through the years. During that time, I have heard pastors and staff members make thousands of public announcements from the platform. But I have never heard one of them say, "Ladies and gentlemen, we don't need any more nursery or preschool volunteers, we have more than enough helpers. We don't need any more teachers, because we have a long waiting list. We are never going to take another offering, because we have more money that we can spend in a lifetime." I have never heard any words like that. But conversely, more times than I could possibly count or recall, I have heard frustrated pastors beg for people to serve the Lord.

James 2:26 says, *faith without works is dead.* A true believer consistently bears fruit for God's glory and works to please Him. When we "sign up" to follow Christ, we sign up to live our lives the way He did. We sign up for servanthood. It's non-negotiable, and it's a lifetime commitment. Think about it this way – salvation is the work God does for us, sanctification is the work God does in us, and service is the work God does through us.

OCTOBER 7

LOOKING AT THE FUTURE

(Ezekiel 39:1-16)

Michel Nostradamus was a French astrologist and seer who lived in the sixteenth century. The legend of Nostradamus has been greatly popularized in this generation. Books, films, videos, and *The History Channel* have suggested that the Frenchman may have actually looked five hundred years into the future and seen shocking historical events such as the Kennedy assassination and the falling of the World Trade Center. Intelligent people around the globe believe that Nostradamus could actually see the future. It's amazing that folks will accept things like this but not believe that God spoke through His prophets as they foretold incredible future events.

The prophet Ezekiel saw Russia thousands of years before there was a Russia. In Ezekiel 38 and 39, he describes the battle of Gog and Magog that will take place on the planet after the rapture of the church. Most scholars believe this battle will occur during the first three and a half years of the tribulation. Ezekiel 38:2 specifically names two Russian cities, Meshech (possibly Moscow), and Tubal (perhaps Tobolsk). Ezekiel looked into the future and saw it happen. You can believe it because the Word of God is irrefutable. Unlike man's human, fallible prophecies, God's Word will always come to pass and testify of Him.

OCTOBER 8

THE REAL DEAL

(Acts 5:17-42)

When my son, Jonathan, was a little guy, our family was out walking in a mall one evening. He saw one of those electrical, mechanical rocket-ship rides and asked, "Dad, can I ride that rocket? It only costs fifty cents." So I gave him two quarters to ride it while I did a little window-shopping. My son was on that rocket ship for at least a full five minutes. When he finally got off and came back over to me, I said, "Son, that was a pretty long ride for fifty cents." My boy looked at me and replied, "Oh no, Dad, the ride was broken. But there were some people standing around watching. So I just jumped up and down on it for a while so everybody would think I was having a good time."

Unfortunately, that is a picture of some Christians. They go through the motions, but have no power and no joy. In the first century, the believers were authentic. Acts 5:17-42 tells the story of apostles who were persecuted, but they kept serving God with joy. Their testimony was so impressive, a Pharisee named Gamaliel took note (vv. 34-39). Those believers were the real deal and their authenticity changed the world.

NO DOUBT

(Malachi 1:1-14)

All doubt comes from the Devil. One of his main objectives and goals is to bring doubt of some kind into your mind. Firstly, he constantly casts doubt on the Word of God. That is how the snake got Eve to eat of the forbidden fruit in Eden. Then, even after you believe God's Word and get saved, the Devil works overtime in an attempt to make you doubt the eternal salvation you have received. He doesn't want you to claim and hold onto the promises of God. Finally, when any trouble or difficulty comes your way, the Devil will try and get you to doubt God's love for you. That is what the Enemy did to Israel in the last book of the Old Testament.

In the first chapter of Malachi, the people doubt God's love. Malachi responds by telling Israel that God promised them a land of milk and honey, but their sins and the sins of their priests had polluted the land (vv. 7, 12). However, in the end, their loving God graciously restored them to their land and delivered them from captivity. Doubt is a sin, but there is no doubt that God's love is greater than our sin.

OCTOBER 10

THE CONTRACT

(Galatians 3:15-29)

On September 21, 1957, CBS debuted a legal show on primetime television. Many of the executives at the network later confessed that they thought the show would be a flop because nobody would want to watch a sixty-minute legal drama. But the courtroom drama became an instant hit that ran for 271 episodes over nine seasons. It was a program called *Perry Mason*. Almost sixty years later, television shows about lawyers and court cases remain very popular. Programs such as *Matlock, L.A. Law, The Good Wife, Law & Order, Boston Legal*, and *The Wire* are award-winning, highly watched legal dramas. Americans have always found something compelling about a lawyer passionately arguing a case in a court of law.

Paul is making a strong legal argument in Galatians 3. He is comparing the law to a human contract. God made a contract with and a promise to the seed of Abraham. The contract with Abraham was made over four hundred years before the law was ever given to Moses (v. 17). The law could never cancel that contract. The seed of salvation is Jesus Christ (v. 16). Jesus Himself mediated our case and suffered our punishment, making it possible for us to be declared "not guilty." Case dismissed.

A DRY BROOK ... A DEPLETED BARREL ... A DEAD BOY

(1 Kings 17:1-24)

Our God is a God of miracles. In First Kings 17, Israel is in the middle of a horrible three-and-a-half-year drought. God sent the prophet Elijah to a brook, and fed him with water, meat, and daily bread. But the water eventually dried up (v. 7), and God led His preacher to the house of a poor woman who was about to prepare her last meal. However, when she faithfully obeyed the word of the Lord (vv. 15-16), she and her son had plenty to eat for days. However, later on, the son died, and gloom filled the house. In the first recorded resurrection in the Bible, Elijah carried the boy's corpse to his room and raised him from the dead.

There are many lessons in this one great chapter. All of us experience a dry brook from time to time, a time of testing just as it was for Elijah. But he trusted God and enjoyed the provision of the Lord through a poor widow. The widow, who was running out of food, took a step of faith and experienced blessings. Yet great blessings are often followed by times of testing. In the end, God was glorified through a brook, a barrel, and a boy.

OCTOBER 12

GET YOUR EXERCISE

(1 Timothy 4:1-8)

America is a very unhealthy nation. The Centers for Disease Control and Prevention (CDC) reports that six out of ten people in the United States are either overweight, obese, or engage in unhealthy behaviors like smoking, heavy drinking, or lack of exercise. According to the latest Gallup Poll, in the last five years, less than 50 percent of all adult Americans get any type of extended and healthy cardio workout. Only one in five people in this nation meet the federal guidelines of effective aerobic activity. The CDC affirms that this is one reason why the soaring rates of heart disease, diabetes, and other chronic illnesses are reaching record numbers in this country.

Verse 4 has often been misinterpreted that Paul disdained physical exercise. The verse actually reads, *For bodily exercise profiteth little.* Paul already said that our body is the Lord's temple (1 Corinthians 6:19). We should care for it. His point is that spiritual exercise profits us both in this life and in the life to come. Be sound in doctrine, feed on the Word, and exercise. The spiritual life is about balance. While we are in this body, we should care for it. A healthy body enables a healthy spirit.

OCTOBER 13

THE FAMILY PET

(Exodus 12:21-36)

I once spoke with some college students at a church. There was a girl in that college group who owned a four-foot-long pet iguana. She was proud of the fact that the iguana slept in her bed and snuggled with her. The young lady told us that she awakened out of a deep sleep one dark night because she felt pressure on her throat. That big lizard stood on top of her with his mouth an inch from her nose. When she regaled all of us with that story, I asked what she did. The young woman smiled and exclaimed, "I kissed him!" If I woke up with an iguana standing on me, I sure wouldn't kiss him. I believe I would kill him.

Of course, none of us could imagine willfully killing a beloved family pet. But that is precisely what the Israelites did in Exodus 12. God commanded them to *draw out ... a lamb,* and kill it. The word *lamb* comes from a Hebrew word that literally means "a little pet lamb." Each father took a lamb that was considered a family pet and killed it so his family could be saved. A sacrifice only has relevance if it has special meaning.

OCTOBER 14

THE MAN WHO BAPTIZED JESUS

(Mark 1:1-13)

John the Baptist was a preacher who didn't care much about public opinion. He wasn't running for denominational office or trying to climb an evangelical ladder. John was not the kind of preacher most folks would be comfortable taking out to dinner. After all, the guy's wardrobe was a bit unusual. He wore camel-skin clothes and leather underwear. Have you ever smelled a camel up close and personal? In addition to that, John ate locusts seasoned only with wild honey. Finally, John's message was a bit abrasive to the high-brow religious leaders who came to his services. He called them *snakes*, and used words like *repent* and *unquenchable fire*.

But this was the man chosen to baptize the Son of God. Jesus came to the banks of the Jordan River one day and asked John to baptize Him. After the Lord was immersed, the heavens immediately opened up. The Spirit flew down in the form of a dove (v. 10), and the Father spoke out loud (v. 11). John was a living example that God uses the foolish to confound the wise. He also reminds us that anyone who defies worldly expectations to be obedient to God will be used mightily in His service.

OCTOBER 15

UNDER THE ANOINTING

(Leviticus 8:1-13)

After I preached one evening at our student camp, a sixteen-year-old girl approached me sheepishly and said, "Brother Rick, I want to ask you a question, but I don't want to offend you." When I gently assured her that she would not offend me, she asked, "I was wondering why the top of your head always shines while you are preaching." Of course, I am sure the shine comes from a combination of hot lights, perspiration, and follicle impairment. But I thought I would have a little fun with my explanation to this young lady. So I smiled and replied, "That shine is from the shekinah glory of God." Although I was joking with her, I pray that I never stand to preach without God's anointing.

In Leviticus 8, Moses anoints Aaron for ministry. It was a very significant Old Testament ceremony. First, Aaron was covered with the outer girdle, coat, robe, breastplate, and crown (vv. 5-9). Then Moses anointed the altar and poured oil on Aaron's head. The word *anointing* means "to consecrate," which in turn implies being completely set aside for God's purposes. Having the anointing means dying to self and living only for the will and purposes of God.

OCTOBER 16

RESCUED FROM SIN

(Romans 3:21-31)

The legacy of the RMS *Titanic* has been publicized and romanticized countless times in books, documentaries, and a blockbuster motion picture. Declared the "unsinkable ship," the *Titanic* struck an iceberg on her maiden voyage at 11:40 p.m. on April 14, 1912. About three hours later, the huge ship slipped under the water and settled on the bottom of the ocean. There were twenty-two hundred people on board, and over fifteen hundred of them lost their lives in the freezing Atlantic that terrible night. Seven decades after the ship went down, Titanic was discovered in 1985 off the coast of Newfoundland. Radar indicated that the ship was buried two and a half miles deep. Little wonder that so many lost their lives.

But do you know that more people have drowned in eight feet of water near shore than have drowned in thirty thousand feet? What a perfect picture of sin. It is not the type of sin that kills, it is the fact of sin. One small sin has the same power to destroy as a deep ocean of many sins. Romans 3:23 says, *For all have sinned.* But the very next verse declares, *Being justified freely by his grace.* Christ has rescued you from drowning in the depths of sin.

THE EARTHQUAKE THAT WILL SHAKE THE WORLD

(Zechariah 14:1-21)

In the 1930s, physicist and seismologist Charles Richter developed a scale for measuring the power and intensity of earthquakes. It was appropriately named the Richter Scale. According to the scale, an 8.0 quake is ten times greater than a 7.0 quake. The biggest earthquake in world history was the Great Chilean Earthquake of 1960. It measured 9.5 on the Richter Scale. The quake killed seventeen hundred people, destroyed $800 billion in property, and left over two million people homeless. The most powerful earthquake in the Unites States was the Great Alaskan Earthquake of 1964. That monster quake measured 9.2 on the scale. But one day, the biggest quake of all time is coming to this planet. It will be an earthquake that will shake the whole world.

The last place Jesus stood on this earth was on the top of the Mount of Olives. When He returns to earth, He will put His foot down on that same mountain. Zechariah says the whole mountain will split in two (v. 4). *Jerusalem shall be safely inhabited* for the first time in history (v. 11), and we will all worship in the great city (vv. 20-21). The return of the King of Kings will shake the entire world.

OCTOBER 18

THE THRILL IS GONE

(Revelation 2:1-7)

If the great church at Ephesus existed in the twenty-first century, it would be considered a very successful, exciting church. They would have a state-of-the-art website advertising and extolling the virtues of the church. The church calendar would be constantly packed with big events and promotions for children, students, young couples, and senior adults. It would be a church known for its gifted preaching, great music, and grand presentations. The church would have the reputation for speaking out against the social sins of the culture and standing against wickedness. No doubt, the great church at Ephesus would be the talk of the town. It would be the place you would want to call your home church.

But Jesus Christ was not pleased with them. They had grown cold and lost the thrill of loving Him (v. 4). It is a commendable thing to be busy for the Lord and to seek excellence in everything you do for Him. However, labor and excellence are never substitutes for a real relationship with the Lord. Without passion for and direction from the Lord, the work is meaningless. Christ counsels the church to remember, repent, and return (v. 5). Don't get so busy working for the Lord that you forget about the Lord you are working for.

OCTOBER 19

THE BOOK THAT
CAN'T BE BURNED

(Jeremiah 36:21-32)

Thousands of years have rolled off the calendars of time since the Bible was written. During those thousands of years, empires have risen up and fallen down. Great civilizations have come and gone. Ordinary books have turned to dust, but the Bible is still standing. Emperors, rulers, and kings have tried to exterminate the message of the Bible. Atheists and agnostics have tried to eliminate the majesty of the Bible. Liberals and skeptics have tried to erase the miracles of the Bible. But the Bible is still standing. It has been relentlessly attacked, ignored, sneered at, lampooned, and made fun of. But the Bible is still standing. It is the one book that is absolutely unalterable, indestructible, and invincible.

Just ask a godless king named Jehoiakim. When he heard the inspired Word given to Jeremiah, the king cut up the scroll and burned it in his fireplace (v. 23). He thought he would destroy the Word, but the Word destroyed him (vv. 30-31). Jeremiah inscribed a new copy of his book to Baruch (vv. 27-28). It is still standing. In fact, you read a copy of it today. God says that everything will pass away, but His Word will remain forever. It is truly a living Word.

Kneeling Before The Lord

(Philippians 2:1-11)

A young woman brought her boyfriend home to meet her father. The dad took him into his study for a private chat. Immediately, the young man fell on his knees before the father and said, "Sir, I bow to your authority, and I humbly ask for your daughter's hand in marriage." The shocked dad asked, "Do you have a job?" Still on his knees, the trembling boy answered, "No, but God will provide." The father inquired, "How do you plan to take care of my daughter, and give her a nice place to live?" Once more, the young man answered, "I have no worries. God will provide." Later that evening, father was talking with his wife, and she asked how the interview went. The man replied, "Well, he has no job and no plans. But he believes in miracles. In fact, he thinks I am God."

There is only one God. Sadly, we live in a world that bows before earthly celebrities and superstars and places man in the authority only God deserves. There is only one worthy of worship. Paul reminded the Philippians that *every knee [will] bow* before Jesus Christ. We do not worship a baby in a manger or a man on a cross. Our mighty God alone holds all authority in heaven and on earth.

OCTOBER 21

DOING WHATEVER YOU WANT TO DO

(Judges 21:13-25)

The annual Florida-Georgia football game is held in Jacksonville, Florida, each year. The game is a big rivalry. There are forty thousand blue-clad Florida Gators fans, and forty thousand red-clad Georgia Bulldogs fans sitting in the stands. Let's say that I go to the game and sit down in the stands. As I look to my right, I see a Bulldogs player sitting next to me. I say to that guy, "Aren't you supposed to be on the field?" He quickly answers, "No. I am a wide receiver. They can't cover me or tackle me if I sit way up here." Then I look on the field and notice that there are no boundaries, yard markers, or end zones. In addition to that, there are no rules or referees. Of course, that wouldn't be a game. It would be uncontrolled, unaccountable, unofficiated madness.

That is not unlike the culture in Israel at the end of the book of Judges. Sanctity in marriage and the family had all but disappeared. In other words, the standards were erased. Verse 25 is a synopsis of where America is headed. When God is not in charge, people will make their own rules. Without the perfect will of God, chaos will prevail in every situation.

A FISH STORY

(Luke 5:1-11)

My father always wanted to catch a trophy bass. Some of my fondest memories are of vacation mornings spent as a boy in a boat with him. We always caught plenty of fish but never the trophy. One morning, after fishing for about three hours, Dad said, "Before we go in, let me try one more cast on the other side of the boat." He tossed his line beside some grass and quickly got excited as the rod bent with what was obviously a big fish. Finally, he got the fish near the boat and yelled for the net. Instead, I grabbed the tight line, and the fish fell off. We watched that trophy bass swim away. I think my dad thought briefly of letting me swim back to camp.

No fish story compares with the one Luke told. Jesus Christ borrowed a boat and used it as His pulpit (v. 3). After His sermon, He told the men to cast out their nets. Peter, tired because they had fished all night and caught nothing, obeyed, and they caught more fish than the nets could hold. Jesus told them to follow Him and fish for men (vv. 10-11) – the greatest "trophy catch" in the world.

THE PRAYER WARRIOR

(2 Samuel 5:1-25)

What else can be said about the illustrious life of David? After all, God called him *a man after mine own heart* (Acts 13:22). Think about David's résumé – singer, author, and military genius. While still a young shepherd boy, David accomplished one of the most notable victories in Israeli history when he conquered a giant with a slingshot and a stone. But by that time, he had already killed a lion and a bear. Yet even after all of those renowned victories, the best was yet to come. Second Samuel 5:10 says, *And David went on, and grew great, and the LORD God of hosts was with him.* David became the king of Israel and reigned for forty years.

One of his first acts as king was to take back Jerusalem and make it the capital. But right after the victory, the Philistines came, ready to attack (v. 18). David defeated them also. However, he didn't win his battles as a military warrior. He won them as a prayer warrior (v. 19). David may have sat on the throne in Jerusalem, but the secret of his success sat on the throne in heaven. David knew that God was the source and substance of everything he had or did.

SAVED ONCE

(Hebrews 6:1-12)

During a crusade service one night, a woman walked down the aisle, professing Christ. Later that evening, she walked up to me and said, "I am so glad that is settled. I was saved when I was a little girl, but I needed to get saved again." I talked with her for quite a while. However, that frustrated lady couldn't grasp the fact that she could only be saved once. Sadly, there are many people who have a theology just like hers. Opponents of eternal security will often quote verses such as Hebrews 6:5-6 as the reason they believe salvation can be lost. In fact, this passage has probably disturbed and confused more believers than any other passage in the Bible.

Hebrews 6:6 is not about salvation, it is about repentance. If it were about salvation, it would mean that lost salvation can never be regained. The words *fall away* mean "to wander, or fall beside." The verse describes a believer who slips into sin. If a sinning believer continues in sin, he puts Christ to shame. You cannot lose your salvation, but you can lose your holiness. You cannot lose your identity in Christ, but you can lose your reward in Christ.

FILTHY RAGS

(Isaiah 64:1-12)

I once preached revival at a country church. I flew to the engagement, and the pastor provided me with the church van to use during the week. On Sunday morning, I wore a nice beige suit with color-coordinated shoes, shirt, and tie. After the first service finished, folks came to me and encouraged me about the message. I felt pretty good about myself until a woman from the choir walked up and said, "Preacher, I don't know if anybody told you, but you have an ugly grease stain on the back of your coat." She was right. I had somehow managed to rub my coat up against some grease inside the door of that old van as I got out. That woman didn't hear anything I had to say because of my dirty clothes.

Isaiah 64:6 is one of the most familiar and often-quoted verses in the entire Bible. The words *filthy rags* are really pretty gross and disgusting. Literally, that Hebrew phrase is used in describing a "bloody, stinking, rotten pile of bandages." God is telling us that *all our righteousnesses* (righteousness or religious acts) are sickening to Him outside of Jesus Christ. He alone is our hope of glory.

TELL SOMEBODY

(Matthew 28:1-20)

A pastor told a compelling story. He was on a Middle Eastern tour and began witnessing to his Arab guide. The man was not interested, but the determined pastor was very persistent and continued to share his faith. Finally, the guide asked, "Why are you bothering me with this?" The pastor answered sincerely, "Because I love you. I want you to be saved and know Jesus Christ." Upon hearing those words, the Arab replied, "You just don't want to commit the sin of the desert." Puzzled, the pastor asked, "What is the sin of the desert?" The Arab guide said, "The sin of the desert is to know where water is, and not tell someone who is dying of thirst."

This is a beautifully appropriate reminder that Jesus is the living water. Matthew 28:19-20 is the Great Commission. Jesus Christ has commissioned all of His disciples to spread the gospel to the world. The first example of witnessing was given earlier in the twenty-eighth chapter of Matthew. When the two Marys saw that their Lord was alive, they were told by the angel to *go quickly* (v. 9) and tell the good news. Tell somebody today that Jesus saves, revives, and quenches every thirst.

JEALOUSY

(Genesis 37:18-36)

Channelview, Texas, is a middle-class suburb of Houston. Two teenage girls named Amber Heath and Shanna Holloway lived in the same neighborhood and attended a private Christian school together. Their mothers were friends who attended the same church and served as officers on the school board. But one day, Amber beat Shanna for a place in the cheerleading squad. Earlier in the year, she had also beaten Shanna in a beauty contest. Shanna's mother was so jealous, she tried to hire a hit man to kill Amber and her mother. Her plan was foiled and she was arrested for solicitation of a capital murder. The woman was sentenced to fifteen years in prison, but only served six months due to a technicality.

Jealousy has been called the green-eyed monster. It causes hatred, bitterness, and even violence. A seventeen-year-old boy named Joseph was the favored son of his daddy, Jacob. One day, Jacob gave Joseph a beautiful coat, and it incensed his brothers (Genesis 37:3-4). They put him a pit, sold him into slavery, and lied to their father that he was dead. Jealousy is entirely focused on self-gratification and is very destructive, both to the target of jealousy and to ourselves.

OCTOBER 28

THE POWER OF FAITH

(1 Corinthians 2:1-16)

O n a windy, cloudy, summer day, a little boy flew his kite in the park. It flew up so high, it was completely hidden in the clouds, but the boy held tightly onto the string. A man walked by and asked, "Hey buddy, what are you holding onto up there?" Without hesitation, the boy replied, "I am flying my kite today. It flew so high that it disappeared in the clouds." The man thought he would have a little fun with the kid, so he said, "Well, maybe your kite flew so high, it flew away. What makes you think your kite is still there?" The boy exclaimed, "I know that my kite is there because I can still feel the tug."

Even though I cannot see Him visibly, I know my God is there because I feel the tug of the Holy Spirit on my heart. The Christian life is a journey of faith. In Paul's day, there were many Christians in Corinth who thought that the church should rely on the philosophies and wisdom of men. Paul reminded them that our faith stands on God's power (v. 5). Be sure to follow the tug today. He will pull you on the right path.

OCTOBER 29

FROM FAMINE TO FEASTING

(2 Kings 7:1-20)

An amazing story is tucked away in the seventh chapter of Second Kings. Israel was under siege by the Syrian army. All supplies had been cut off, and there was a severe famine in the land. The worst kind of food sold for ridiculous prices. For instance, donkey heads sold for fifty dollars apiece, and the people also ate dove dung (2 Kings 6:25). Can you imagine someone placing an order: "Give me a donkey burger, and hold the dove dung"? Seriously, the people were even resorting to cannibalism (2 Kings 6:28-29). Yet, in the middle of all this despair, God did something unexpected and impossible.

Four lepers sat at the gate of the city. They reasoned that if they sat there, they would die, and if they waited for the Syrians, they would die (vv. 3-4). So they decided to go to the Syrian camp. When they arrived, no one was there. The Syrians were still running from the angels of God. The lepers stuffed their bellies with food, their pockets with gold, and then told everyone else where the food was (vv. 8-10). God used four lepers to feed the whole city. When man creates impossible circumstances, God responds with incredible miracles.

WANTING THE WILL OF GOD

(Acts 9:1-18)

A wandering vagabond spent his entire life and existence walking randomly across the country and living from place to place. One day, a man asked him, "How do you decide where you are going to go?" The hobo answered, "I just go." Curious, the man asked, "But what do you do if you are walking down a road and you come to a fork in the road?" The homeless man replied, "Well, in that case, I just pick up a stick and throw it straight up into the air. Whichever way it lands, that's the way I go." Then he added, "Sometimes I have to throw it up in the air six or seven times for it to land right."

Regrettably, there are a lot of people with the same attitude. Sometimes we say, "I really want the will of God in my life." But we keep throwing the stick up in the air until it lands in the direction we want. Immediately after Saul met Jesus on the Damascus Road, he asked, "Lord, what do you want me to do?" (v. 6). God is the divine GPS who has the only right directions for your life, but you have to obey, whatever He decides.

DRESSED UP FOR DEATH

(1 Kings 22:29-40)

It is astounding that Americans spend almost $8 billion per year on Halloween cards, candy, costumes, and decorations. Close to $1.5 billion is spent annually on adult costumes alone each year in this country, more than that spent on children's costumes. Nearly 45 percent of all adults dress up for Halloween. The average adult spends about $93 on their costume. By far, the most-popular costumes are death-related such as witches, zombies, and vampires. In the Bible, the king of Israel tried to disguise himself one day in order to trick God and escape death.

King Ahab was the wicked king married to Jezebel. He led the nation of Israel into immorality, Baal worship, and demonism. But Ahab crossed God's line when an innocent man (Naboth) was killed so the king could steal his vineyard (1 Kings 21). Elijah pronounced judgment, and Ahab disguised himself in battle (v. 30). However, an archer *drew a bow at a venture* (v. 34), and Ahab was killed. He tried to trick God, but he received the "treat" he really deserved. No costume or disguise can hide our true selves from God. Unless we "wear Jesus," we get what we deserve.

THANKSGIVING & CHRISTMAS

We have now come to the last two special months of the calendar year. Thanksgiving and Christmas are not far away. I love this time of the year. It is a special time indeed. November, the month of Thanksgiving, is a great month for believers. Christians should be the most thankful and grateful people living on the planet. Over one hundred times in the Bible, God's saints are commanded to be grateful and give thanks unto the Lord. For the thirty days of November, each day's devotion will be specifically about thanking God for the blessings He has given us.

Starting the first day of December, and going through December 25, we will count down to Christmas and the glorious birth of our wonderful Savior. December is an exciting month because it is the celebration of Christ's birthday. Every day will be directed to the miraculous prophecies, promises, and arrival of Jesus in the manger in Bethlehem. December 24 and 25 will be dedicated to the New Testament Christmas story in Luke 2. I pray that these last sixty-one devotions of the year will be a blessing, challenge, and encouragement to you.

NOVEMBER 1

ALWAYS GIVE THANKS

(Philippians 4:1-9)

Rudyard Kipling was a great British poet of the late-nineteenth and early-twentieth centuries. At the height of his fame, Kipling's poetry made him a great deal of money. A newspaper reporter once interviewed him and said, "Sir, it has been calculated that the money you make from your writing comes to about one hundred dollars per word." Rudyard Kipling responded, "I was unaware of that fact." The reporter cynically pulled a hundred-dollar bill from his pocket, handed it to the great poet, and said, "Now, I want you to give me a word that is worth a hundred dollars." Kipling folded the bill, put it in his wallet, and said, "Thanks."

Thanks is a powerful word of immeasurable value. Paul told the Philippians not to worry, fret, or be anxious, but to pray with thanksgiving (v. 6). The word *thanksgiving* means to "express gratitude to the Lord." God tells us to always give thanks. We spend a lot of time teaching our children the value of giving thanks, yet we so often forget to do the same for the manifold blessings God has given us. Thanksgiving is an indication of the value we attach to God and His provision for us.

THE BLESSING OF ISRAEL

(Genesis 12:1-9)

Frederick the Great of Prussia was a very devout Christian, but became enthralled with the writings and philosophies of a French atheist named Voltaire. As he plunged deeper into Voltaire's misguided teachings and ideas, doubts about God's inerrant Word started to creep slowly into Frederick's mind, heart, and faith. One day, he became so overwhelmed with doubt that he sought spiritual counsel from his pastor. The pastor said, "If you are questioning whether God's Word is true, look no further than the Jews. The miracles and preservation of the Jewish nation tell us that God always keeps His promises."

In Genesis, God made a promise to Abram. He said, *And I will make of thee a great nation .... And I will bless them that bless thee, and curse him that curseth thee* (vv. 2-3). God has kept that promise. No nation on earth has blessed Israel like America, and no nation has been as blessed as America. We had better keep on doing it. Thank God for Israel. After all, Israel gave us the Son of God and the Word of God, and became a living example of God's faithfulness towards His people. Take time to thank God for Israel, and pray for them today.

I CAN SEE

(Mark 10:46-52)

When I was a boy preacher, one of my heroes was Dr. Homer Lindsay Jr. He was the pastor of the great First Baptist Church of Jacksonville, Florida. I once heard him preach a powerful sermon about giving thanks. In the message, he said he once encountered a man who complained by saying, "I have nothing to be thankful for." Dr. Lindsay asked, "Aren't you are a millionaire?" The griper responded, "No, I am not a millionaire." Smiling, the preacher replied, "God has blessed you with two healthy eyes. Would you sell your eyes for a million bucks?" The man answered, "Absolutely not." Dr. Lindsay quickly said, "You have something worth more than a million dollars. Get on your knees, and thank God for your sight."

There are many blessings that we take for granted or overlook. In Mark 10, a blind man named Bartimaeus was begging by the side of the highway one day. Suddenly, he heard that Jesus was passing by. Verse 47 says that he cried out for *mercy* (compassion). Jesus stopped and healed him. If you are reading these words, you have the gift of sight, something so many others do not have. Thank God for your eyes today.

WHAT GOD WANTS

(1 Chronicles 16:1-15)

What does God want from you? I want you to stop and really let that question soak in for just a moment or two. What does God want? Well, God doesn't want your money. He demands our tithes and offerings, but God surely isn't in a financial crisis. After all, He owns it all. God certainly doesn't need your help. I am glad that He chooses to use us in His service. Christians are His hands and feet in the world. But let's be honest. God survived without your help before you got here, and He will do just fine after you are gone. Finally, God doesn't need your advice or counsel. He doesn't need to pick your brain, run anything by you, or get your take on it. So, if God doesn't want your money, help, or advice, what does God want from you?

Almighty God wants your praise and thanksgiving. When the ark of the covenant was carried into Jerusalem, it was a time of great euphoria and national celebration. Yet, in the midst of it all, David reminded the people to stop and give thanks to God (v. 8). That is what God wants – hearts that overflow with thanksgiving and praise.

Say Your Blessing

(John 6:1-13)

I love it anytime I get to spend precious moments in the company of my sweet granddaughters. But one of my favorite occasions is always mealtime. Those hungry little girls will sit down at the table and invariably, one of them will reach for their food. At that moment, one of their parents will speak up and say, "Wait a minute. Before you eat, you need to say your blessing." Our two-year-old will almost always pray while she squints her eyes. I have always thought she was watching her food to be sure no one else took it off her plate. At any rate, what a great joy it is to see their parents teach them to fold their hands, bow their heads, and say a blessing to the God who provided a meal.

No matter how busy we are, we should never enjoy a meal without thanking the One who has provided it. Jesus taught us that lesson in the midst of a huge and very hungry crowd. When He took the small loaves of bread in His miraculous hands, the first thing Christ did was give thanks (v. 11), and doing so released a miraculous provision. Be sure to say your blessing today.

Time For The Offering

(Psalm 50:14-23)

It is both astounding and heartbreaking at the same time that, according to the latest statistics, the average church member in America gives only 2 percent of their income to God. Only 3 percent of all evangelical church members give at least 10 percent. Approximately 50 percent of all active church members do not give one penny all year long in any offering. Sadly, 70 percent of the members who die never leave anything in a will or an inheritance for kingdom ministry. It has been estimated that if every church member in America tithed (10 percent), there would be a surplus of $165 billion in our churches. That would be more than enough to clothe the destitute, feed the hungry, shelter the homeless, and reach the world with the gospel.

But the offering is not just something that is given on Sunday. Believers are expected to give an offering of thanksgiving every single day. Psalm 50:14 says, *Offer unto God thanksgiving; and pay thy vows unto the most High.* The word *offer* is a picture of slaughtering an animal on the altar. The act of thanksgiving is a sacrificial offering that we give to the Lord in response to His infinite grace and goodness.

THE BLESSING OF THE BLOOD

(Matthew 26:26-35)

Since 1881, the American Red Cross has been giving and distributing lifesaving blood to people in need. Every two seconds, somebody somewhere in America needs blood. If there is no blood, there is no life. One out of every ten people admitted into the hospital must have a blood transfusion or they will die. A single car accident victim can require as many as a hundred units of blood. Because of that, there are about forty-three thousand pints of blood given every day. The Red Cross claims that one pint of blood can save up to three lives. That is a very impressive statistic, but I've got one that is a whole lot better. One single drop of the blood of Jesus Christ can save the whole world!

At His final meal with the disciples, Jesus took a cup, and gave thanks. He said, *For this is my blood of the new testament, which is shed for many for the remission of sins* (v. 28). Jesus is a living testimony to God's Word, which says that *life … is in the blood*. Eternal life can only be found through the blood of Christ. Every single day, every believer should stop and thank Jesus Christ for His lifesaving blood.

PROTECTED BY THE FATHER

(2 Samuel 22:1-14)

One of the priorities of parenthood is protection. When our children were small, we had to childproof our house. You know what I'm talking about. My wife and I put those pronged plastic caps in the electrical outlets and plastic locks on the cabinet doors. The iron was always put away so that the cord couldn't be pulled and cause it to fall on a child. Anything small enough to be put in the mouth was always hidden or thrown in the garbage. Our children freely crawled, romped, and toddled around the house, never realizing that Dad and Mom had probably saved their lives that very day. Countless dangers surround us in our Christian walk, but we are safe under the watchful eye of our heavenly Father who loves us and cares enough to take care of even the smallest detail of our lives.

In Second Samuel 22, David praises God for His watchful care over his life. Verses 2-5 are very descriptive. David worshipfully calls God his rock, fortress, deliverer, shield, horn, high tower, refuge, and savior. Do you realize that God protects us even when we aren't aware of the danger around us? Have you thanked God for His protection on your life today?

Murmuring Mouths

(Philippians 2:12-24)

A woman had been married for twenty years to a man who was hard to please. All that the husband did for their entire marriage was gripe, grumble, complain, and criticize her. Early one morning, she asked her husband what he wanted for breakfast. He grunted, "I want two eggs, one scrambled and one fried, and I want a fresh cup of coffee." Determined, she made up her mind to please him, no matter what. She went to the store and purchased his favorite brand of coffee. Then she stopped by a farm for two fresh eggs. She cooked the eggs exactly as he requested, poured the coffee, carried a tray, and served her husband breakfast in bed. He looked at the plate and scowled. "You scrambled the wrong egg."

This is the attitude of many believers. They look for something to complain about and never enjoy the wonderful things that come their way. Christian mouths should not be critical. Last month (October 20), we discussed bowing to Christ's lordship in Philippians 2. When Christ is the absolute, undisputed Lord of our lives, there will no murmuring (grumbling, complaining). Christians should use their mouths to encourage each other and give praise and thanksgiving to God.

GIVING GOD THE GLORY

(Nehemiah 12:27-43)

Nehemiah and the citizens of Jerusalem had just finished the great task of rebuilding the walls of Jerusalem, a monumental undertaking. The historian Josephus said the circumference of the city in his day was thirty-three stadia. That equals about 4.5 English miles that would surround 960 acres. Yet, the whole task was completed in just fifty-two days. It would have been easy for the workers to sit back, admire their work, and take the credit for what had been accomplished. But they did not take any glory or accolades for rebuilding a massive wall that had eight gates and thirty-two watchtowers. Instead, the people of Jerusalem celebrated, praised, and gave all of the glory and thanksgiving to the Lord.

Ezra and Nehemiah divided the people into two groups and marched. It was similar to the victorious march around Jericho with Joshua. But this wasn't just a victory march. This was a march of thanksgiving (v. 27). It was a big human accomplishment, but it had been done with supernatural intervention. God got the glory, and the celebration was heard far away (v. 43). Thanksgiving is actually giving glory to God for everything, both the great achievements and the small daily blessings.

SALUTING THE SOLDIERS

(2 Timothy 2:1-13)

My weekends are usually filled with flight schedules, rental cars, and hotel check-ins. One rare free Saturday, my son and I attended a college football game together. During halftime festivities, U.S. Marine Sergeant Robert Blumenberg and his family were introduced to the crowd. Robert was being honored by the Wounded Warriors Project. As he walked onto the field with a prosthetic left leg, ninety thousand grateful fans stood and applauded for almost two full minutes. Tears filled my eyes to see the outpouring of appreciation. The huge crowd did not cheer a long touchdown run or a great defensive play. Instead, they saluted a soldier who had valiantly fought for his country.

Today is Veterans Day, a day to say thank-you to the courageous veterans who have fought for our freedom. Second Timothy 2:3 reminds us that Christians are soldiers in the army of the Lord. We are engaged in an intense spiritual war, and sometimes it is hard. But we cannot become entangled with the world (v. 4). Our main task is to love God and those we know. When we give thanks to Him today, let us be sure to include our fellow soldiers in Christ whose prayers have aided us along the way.

FOUL-WEATHER FRIENDS

(Proverbs 18:6-24)

The definition of a fair-weather friend is "a friend who only wants to be around when it is convenient, pleasant, or profitable." In actuality, the term *fair-weather friend* doesn't really mean a friend at all. Someone has well said, "A real friend is someone who walks in when everybody else in the world walks out." That rare type of friend can be correctly classified as a foul-weather friend. Everybody needs real friends who know everything about you and still love you anyway, even when the going gets tough. A foul-weather friend believes in you even when you don't believe in yourself. They stick by you after you mess up or make a mistake.

Proverbs 18:24 is talking about foul-weather friends, *a friend that sticketh closer than a brother.* The Hebrew word for *sticketh* is used to describe "skin sticking tight to the bone." In other words, a real friend sticks through thick and thin. We have many acquaintances in life, but God brings special people into our lives to love and support us. Be thankful for the real friends God has put into your life and take time to pray for them today. They are God-given, raised up for you as you are for them.

HALLELUJAH FOR HEAVEN

(Revelation 22:1-21)

Aman left the frozen, snow-covered streets of Chicago for a relaxing vacation in warm and sunny Florida. His wife was away on a business trip and was scheduled to fly to Florida and join him the next day. After arriving at his luxury condominium, the man sent his spouse a quick email. He couldn't remember her exact email address, and he missed it by one letter. The communication was mistakenly sent to an elderly woman whose husband had just passed away. When the grieving woman opened it, the email said, *Just checked in. Everything is prepared for your arrival tomorrow. Signed, Your Loving Husband.* Underneath those cheery words, the man wrote, *P.S. – It sure is hot down here.*

People find it regretfully easy to joke about the afterlife and our future in eternity. There are only two destinations after death. One is a place of eternal torment. The other is a glorious home called heaven. In heaven, *there shall be no more curse* (penalties or condemnations). Your glorious future has been secured for you by the grace and the blood of Jesus. Give God thanks today for the place He has prepared for you, and take time to pray for the unsaved.

GRATEFUL FOR THE PASTOR

(Psalm 105:8-25)

One of the greatest blessings I have as a traveling evangelist is hearing people brag about their pastor. I was preaching at a church in Tennessee when a man and his wife walked up to me after the service one evening. Both of them spoke very encouraging words to me about my ministry and the revival that week. Then, without hesitation, the man smiled and enthusiastically said, "But I want you to know that we hear the Word of God preached here every week. We really love our pastor." It was music to my ears. Thank God for faithful church members who love, encourage, appreciate, and pray for their pastor. Conversely, it is a tragedy when folks attack, abuse, criticize, and plot against their pastor.

God specifically warns us to *Touch not mine anointed [consecrated], and do my prophets no harm* (v. 15). It is a dangerous thing to speak out against or try to hurt the man that God has called to be your shepherd. Take a moment each day to pray for the pastor that God has placed in your life. Be grateful and thankful that you have a loving shepherd who feeds and guides you and is faithful to his divine calling.

Thank God For The Gospel

(Romans 1:1-17)

In the early evening of May 6, 2013, Charles Ramsey of Cleveland, Ohio, sat down to eat his meal. Suddenly, he heard a desperate scream coming from a neighborhood house. He walked across the street and saw a woman on her knees, weeping behind the locked glass door. The fifty-two-year-old owner of the house had been secretly and sadistically holding three young women hostage for ten years. They had been starved, raped, beaten, and chained in his dark basement. Charles Ramsey kicked open the bottom of the door and set the women free. The amazing news story instantly hit social media and circled the globe. In a world of constant bad news, the rescue was the good news of the day. Three women had been set free.

Paul uses the word *gospel* three times in the first chapter of Romans (vv. 1, 9, 16). *Gospel* means "good news." The good news is that Jesus saves. Aren't you glad that you heard the gospel of Christ one glad day and were saved? Take some time today and thank God that someone took the time to share His great gospel with you. Where would you be if they hadn't had the courage to intervene?

NOVEMBER 16

THE LOVE OF GOD

(Deuteronomy 7:6-21)

In 1917, Frederick Lehman wrote the lyrics to a song called *The Love of God*. The famous hymn is one of the most beloved gospel songs ever written. Although he penned the first two verses, Mr. Lehman credits the third verse of the song to a rhyme found penciled on the wall of a patient's room in an insane asylum. The words were discovered after the patient died and had been carried to his grave. Those incredible words are: *Could we with ink the oceans fill, And were the skies of parchment made, Were every stalk on earth a quill, And every man a scribe by trade; To write the love of God above would drain the ocean dry; Nor could the scroll contain the whole, though stretched from sky to sky.*

The love of God cannot be fathomed. In Deuteronomy 7, Moses reminds Israel how much God loved her. The same is true for God's chosen people of the New Testament covenant. We cannot adequately describe God's amazing love, a love which can reach out and touch even a tormented soul locked away in an asylum. We can only thank Him for loving us so completely that it cost Him His life.

SHARING THE FRAGRANCE

(2 Corinthians 2:1-17)

Most everybody enjoys the pageantry, color, and excitement of a parade. In the days of the Roman Empire, parades were a really big deal. After the conquering Roman army achieved a great victory, they would publicly march in a parade of glory and honor. When the victorious army entered the city, the trumpets would blow and the captives would be led down the streets as the thick smoke and smell of incense filled the air. To the victors, the fragrant incense was the aroma of life. But to the prisoners, the smell was a reminder of their coming death. In Second Corinthians 2:14-17, Paul uses the smell of incense to illustrate the victory that we have in Christ.

As Christians, we have the fragrance of Christ. The *savor* (perfume) that surrounds us is the sweet smell of eternal life. However, the lost world is headed for death. In verse 14, we are commanded to share the fragrance as we march through this procession of life. Be thankful today that you are blessed with the savor of salvation. But also be thankful that you have the amazing privilege to share the fragrance with everyone around you as your life displays the victory of Christ.

MORE BLESSINGS THAN YOU CAN COUNT

(Genesis 28:10-22)

Before entering evangelism ministry, I had the privilege of pastoring two wonderful churches. But in the very first church I pastored, there was a pessimistic woman who greeted me almost every Sunday with the same five words. "Preacher, I've got a problem." She seemed to always find me right before the worship service started. After spending a few moments with that discouraging lady, I would always enter church in a defeated mood. One Sunday, I tried to avoid the negativity by hiding in the baptismal changing room. But right before the service, she found me. At least on that day, the lady didn't start the conversation with the same five words. This time she said, "Preacher, I'm glad I found you. I've got a problem."

In Genesis 28, Jacob was in the wilderness, fleeing for his life. But at that dismal moment, God opened up heaven to him. Jacob got his eyes off his circumstances and focused on the blessings and promises of the Lord (vv. 12-15). We become what we speak and what we focus on. We choose to see either blessings or problems. You have blessings beyond number. Don't count your problems today. Thank God for your blessings.

THE FATHER'S FAMILY

(Acts 11:19-30)

Thanksgiving is a time for families to gather together. I cannot imagine how sad it would be to spend the Thanksgiving season away from my loved ones. My heart always goes out to those who are serving God or country on foreign fields and are away from home during the holidays. It is always a sweet time of celebration just to be near the people who are dearest to you. Have you ever considered the fact that each Sunday is a time for God's family to assemble and give Him praise and thanks? Yet we live in a culture in which church attendance is on the decline. God expects His children to be together in church. We need each other. Our church family has a divine purpose. They love us, support us, mourn with us, and celebrate with us.

In Acts 11, God's infant church was growing (v. 21), and the heavenly Father gave His young family a name. It is a title that we are still called today (v. 26). I am so thankful that I have many loving brothers and sisters who belong to the same Father and who share an eternal unity found only in Jesus. Thank God for the church.

It Is A Privilege To Give

(2 Chronicles 31:1-21)

Several years ago, I preached in a revival crusade at a church. During the very first service of the week, the pastor stood and said, "I am going to ask our ushers to come and receive the offering." Without coercion, the entire congregation of five hundred people stood and applauded. Now, mind you, this was not polite, casual applause. These people were spontaneously clapping and shouting praise to God as the ushers made their way to the front of the church. The pastor then announced, "If you are visiting with us, this is not a show. Our people get excited when it is time to pass the plates and give an offering." At that very moment, I realized that I was not in a typical church. Needless to say, we experienced Holy Ghost revival that week.

King Hezekiah was the thirteenth king of Judah. Under his bold leadership, Israel experienced a great awakening. Second Chronicles 31 describes the removal of idols from the land (v. 1). Then, the people gave thanks and praise to God (v. 2). After that, they brought in abundant offerings by the heaps, and gave them to the Lord. Be thankful and give back to the gracious God who has blessed you.

TELLING THE TRUTH

(John 8:31-47)

There are many sweet perks to being a grandparent. One weekend, my wife and I had the joy of entertaining two of our precious grandchildren while their parents celebrated their wedding anniversary. We spent a delightful couple of days watching movies, playing games, and going to the park. On one of the nights, our energetic three-year-old didn't want to go to bed. Nana was trying to rock her as I was preparing to start packing and preparing for a revival trip the next day. As the child finally closed her eyes, I got up from the couch and announced to my wife, "I still haven't cut my hair." Without hesitation, my youngest granddaughter opened her eyes, and replied, "Granddaddy, you don't have much hair."

Sometimes, the truth hurts. But in John 8:32, Jesus said that *the truth shall make you free.* He was talking with Jews who were in spiritual bondage. Christ reminded them that there is a distinction between Abraham's physical seed and Abraham's spiritual children (vv. 37-39). The truth has set you free and brought you into God's spiritual family. That glorious truth alone is cause for joyful thanksgiving every day.

NOVEMBER 22

THANK GOD I'M AN AMERICAN

(Psalm 33:12-22)

Y ou had nothing to do with being an American. Think about it. You could just as easily have been born in the war-torn Middle East or in a nation that promotes and practices terrorism. You could have been born in an impoverished third-world country in which the greater part of the population goes to bed starving every night. You could have been born in a land that forbids the worship of God and prohibits the teachings of Jesus Christ. Instead, our sovereign God placed you right in the middle of the greatest nation on the globe. You have been born and bred in the United States of America. When you drop to your knees in prayer today, don't forget to pause and give God thanks for the nation that you call home. God bless America.

The psalmist said, *Blessed is the nation whose God is the Lord.* Every day, we see the wonderful truth that God abundantly blesses His people who are called by His name. Our great nation has been immeasurably blessed only because it was founded in God's name, on God's Book, and by God's standards. Let us thank Him and never forget that America needs God more than God needs America.

How To Turn Thanksgiving Into Thanks-Living

(Romans 14:1-11)

In this day of instant social media, there are no secrets. One recent Christmas Eve, an American teenager exchanged gifts with her family, then immediately picked up her phone and told everyone about it on Twitter. The ungrateful girl belligerently tweeted, *I hate my mom. She got me a black iPhone 5 and I told her that I wanted a white phone. Being an upper-middle-class suburban kid is so rough. I only got about 800 dollars' worth of gifts for Christmas this year. My life stinks.* Sadly, that young girl's cyberspace comments reveal an attitude that is all too common in this entitled generation. We live in a country and a culture that takes for granted the abundant blessings that we receive.

Christians should be the most grateful and thankful people in the world. The fourteenth chapter of Romans reminds us that Jesus is Lord, and we live daily to please Christ and not ourselves. One of the ways that we please our Lord is by giving thanks to Him (v. 6). Thanksgiving is not a celebration that occurs just once a year. We give thanks each day of the year because God deserves and requires it. That is called "thanks-living."

OFFERING THANKS

(Leviticus 7:1-17)

Thanksgiving Day is exclusively an American holiday tradition. In the cold and brutal winter of 1621, half of the pilgrim settlers died of starvation or disease. Colonial leader William Bradford called for the pilgrims to set aside three days in December to praise the Lord for the bountiful harvest. One hundred and sixty-eight years later (1789), President George Washington proclaimed November 26 a National Day of Thanksgiving to the Lord. In 1863, Abraham Lincoln formally declared that the last Thursday of November be set aside as a day for Americans to give thanks. Finally, in 1941, the U.S. Congress decreed that the fourth Thursday of November would always officially be recognized and celebrated as Thanksgiving Day.

Offering thanks was a way of life for Israel. In the first seven chapters of Leviticus, Moses describes five different offerings that the Hebrew people gave to the Lord. The word *offering* is found sixteen times in the first seventeen verses of Leviticus 7. It literally means "to give a sacrificial present." God requires us to give thanks in all circumstances, not just the good ones. Giving thanks in the hard times is a sacrificial offering of faith. Stop for a moment today and offer God thanksgiving for His blessings to you.

November 25

Rejoicing Over The Rapture

(Revelation 4:1-11)

The dictionary defines the word *rapture* as "an expression or manifestation of ecstasy, or being carried away with emotion." *Rapture* has become a well-used word in our society. Victoria's Secret has a best-selling product called Rapture Perfume. There is a popular rock band from New York named The Rapture. Many books, novels, and movies are now using the word *rapture* in their titles. There is even a sporting-goods company that manufactures a special line of golf clubs that are known as Rapture Clubs. Using the word for worldly things to distract us from its real spiritual significance is a good indication that the real rapture is not too far off.

The fourth chapter of Revelation gives us a vivid picture of the real rapture. John hears a trumpet and is immediately caught up into heaven (vv. 1-2). Around the glorious throne of God, John sees all of the creatures and saints giving thanks and praise to the Lord who sits on the throne (vv. 8-11). In addition to thanking God for our present blessings, we should give thanks for the immeasurable blessing we all wait for with eager expectation. Rejoice and give Him thanks. This could be the day that Jesus takes you away.

NOVEMBER 26

WEARY OF THE WHINING

(Numbers 11:1-15)

A monk named Peter joined a monastery and took a vow of silence that permitted him to speak once every seven years. After seven long years, he stood before the bishop who said, "You may now speak." Peter answered, "My bed is hard." Seven more arduous years dragged by, and Peter was once again allowed to speak. He told the bishop, "My room is cold." After speaking his piece, he resumed his vow of silence. Seven years later, Peter spoke up and told the bishop, "The food is bad. I can't take this anymore. I quit." The bishop looked at him and replied, "Well, it doesn't surprise me. You have whined and complained ever since you got here." Unfortunately, many of God's children are always whining and complaining.

It seemed the children of Israel only opened their mouths to whine and complain. Even when God provided manna in the wilderness, they complained and tried to improve it (vv. 5-8). Finally, Moses was so weary of the complaints, he asked God to kill him (v. 15). Nobody likes to hear people whine all the time. I've got news for you. God doesn't like it either. Don't whine to God today. Worship and give Him thanks.

UNDER HIS FEET

(Ephesians 1:15-23)

As a young boy, I loved to play at my grandparents' house in the country. They had a garden, a chicken house, and a pigpen, and all sorts of cool things for a kid to do on visits. One day, while playing near the garden, I saw a small snake lying on a rock. Of course, it looked like a python to me. Immediately, I called to my grandfather, who was standing nearby. Granddad walked over and looked down at the small snake. He didn't grab a shovel, an ax, or a gun, but simply raised his foot, stomped on the snake's head, and killed it. I looked admiringly at my grandfather as if he was some kind of superhero. He had killed a snake by just stepping on its head.

Jesus Christ stepped on a bigger snake than that. He put His mighty foot on the Devil's head and crushed him. Paul told the Ephesians that every principality and power is under the feet of Jesus (vv. 21-22). Give Him thanks for His mighty authority in your life. Every single storm, situation, sickness, and struggle you face today is under His feet. And because you are in Him, those things are under your feet as well.

GOING THROUGH
THE MOTIONS

(Amos 4:1-13)

Some people believe that they are right with God simply because they regularly attend church services on Sunday. Unfortunately, nothing could be further from the truth. You can sit in a beautiful stained-glass sanctuary, open your wallet and give a generous offering, listen to a choir that sings like angels, hear a sermon that rings the bells of heaven, and still not be tuned in to the Lord and His purpose for your life. Attending church is not a guarantee of salvation, and participating in church activities does not make you a "real Christian." America is a land that seems to have churches on every corner. We are surrounded by and bombarded with a proliferation of Christian symbols, music, bookstores, and materials. Yet we live in a nation that is far from God and moving ever farther away.

In his fourth chapter, the prophet Amos addresses a nation that faithfully attended church and gave thank offerings to God (vv. 4-5). But they were just going through religious motions. Relationship had become ritual, and the people had lost their love for the Lord. It wasn't real at all. God doesn't want our religious motion. He wants our righteous devotion. He wants our pure, humble, and unreserved thanksgiving.

Celebrating The Savior

(John 7:25-39)

Americans love to celebrate holidays. I don't think anyone would argue the fact that three of our biggest holidays are Christmas, Thanksgiving, and the Fourth of July. At Christmas, we celebrate our spiritual faith. At Thanksgiving, we celebrate our material blessings. On the Fourth of July, we celebrate our political freedom. Did you realize that the Jews also celebrated three main holidays or feast days? They were the Passover Feast, the Feast of Pentecost, and the Feast of Tabernacles. The Feast of Tabernacles was like Christmas, Thanksgiving, and the Fourth of July all rolled into one. At this feast, the high priest would dip a golden pitcher into the Pool of Siloam. He would then carry that water to the temple and pour it on the altar.

When the water hit the altar, the Levites would blow their trumpets. At that moment, the people would shout, sing, and dance in the streets. In John 7, Jesus attended the Feast of Tabernacles. He stood and told them that He was the only living water that could quench their thirst (vv. 37-39). Today, we don't celebrate a ritual. We celebrate and give thanks to a Savior whose body was broken to release the living water which brings eternal life.

GOD BLESSES FAITHFULNESS

(Proverbs 28:18-28)

When God called me into evangelism, I was pastoring a great church that paid me a wonderful salary. With a wife and two little girls, I wasn't thrilled about stepping into the unknown. After seeking God's direction, our family took a step of faith in the fall of 1988. In early January of 1989, however, doubt crept in. I had no revivals scheduled until February, and we were financially tight. As I wept before the Lord, He encouraged me to stay faithful. One cold morning, I walked to the mailbox. Along with the mail, there was a plain, unaddressed, unstamped envelope that an anonymous person had put into the box. Inside the envelope were ten one-hundred-dollar bills. That money covered our bills until the revival schedule started.

God honors and blesses faithfulness. In Proverbs 28, Solomon is writing about the blessings of a faithful man. Our Father expects us to diligently labor (v. 19). But God also promises to bless that faithful labor (v. 20). Solomon closes the chapter by reminding us that God also provides for those who are givers (v. 27). He blesses faithfulness because He is faithful. Give thanks today, because He recognizes and rewards obedience and multiplies what we sow.

REASON FOR THE SEASON

(Matthew 1:18-25)

Every year at the beginning of December, stores and retailers across this nation issue strict guidelines on how employees should address shoppers. Some merchandisers adamantly demand their staff greet customers with the words *Happy Holidays* or *Season's Greetings* instead of *Merry Christmas*. The words *Merry Christmas* are considered offensive. It is now estimated that 49 percent of all Americans believe that saying "Happy Holidays" is more appropriate than saying "Merry Christmas." In the state of Maryland, public schools recently changed the words *Christmas Break* to *Winter Holidays*. It is tragic when Christ is removed from Christmas. What is even more tragic is that these advocates of politically correct terminology, who advocate the offensiveness of the word *Christmas*, still enthusiastically celebrate the holiday they demean and mock. If they don't believe it, why celebrate it at all? Yet they don't see the hypocrisy.

Christmas is a celebration of the birth of our Savior. In Matthew 1, the angel of the Lord visited Joseph. The angel told him that Mary was going to give birth to a son named Jesus, and He would *save* (deliver) the world from their sins (v. 21). Jesus Christ is the reason for the season. Without Him, there is no reason to celebrate.

DECEMBER 2

THE JESUS BOOK

(Genesis 3:14-24)

From cover to cover, God's written Word speaks of God's living Word. The Bible is the Jesus Book. It has been said that if you want to know about roses and lilies, read a book about botany. But if you want to know about the Rose of Sharon and the Lily of the Valley, read the Bible. If you want to know about the stars, read a book about astronomy. But if you want to know about the Bright and Morning star, read the Bible. If you want to know about the ages of rocks, read a book about archaeology. But if you want to know about the Rock of Ages, read the Bible. Open your Bible to any of its sixty-six books, and Jesus Christ will step out. The Bible is not just a history book. It is the book that tells His story.

The first prophecy in the entire Bible is found in the first book of the Bible. In Genesis 3:15, God told the serpent that He would bring forth a man through the woman who would crush Satan's power. Redemption's plan was unfolded thousands of years before Jesus Christ was born in Bethlehem. God warned the Devil that Christmas was coming.

December 3

Cutting Down The Christmas Tree

(1 Peter 2:13-25)

We have had artificial Christmas trees in our home for many years now. But when my three children were growing up, we often made a family excursion to a tree farm to cut down a real live Christmas tree. One year, our family loaded up the trusty minivan and headed to the Candy Cane Christmas Tree Farm to pick out our tree. After cutting it down, we carefully wedged the seven-footer between the seats of the van and our three kids. On the ride home, the Coram family was really in the Christmas spirit. We sang and serenaded one another with the songs of the season. At the height of the euphoria, a big spider crawled out of the branches and escaped into the van. Needless to say, that minivan started rocking.

Beautifully decorated trees are an important part and focal point of every home during the Christmas season. Around the brightly lit trees are the gifts that we give and receive. While we enjoy our trees this year, let's never forget that the greatest Christmas gift was given so that He could die on a tree to save our souls (v. 24). Jesus, the gift of grace, was born to die for our sins.

WONDERFUL

(Isaiah 9:1-7)

S everal men were in a golf club locker room when a cell phone rang. A man picked it up from the bench, engaged the speaker, and said, "Hello." Everyone in the room heard a voice answer, "Honey, it's me. I'm at the mall and I found a beautiful leather coat for only one thousand dollars. Can I buy it?" The man said, "Sure." Excitedly, the lady said, "You are the best! I also stopped by the Mercedes dealership. The new models are out. I picked out the color I like, and it is only ninety-nine thousand dollars. What do you think?" Once again, the man said, "Sure." The woman exclaimed, "Oh, honey, you are the most wonderful husband in the world! Bye." After hanging up, the man looked at the other guys and said, "Does anyone know whose phone this is?"

That woman misunderstood the word *wonderful*. Isaiah 9:6 covers the entire life of Jesus from His birth (*Wonderful*) to His return (*The Prince of Peace*). *Wonderful* in Hebrew means "a miracle and a marvel." That is a great description of the birth of Christ. It was wonderful because it was the greatest miracle of grace the world has ever known. God Himself came to save His people.

DECEMBER 5

MAKING A LIST

(John 3:1-17)

I t is that time of the year once again. The time has come for making a Christmas gift list. My grandchildren and children have already given my wife and I their lists. One of my youngest granddaughters wants a Kindle, and has repeatedly specified that it must be a blue one. Another grandchild wants the very latest American Girl doll. Both of my daughters have requested kitchen pots and serving dishes. All the individual gift lists are diligently written down and checked twice. Whenever an online purchase comes to the door, or something is picked off the shelf at a store, Judy checks that special gift off the list. She wants to be sure that our family is getting the gifts that they requested.

If sinful mankind had been permitted to make a Christmas wish list for God, what gift do you think would have been first on that list? Wise men would ask for a Savior. In John 3, Jesus had a nighttime interview with Nicodemus. Christ told the religious man that he must be born again (v. 3). Then Jesus explained that He is the only gift that gives everlasting life (v. 16). .

DECEMBER 6

KNEELING BEFORE THE KING

(Psalm 72:1-11)

Have you noticed all the new Christmas yard art that pops up each year? The stores are filled with everything from huge, inflatable characters to elaborate, music-synced laser lights. Some people spend a great deal of time, effort, and money to showcase their homes to passers-by. One of the greatest outdoor Christmas displays I have ever seen was in front of an office building in Ocala, Florida. It was a beautifully lit manger display. The lights and focus were brightly reflected on the Christ child in the cradle. But the captivating sight of the display was a six-foot-tall Santa Claus, humbling kneeling with his head down in front of Jesus in the manger. Santa knelt before the King. What a testimony in a world where Santa has replaced Christ as the heart of Christmas.

Christmas is a celebration of the birthday of the King of Kings. In Psalm 72, Solomon writes about a prophetic event. Verses 10-11 describe kings bringing gifts and kneeling down in front of the greatest King of them all. That grand event will happen one day when every knee bows before King Jesus. But it also occurred long ago when three wise men first came to see the Christ child.

DECEMBER 7

NO BABY QUITE LIKE THIS ONE

(Luke 1:26-38)

It was Christmas night, and a little four-year-old girl was tired out after a very busy day. It all began when she had awakened early that morning and rushed into the living room to see all the beautiful gifts under the tree. During the course of the thrilling day, she had opened all her presents, eaten her favorite food, spent the day playing with her cousins, and enjoyed every exciting and exhausting minute of Christmas. Now, as her mother gently tucked her into bed, the mom kissed the child and asked, "Did you have a lot of fun today?" With a radiant smile, the little girl looked up at her mom and replied, "Yes, Mommy, Christmas was so much fun. I really hope Mary and Joseph have another baby next year."

Mary and Joseph did have other babies, but none like Jesus. That is because the Father of baby Jesus was God (v. 35). Jesus Christ was virgin born (v. 27). His was the most miraculous birth in history. There has never been a baby quite like Him, nor will there ever be again.

DECEMBER 8

SONGS OF THE SEASON

(1 Chronicles 15:15-29)

I love Christmas music. Whenever we drive long distances to see family during the holidays, I always have the radio tuned to the songs of the season. I can't think of a holiday song that I really don't like. In fact, I even enjoy *Rockin' Around The Christmas Tree* by Brenda Lee. Recently, I read an article that listed the five most-popular Christmas songs in history. Those famous songs are: 1) *The Christmas Song ("Chestnuts Roasting on an Open Fire")*; 2) *White Christmas*; 3) *Winter Wonderland*; 4) *Silver Bells*; and 5) *I'll Be Home for Christmas*. Of course, I appreciate all of those songs. But I couldn't help but notice that none of those tunes mention the real meaning of the season. Christmas is about Jesus Christ.

God gave us music to praise Him. In First Chronicles 15, David brought the ark of the covenant into Jerusalem. He appointed the Levites to play, sing, and celebrate with the sound of music (v. 16). Even criticism and jealousy could not stop David from praising the name of the Lord (v. 29). Raise your voice and sing songs of praise and exaltation as you celebrate Jesus this season. The angels did, and so should we.

LOOKING FORWARD

(Galatians 4:1-11)

A pastor worked on his Sunday sermon one evening in his study at home, when his energetic little girl came bursting into the room and asked, "Daddy, will you please play with me?" Smiling, the pastor said, "Baby, please be patient with me for a few more minutes. As soon as I finish my sermon, I promise you that I will spend time with you." The small girl answered, "Okay, Daddy." As she walked out of the study, the precious child did a U-turn and ran back to her father. She jumped into his lap, squeezed him tightly, and sweetly kissed his cheek. Then, with bright blue eyes, she looked at her dad and said, "Daddy, I just wanted you to know what you have to look forward to."

For centuries, the Jews had looked forward to the coming of the Messiah. In Galatians, Paul explained that Christ had come. In verse 4, he said that the Son of God came to earth in the fullness of time. That describes "a container that is completely filled up." Christmas celebrates the fulfillment of a promise. Jesus has come to the earth. His first coming reveals what we look forward to – eternity with Him.

NAMING THE CITY

(Micah 5:1-15)

My oldest daughter was born in a hospital in Tampa, Florida. At that particular time, my life and ministry were located in that Central Florida city. I had no intention of ever leaving there. After all, I had spent most of my life in that area. Even when I attended Bible college, it was not far from where I was born. All of my parents, relatives, and in-laws were living close by in that familiar place. So, if someone had told me that ten years after the birth of our oldest daughter in Tampa my youngest child would be born one day in a hospital in Jacksonville, Florida, I would have looked at them as if they were completely out of their mind.

None of us can possibly know where the future will take us. Yet Micah recorded the name of the exact town that Jesus would be born in 750 years before it happened. In verse 2, the prophet named the small, anonymous hamlet of Bethlehem as the city that would see the birth of Jesus Christ. Only God could accurately pinpoint the exact place 750 years before it happened. Jesus came to us as living proof that God always keeps His Word.

JOY TO THE WORLD

(Revelation 19:11-21)

An English hymn writer named Isaac Watts wrote one of our most popular Christmas carols almost three hundred years ago. It is the beloved song called *Joy to the World*. But do you realize that it was not written about the birth of Jesus Christ? Think about it. There is absolutely no mention in the song of Mary, Joseph, angels, shepherds, or a manger. The chorus of the beloved hymn simply says, *Joy to the world! The Lord is come; Let earth receive her King*. Before his death, Isaac Watts testified that the words of the song are based on the second half of Psalm 98 and do not refer to the birth of Christ in Bethlehem. Instead, they are describing His triumphant return to earth at the end of the age.

Please don't stop singing *Joy to the World* this Christmas season. After all, it is a glad song with a glorious message, and Christmas is a time of great joy. But remember that Jesus' first coming was the preparation for His second coming. He is coming again. In Revelation 19, John describes our victorious King riding back to earth on a white stallion. Joy to the world. Jesus is coming again.

DECEMBER 12

GOD IS NOW HERE

(Isaiah 7:1-14)

A certain man was a devout and defiant atheist. He was determined to raise his children to denounce the existence of God. The atheist hired an artist to paint a script on the wall of his study. In big letters, the words said, *GOD IS NOWHERE.* One day, his young son played in the study while he read his newspaper. The small boy saw him reading, and said, "Daddy, I can read too." His father replied, "That is great. Why don't you practice right now? Read these words on the wall." The little guy looked up at the big words *GOD IS NOWHERE* for a moment. Then he proudly said, "God is now here." From that day on, the atheist could never look at those words in the same way. Through a child's vision, he discovered that God is now here.

The prophet Isaiah looked down through time and saw the coming of the Lord. Isaiah 7:14 is an amazing Old Testament prophecy concerning the birth of Christ. It was fulfilled in Matthew 1:23. Isaiah declares that the coming child would be called Immanuel, which literally means "God is with us." This is the real message of Christmas. Christ has come. God is now here.

DECEMBER 13

ANCESTRY.GOD

(Matthew 1:1-17)

In 1990, two enterprising young men started a small Internet genealogy company based in Provo, Utah. The company is called *Ancestry.com*. It is the largest for-profit genealogy company in the entire world. Because there are so many people today who are interested in finding information concerning their genealogies and family trees, *Ancestry.com* is now worth about $450 million. As of 2016, *Ancestry.com* has well over two million paid subscribers. The company has access to seventy million family trees, sixteen million historical records, and well over two hundred million photographs available to those looking for their ancestors. God's ordained social structure for His people included a detailed and accurate record of births, deaths, and marriages. The family tree was an integral part of Jewish individual, family, and tribal identity. It defined who they were.

The Bible is filled with listings of family trees. But did you know that the last recorded birth in Scripture is Jesus Christ's? The final genealogy in the Bible is found in the first seventeen verses of Matthew 1. It really is amazing. The entire Old Testament is full of long genealogies and family trees. However, the very top branch of the family tree is Jesus. You could call it *Ancestry.God*.

STEALING CHRISTMAS

(Genesis 4:1-26)

Many years ago, our family attended a Christmas Eve service. When we returned home, there were two police cars in our driveway and our front door was open. My wife exclaimed, "Our house has been broken into!" My children were upset. Our youngest son immediately thought the gifts under the tree were stolen, and he burst into tears. He screamed out, "Somebody stole my presents!" The whole thing was a bit disconcerting until the officer assured us that there had not been an intruder at all. Evidently, we had failed to lock the front door. It was windy that evening, and it appeared that the door had been blown open and triggered the security alarm. But for a brief moment, my children thought someone had stolen their Christmas.

In Genesis 4, God accepted Abel's offering over Cain's (v. 4). Satan prompted jealous Cain to kill his own brother. Some have suggested that perhaps the Enemy thought the prophesied messianic seed (Gen. 3:15) was coming through Abel. Whether or not that is true, one thing is clear. The thief could never steal Christmas. The promised seed came through Seth (v. 25). God's covenant cannot be broken. His promises cannot be stolen.

ALL ARE WELCOME

(Acts 10:34-48)

Every year, the Rock Center Café in New York City hosts Breakfast with Santa. The huge event is held every weekend from Thanksgiving to Christmas. It is one of the most-popular Christmas attractions in Manhattan. Those children who are fortunate enough to attend Breakfast with Santa enjoy a family-style meal, gifts from Santa's elves, and a personal visit with Santa Claus himself. There is one catch, however. The big event is not open to the general public. Not everyone is welcome to just walk in and sit down on Santa's lap. Reservations and tickets must be purchased well in advance. The reservations fill up very early, and there is a long waiting list for those who don't apply in time. Many will not get in.

There is no waiting list to meet Jesus. All are welcome to sit at the feet of the King. Acts 10 is one of the most important chapters in the entire book of Acts. It records the opening of the door of faith to the Gentiles. Peter preaches a "whosoever will" gospel (v. 43). Your reservation into heaven must be made through Jesus Christ. But all are welcome. You only need to accept the personal invitation from God.

CHRISTMAS IS GETTING CLOSE ON THE CALENDAR

(Malachi 4:1-6)

When I got up this morning, I had to check my calendar to book some airline reservations for next year. As I thumbed through the calendar, a thought occurred to me. Do you realize that every time you scroll through your calendar to write down a date or pencil in an event, you are using Jesus Christ as your point of reference? After all, it was Jesus who divided history into BC (before Christ) and AD (anno Domini, "in the year of our Lord"). Every moment and event on your calendar is marked by how many days and years it has been since Jesus Christ walked this earth. Even your very own birthday is dated by the birthday of Jesus Christ.

Malachi ministered about four hundred years before Christ. In chapter 4, Malachi refers to Christ as the *Sun of righteousness* (v. 2). The very last word in the Old Testament is *curse* (v. 6). At the end of the New Testament are the words *no more curse*. Malachi's day was one of darkness. Israel had no more prophets until the coming of the One who would break the curse forever. But Malachi knew the Son was coming. God's calendar was poised for change.

HE DOES ALL THINGS WELL

(Mark 7:24-37)

My wife, Judy, and I recently needed some work done on our house. The work was well beyond my skill set. Now, I am a hard worker and will sweat with anyone. But outside of preaching the gospel, I have extremely limited skills. Some might say I am limited even when it comes to preaching. At any rate, a trusted friend recommended a very competent handyman to us. Our friend testified, "He can fix anything, and he can build anything." We phoned the handyman, and I am happy to report that he was masterful in his craft. One day, I watched him skillfully laying tile on our front porch. I commented, "You can really do anything, can't you?" He answered, "No sir. I can't preach a lick." God has given each of us different gifts and talents.

There is only one person in history who did all things well. In the last part of Mark 7, Jesus performed miracles over demons and deafness. The people marveled and testified, *He hath done all things well* (v. 37). From the cradle to the cross to the crown, Jesus did all things well. He still does all things well.

DECEMBER 18

THE RIGHTEOUS BRANCH

(Jeremiah 23:1-15)

As I walked into a revival service one evening, a troubled woman greeted me in the church vestibule. She told me that her grown, married daughter had completely turned her back on God, the Bible, and the local church. Sadly, the young woman was no longer interested in attending church or even letting her children go to church with their grandmother. The daughter told her mother that she had listened to a well-known radio preacher who had said, "There are many ways to God. You don't necessarily have to come through Jesus Christ." My heart broke as I prayed with and counseled that dear woman. Once again, I was reminded of the great responsibility to open the Bible and preach the truth, even if it's unpalatable to those listening.

In Jeremiah 23, the pastors of Israel had become negligent shepherds (v. 1). But although the remnant was scattered, God reminded them that the *righteous Branch* (a sprout that buds) was coming (v. 5). Jeremiah is giving a messianic prophecy about the birth of Christ. Jesus is the only way to God. We are righteous before God only because Christ is our righteousness. God would not send His Son to die for no reason.

MISSING THE PARTY

(Acts 3:1-16)

I heard a story about a little boy who completely forgot all about his dear grandmother's birthday. A few days passed, and the boy's mom asked him, "Did you remember to wish Grandma a happy birthday the other day?" The boy's heart sank, and he replied, "Oh no. I forgot all about it." So he quickly wrote his grandmother a very special belated birthday message and immediately mailed the card. When his grandmother opened the card, it said, *Grandma, I am very sad I forgot your birthday last week. It would serve me right if you forgot about mine coming up next Tuesday. Love, Johnny.*

Acts 3 records the healing of a lame man (vv. 7-8). After the public healing, Peter told the crowd about Jesus (vv. 12-16). They had no idea that the prince of life had been in their midst, and they missed Him for a murderer (v. 14). During this season, millions of Americans will not realize that Christmas is all about the birth of a Savior. Sadly, they will miss the real party because they see things from the wrong perspective.

THE MESSIAH IS COMING

(2 Samuel 7:12-21)

King David always had one great burning desire: to build a beautiful temple for God in Jerusalem. It was the life ambition of Israel's great king to construct a magnificent, palatial home to honor and glorify God. But the Lord never permitted David to build His temple. God had a different kind of house in mind. He wanted David to build a royal human house that would stand forever. Second Samuel 7:13-16 is a messianic prophecy of the Old Testament known as the Davidic covenant. God promised David that the Messiah would be birthed from his family tree. David wanted to build God a house of stone. However, when Christ was born, God built David a royal family that would stand for all of eternity.

In Second Samuel 7, God states that the throne would be forever (v. 13), and David's house and kingdom would be forever (v. 16). Skeptics argue that the promise was broken because David doesn't have a descendant on his throne today. But Christ will fulfill the Davidic covenant when He sits on David's throne and rules during the millennial kingdom (Revelation 20:1-6). In the meantime, He remains King of the Jews. No one can remove His right or title.

GOD'S GLORY IN HUMAN FLESH

(John 1:1-14)

O ur family has always had a wonderful and longstanding Christmas tradition. Before any of the gifts are passed out and opened, someone will turn in the Bible to Luke 2 and read the Christmas story aloud. Without question, the two most familiar and often recited Christmas passages are those beautiful accounts that are found in the second chapters of Matthew and Luke. After all, when we think of Christmas, we always visualize Mary and Joseph, the baby, the manger, the angels, the shepherds, and the wise men. But one of the greatest descriptions about the birth of Christ is written in the first chapter of John. The real miracle and message of Christmas is that God's glory was revealed in human flesh.

John 1:14 declares, *And the Word was made flesh, and dwelt among us, (and we beheld his glory).* The word *dwelt* literally means "to tabernacle or encamp among us." God became flesh and dwelt among us without ever giving up any of His glory. In other words, He never quit being God. The Creator stepped into a cradle, and we saw His indescribable glory. He now lives in us, and His glory remains, dwelling in and reflected by His people.

DECEMBER 22

MARY HAD A LITTLE LAMB

(Exodus 11:1-10)

Can you guess the title of the children's song that is rated the fifth most-popular kids' tune ever written? It may absolutely shock you to know that it is not a song from a hit Disney movie. As a matter of fact, the song was written almost two hundred years ago. Of course, the beloved song I refer to is called *Mary Had a Little Lamb*. The popular song was actually based on a true story. A little girl named Mary Sawyer had a little pet lamb. One day, Mary took her pet lamb to school with her. Someone in Mary's class wrote a poem about it, and the rest is history. The poem went something like this ... *Mary had a little lamb, its fleece was white as snow; And everywhere that Mary went, the lamb was sure to go.* What a wonderful picture of Jesus.

Exodus 11 reminds us of a day when death came to Egypt (vv. 4-7). The only hope was to be covered by the blood of a lamb (Exodus 12:13). The same is true for you and me. We were born under the curse of death, but *Mary had a little Lamb, He washed us white as snow.*

DECEMBER 23

KING SCROOGE

(Matthew 2:1-18)

In December of 1843, a compelling novel authored by Charles Dickens was published in London, England. The name of the novel was *A Christmas Carol*. From the very beginning, the book received instant critical acclaim and international success. Its story has been adapted many times to film, stage, opera, and television. *A Christmas Carol* tells the story of a bitter old miser named Ebenezer Scrooge who summed up Christmas with the phrase "Bah, humbug." In the end, Scrooge was transformed into a kinder, loving man when he was visited by the ghost of his former business partner and the frightening spirits of Christmas Past, Present, and Yet to Come. Ebenezer Scrooge embraced the Christmas spirit. The message of Jesus is one of transformation, of moving from death to life. Like many of us, Scrooge had to be confronted by death before he would accept life. Sadly, some people never seem to get the message.

King Herod was one who was never transformed. In Matthew 2, Herod told three star-gazing wise men (magi) that he wanted to worship Jesus (vv. 7-8), but what he really wanted to do was kill Him (v. 16). So God guided the wise men home in a different direction, and "King Scrooge" failed to kill Christmas.

WRAPPING THE GREATEST GIFT

(Luke 2:1-7)

The Hallmark Corporation is credited with the founding of the modern-day gift-wrapping industry in America. In the early 1900s, people used thin red, green, and white tissue paper to wrap up their gifts. During the Christmas season of 1917, the Hall Brothers store in Kansas City, Missouri, ran out of the red, green, and white tissue paper. In desperation, the store ordered decorative and colorful envelope lining paper from the Hallmark Manufacturing Plant. The next year, the bright paper was sold at twenty-five cents for three sheets. By 1925, bright gift-wrapping paper was all the rage. Today, it is estimated that Americans spend a staggering $3 billion annually on the paper we wrap our Christmas presents in.

One starry night in Bethlehem, Mary wrapped up the very first Christmas gift. She didn't wrap that gift in bright, shiny, expensive paper. Luke 2:7 says that Mary *wrapped him in swaddling clothes.* Swaddling clothes were simply strips of cloth. God gave the greatest Christmas gift, and Mary wrapped the incredible gift of God's infinite grace in cloth, a type of the winding cloths that, after His death, would wrap our Savior for burial. Aren't you glad that the gift had your name on it?

MERRY CHRISTMAS

(Luke 2:8-20)

On Christmas Day 1965, renowned radio broadcaster Paul Harvey told the following story to his audience. A man informed his family he would not attend the Christmas Eve service with them because he didn't want to feel like a hypocrite. Shortly after his family left, it began to snow heavily. Suddenly, the man heard a thud. Then he heard another and another. Opening the front door, he saw a flock of birds huddled in the snow. The birds were freezing, and they had tried to fly through his window. Instantly, the man felt sympathy for the poor creatures. He trampled through the snow and opened his barn. He tried to shoo the birds in, but they would not go. Frustrated, the man shouted, "If only I could become a bird, they would follow me to the warm barn and be saved!" At that instant, the church bells began to ring. The man sank to his knees in the snow. He realized that was exactly what Jesus had done for him.

The angel told the shepherds, *For unto you is born this day in the city of David a Saviour.* Christ did not come to philosophize or educate. He came to save. That is the Christmas story. Have a happy, blessed Christmas.

December 26

The Day After

(Isaiah 60:1-22)

December 26 has never been a very exciting day. After all, it is the day that follows the magic of Christmas Eve and the joy of Christmas Day. Many people will work today. Some folks will work to take their lights and trees down. Others will work by fighting the crowds in traffic, or at the mall, or at the airport. Still others will head back to work to make a living today. I wonder what it was like the day after the very first Christmas. Mary and Joseph basked privately in the heavenly glow of their newborn baby boy. But apart from the shepherds, no one knew of the events in the stable on Christmas night. It would be thirty years before most of the world would be introduced to Jesus.

However, on the day after the second coming, everyone on the face of the earth will know that Christ is here. Isaiah 60 describes what it will be like when Jesus returns and sits on David's throne. There will be wealth, not war (vv. 3-9). Peace will reign, and the gates of Jerusalem will never be locked (v. 11). The day after Jesus comes back will begin an endless celebration, not end one.

CLEARING UP THE CONFUSION

(Acts 17:122-24)

A woman was home baking cookies one day when the doorbell rang. Opening the door, the lady saw a humble man who kindly asked, "Ma'am, do you have any odd jobs around here that I could do?" Thinking for a moment, the woman replied, "Why yes, I need to have my porch painted. The red paint is in the garage. Do a good job and I will pay you well." The grateful man thanked her and went right to work. Two hours later the doorbell rang again. The woman answered the door and asked, "Did you finish painting my porch? Smiling, the weary man replied, "Yes ma'am. It is all painted bright red. But I need to tell you that you are confused. It isn't a Porsche. It's a Mercedes."

Confusion means we're not sure of the truth, and that's a dangerous place to be. When Paul arrived in Athens, he saw a religious city that was confused. After all, there were gods, altars, and idols on every corner. They even had an altar *TO THE UNKNOWN GOD* (v. 23). Paul immediately cleared up their confusion with the truth by declaring that the God they did not know is the only true and living God (vv. 28-31).

DECEMBER 28

ANTIDOTE FOR SNAKEBITE

(Numbers 21:1-9)

I hate all snakes. Red, yellow, black, or white, they are all hideous in my sight. One evening, I attended a churchwide fellowship meal before a revival service at a country church. After dinner, I walked outside for a breath of fresh air. A man standing beside the sidewalk stopped me and said, "Preacher, did you see that snake lying in the azalea bushes you just walked by?" I shuddered. "No. What kind of snake was it?" The man answered, "Oh, just a big 'ole rat snake. He's not poisonous. A snake like that can't hurt you." He didn't realize that I might hurt myself just trying to get out of its way. Although there might some snakes in this world that cannot hurt us, the poisonous snake called Satan is always ready to strike.

After the Israelites spoke against God, He sent fiery serpents to bite them (v. 6). There was only one cure for the snakebite. Moses lifted a brass serpent up on a pole. All who looked upon it lived (vv. 8-9). Brass in the Bible pictures judgment, and the brass serpent depicts Jesus Christ lifted up on the cross (John 3:14). His blood is the only cure for the poisonous snakebite of sin.

OPEN YOUR MOUTH AND TELL SOMEBODY

(Mark 16:9-20)

I have noticed something very strange about cell phones. Everybody in this day and age seems to want to text rather than talk. For example, I can call any of my children, and most of the time, I will not get an immediate answer. But if I hang up and send them a text, I will get an instant response. That is because we live in a generation that is slowly losing the precious art of old-fashioned communication. Our culture never wants to talk. We email, we tweet, we text, and we post, but we don't talk. Although we live in this highly advanced environment of amazing technology, verbal communication is diminishing rapidly. It makes me sad to think that the next generation might never open their mouths to communicate.

God wants us to open our mouths and tell people about Him. Of course, I know that God uses many forms and methods of communication to get the message out. However, in Mark 16:15, Jesus told His disciples to *preach the gospel*. The word *preach* means "to herald with conviction." The best way to do that is to open your mouth and tell somebody with the certainty of absolute faith that Jesus saves.

DECEMBER 30

TAMING TEMPER

(Proverbs 15:18-33)

Violent temper tantrums are not exclusively reserved for little children. Adults can easily lose control and explode. A woman who tried to rationalize her volatile temper once approached evangelist Billy Sunday. The woman said, "Preacher, it is not necessarily a sin to lose your temper. I mean, I may blow up all the time. But after I blow up, it's all over." Billy Sunday replied, "A shotgun blows up too. However, after it blows up, look at the damage that is left behind." How true that is. Anger is very destructive. Just look around you at all of the rage and anger in our world today. Someone has profoundly said, "You can nurse a grudge. But that won't make it better." Unresolved anger will eventually blow up in someone's face with damaging, destructive consequences.

In paraphrased language, Proverbs 15:18 says, "A hot-headed man stirs up contentions and fights, but he that is slow to anger calms down fighting." The word *anger* is a picture of someone whose nostrils are flaring and snorting. God's Word reminds us that a wise child of God patiently puts their temper under His control and listens to His instructions (vv. 28-33) instead of allowing their anger to control them.

RUN WITH DISCIPLINE

(1 Corinthians 9:19-27)

I t is that wonderful time of the year again, isn't it? During the next twenty-four hours, people will be making New Year's resolutions. Surveys say that most folks will make a resolution to lose weight. I heard about a woman who walked into her bathroom one day and saw her husband weighing himself on the scale. She noticed that he was sucking in his stomach. The woman laughed. "That is not going to help," she said. The man responded, "Sure it will. It's the only way I can see the numbers on the scale." Many folks may be sincere about losing weight, but four out of five resolutions are forgotten by the second week of January. This is because so many resolutions are made spontaneously and without careful thought or consideration of the full ramifications involved. We forget that everything requires discipline.

Discipline is important. In the last four verses of First Corinthians 9, Paul uses the Isthmian Games as a comparison to running the Christian race. Greek athletes disciplined their bodies to win a crown (v. 24). If athletes can be disciplined when running for a fading crown, we should be disciplined when running for an eternal crown (v. 25). Run with discipline this coming year.

Meet the Author

Rick Coram, a full-time Southern Baptist evangelist since 1988, accepted God's call to preach as a teenage boy. After college, he served for four years as a minister of students, and for eight years as a senior pastor in two Baptist churches.

His last pastorate became one of Florida's strongest evangelistic churches, baptizing over one hundred people per year for six consecutive years.

Since entering travelling vocational evangelism, Rick has preached in more than thirteen hundred revivals, crusades, and camps. He is a frequent speaker at state and national evangelism conferences. RICK CORAM MINISTRIES is founder and sponsor of PowerLife Student Camps, and the PowerLife Bible Conference. Since 1990, over twenty-five thousand teenagers have attended the PowerLife camps.

Rick, a native of Florida, makes his home in Jacksonville, Florida. He and his wife, Judy, have three children, Rachel Carter (husband, Bryan), Jessica Turner (husband, Patrick), and Jonathan Coram (wife, Amanda). Rick and Judy have four grandchildren (Jadyn, Bralyn, Brooklyn, and Ansley).

Connect with the Author

www.rickcoramministries.com

www.powerlifestudentcamps.com

Learn more about Rick Coram

www.rickcoramministries.com

Enjoy more titles by Rick Coram

www.rickcoramministries.com/store/books